MP3 For Dummies®, 2nd Edition

Cheat Sheet

Winamp Hotkeys

Press this . . .	. . . to do this
F1	See the About box
Ctrl+A	Toggle Winamp to always stay on top of the screen
Alt+W	Toggle main window on and off the screen
Alt+T	Toggle Minibrowser
Alt+S	Select skins
Ctrl+P	Go to preferences
Alt+F	Call up main menu
J	Jump to new song
Alt+3	Edit current song's information
Shift+V	Fadeout and stop
C	Toggle pause of playing song
Up arrow	Turn up volume
Down arrow	Turn down volume
See more shortcuts	Press F1 and click Keyboard shortcuts tab

Best MP3 Sites for News, Software, and Music

Go here . . .	. . . to get this
www.mp3.com	MP3 songs, news, reviews, forum, links
www.rollingstone.com	Songs in all formats, news, artist encyclopedia
www.dailyMP3.com	News, files, search engines, low-price hardware searches, forum, links
www.listen.com	News, MP3 songs reviewed by their staff, radio stations, videos, tour info, and hardware reviews.
www.gnutellanews.com	Tracks the progress of Gnutella and other file-swapping alternatives to Napster
www.askmp3.com	News, beginner's information, lists of MP3 players, product reviews, search engines, links to technical information

MP3 Compression Rates and Sound Quality

Compressing sound at roughly this rate. . .	results in this quality. . .	at this mode. . .	. . . and shrinks the file by this much
8 kHz	Telephone sound	Mono	96:1
32 kHz	AM radio	Mono	24:1
64 kHz	FM radio	Stereo	26 ... 24:1
96 kHz	Roughly CD	Stereo	16:1
128 kHz	Nearly indistinguishable from CD	Stereo	14 ...12:1

For example, shrinking a file at a rate of 8 kHz gives you telephone-quality mono sound. The file is compressed to 96 times smaller than its original size, making it very tiny.

For Dummies: Bestselling Book Series for Beginners

MP3 For Dummies®, 2nd Edition

MP3-related Newsgroups

These newsgroups, which I discuss in Chapters 3 and 4, carry MP3 files or information about MP3. Not every Internet Service Provider carries every newsgroup, however, so don't be surprised if you don't find all of these in your listing. The first eight groups hold most of the posts, and `alt.binaries.sounds.mp3` carries almost everything.

This newsgroup . . .	. . . carries this information
`alt.binaries.sounds.mp3.1940s`	Music from the 1940s
`alt.binaries.sounds.mp3.1950s`	Music from the 1950s
`alt.binaries.sounds.mp3.1960s`	Music from the 1960s
`alt.binaries.sounds.mp3.1970s`	Music from the 1970s
`alt.binaries.sounds.mp3.1980s`	Music from the 1980s
`alt.binaries.sounds.mp3.1990s`	Music from the 1990s
`alt.binaries.sounds.mp3.200s`	Music from the current decade
`alt.binaries.sounds.mp3`	One large collection of music that's posted simultaneously in the newsgroups dedicated to the other decades — the '50s through the '90s.
`alt.binaries.sounds.mp3.beatles`	Beatles songs
`alt.binaries.sounds.mp3.bootlegs`	Usually recordings of live shows
`alt.binaries.sounds.mp3.brazilian`	Brazilian music
`alt.binaries.sounds.mp3.d`	Discussion of mp3 sound files
`alt.binaries.sounds.mp3.indie`	Music from independent labels
`alt.binaries.sounds.mp3.novelty recordings`	Comedy and novelty songs
`alt.binaries.sounds.mp3.requests`	Requests for MP3 songs go here
`alt.binaries.sounds.mp3.video-games`	Videogame-related MP3s
`alt.binaries.sounds.mp3.zappa`	Frank Zappa music
`alt.binaries.remixes.mp3`	Usually famous songs remixed by somebody else

Quick Tips

- To play MP3s in the car, plug a cassette adapter into your car's tape player, and plug the adapter's cable into your portable MP3 player's earphone or line out jack.

- To play MP3 files on home stereos, convert them to WAV files with Winamp's built-in Nullsoft Disk Writer Plug-in. Then use CD-burning software to create a music CD.

- For the latest answers to Frequently Asked Questions, head to `www.askmp3.com`.

Hungry Minds, the Hungry Minds logo, For Dummies, the For Dummies Bestselling Book Series logo and all related trade dress are registered trademarks or trademarks of Hungry Minds, Inc. All other trademarks are the property of their respective owners.

Hungry Minds™

For Dummies: Bestselling Book Series for Beginners

MP3 FOR DUMMIES®

2ND EDITION

by Andy Rathbone

Hungry Minds™

HUNGRY MINDS, INC.

New York, NY ◆ Cleveland, OH ◆ Indianapolis, IN

MP3 For Dummies®, 2nd Edition

Published by
Hungry Minds, Inc.
909 Third Avenue
New York, NY 10022
www.hungryminds.com
www.dummies.com

Library of Congress Control Number: 2001089115

ISBN: 0-7645-0858-X

Printed in the United States of America

10 9 8 7 6 5 4 3 2 1

2O/QZ/QV/QR/IN

Distributed in the United States by Hungry Minds, Inc.

Distributed by CDG Books Canada Inc. for Canada; by Transworld Publishers Limited in the United Kingdom; by IDG Norge Books for Norway; by IDG Sweden Books for Sweden; by IDG Books Australia Publishing Corporation Pty. Ltd. for Australia and New Zealand; by TransQuest Publishers Pte Ltd. for Singapore, Malaysia, Thailand, Indonesia, and Hong Kong; by Gotop Information Inc. for Taiwan; by ICG Muse, Inc. for Japan; by Intersoft for South Africa; by Eyrolles for France; by International Thomson Publishing for Germany, Austria and Switzerland; by Distribuidora Cuspide for Argentina; by LR International for Brazil; by Galileo Libros for Chile; by Ediciones ZETA S.C.R. Ltda. for Peru; by WS Computer Publishing Corporation, Inc., for the Philippines; by Contemporanea de Ediciones for Venezuela; by Express Computer Distributors for the Caribbean and West Indies; by Micronesia Media Distributor, Inc. for Micronesia; by Chips Computadoras S.A. de C.V. for Mexico; by Editorial Norma de Panama S.A. for Panama; by American Bookshops for Finland.

For general information on Hungry Minds' products and services please contact our Customer Care Department within the U.S. at 800-762-2974, outside the U.S. at 317-572-3993 or fax 317-572-4002.

For sales inquiries and reseller information, including discounts, premium and bulk quantity sales, and foreign-language translations, please contact our Customer Care Department at 800-434-3422, fax 317-572-4002, or write to Hungry Minds, Inc., Attn: Customer Care Department, 10475 Crosspoint Boulevard, Indianapolis, IN 46256.

For information on licensing foreign or domestic rights, please contact our Sub-Rights Customer Care Department at 212-884-5000.

For information on using Hungry Minds' products and services in the classroom or for ordering examination copies, please contact our Educational Sales Department at 800-434-2086 or fax 317-572-4005.

For press review copies, author interviews, or other publicity information, please contact our Public Relations Department at 317-572-3168 or fax 317-572-4168.

For authorization to photocopy items for corporate, personal, or educational use, please contact Copyright Clearance Center, 222 Rosewood Drive, Danvers, MA 01923, or fax 978-750-4470.

Hungry Minds™ is a trademark of Hungry Minds, Inc.

About the Author

Andy Rathbone started geeking around with computers in 1985 when he bought a boxy CP/M Kaypro 2X with lime-green letters. Like other budding nerds, he soon began playing with null-modem adaptors, dialing up computer bulletin boards, and working part-time at Radio Shack.

In between playing computer games, he served as editor of the *Daily Aztec* newspaper at San Diego State University. After graduating with a comparative literature degree, he went to work for a bizarre underground coffee-table magazine that sort of disappeared.

Andy began combining his two interests, words and computers, by selling articles to a local computing magazine. During the next few years, Andy started ghostwriting computer books for more famous computer authors, as well as writing several hundred articles about computers for technoid publications like Supercomputer Review, CompuServe magazine, ID Systems, DataPro, and Shareware.

In 1992, *DOS For Dummies* author/legend Dan Gookin invited Andy to team up on *PCs For Dummies*. Andy then branched off on his own, writing the award-winning *Windows For Dummies* series and dozens of other *For Dummies* books, including *Upgrading & Fixing PCs For Dummies, Multimedia and CD-ROMs For Dummies, OS/2 For Dummies, MORE Windows For Dummies, Dummies 101: Windows 98,* and *Windows NT For Dummies* with Sharon Crawford.

He currently has more than 11 million copies of his books in print, which have been translated into more than 30 languages.

Andy lives with his most-excellent wife, Tina, and their cat in San Diego, California. When not writing, he fiddles with his MIDI synthesizer and tries to keep the cat off both keyboards.

Author's Acknowledgments

Thanks to Dan Gookin and his wife, Sandy; Tina Rathbone; Matt Wagner; Jodi Jensen; Steve Hayes; Nicole Laux; Rich Barker; and everybody who sent material for the book's CD.

Publisher's Acknowledgments

We're proud of this book; please send us your comments through our Online Registration Form located at www.dummies.com.

Some of the people who helped bring this book to market include the following:

Acquisitions, Editorial, and Media Development

Senior Project Editor: Jodi Jensen
  (Previous Edition: Colleen Totz)

Senior Acquisitions Editor: Steven H. Hayes

Copy Editor: Nicole A. Laux

Technical Editor: Rich Barker

Senior Permissions Editor: Carmen Krikorian

Media Development Specialist: Megan Decraene

Media Development Coordinator:
  Marisa E. Pearman

Editorial Manager: Kyle Looper

Editorial Assistant: Jean Rogers

Production

Project Coordinator: Jennifer Bingham

Layout and Graphics: Jackie Nicholas,
  Brent Savage, Jacque Schneider,
  Jeremey Unger

Proofreaders:
  John Greenough, Charles Spencer,
  York Production Services, Inc.

Indexer: York Production Services, Inc.

Special Help
  Jeremy Zucker

General and Administrative

Hungry Minds, Inc.: John Kilcullen, CEO; Bill Barry, President and COO; John Ball, Executive VP, Operations & Administration; John Harris, CFO

Hungry Minds Technology Publishing Group: Richard Swadley, Senior Vice President and Publisher; Mary Bednarek, Vice President and Publisher, Networking and Certification; Walter R. Bruce III, Vice President and Publisher, General User and Design Professional; Joseph Wikert, Vice President and Publisher, Programming; Mary C. Corder, Editorial Director, Branded Technology Editorial; Andy Cummings, Publishing Director, General User and Design Professional; Barry Pruett, Publishing Director, Visual

Hungry Minds Manufacturing: Ivor Parker, Vice President, Manufacturing

Hungry Minds Marketing: John Helmus, Assistant Vice President, Director of Marketing

Hungry Minds Production for Branded Press: Debbie Stailey, Production Director

Hungry Minds Sales: Roland Elgey, Senior Vice President, Sales and Marketing; Michael Violano, Vice President, International Sales and Sub Rights

◆

The publisher would like to give special thanks to Patrick J. McGovern, without whom this book would not have been possible.

◆

Contents at a Glance

Cartoons at a Glance

By Rich Tennant

"Get the cannon ready kids! Your Moms almost got the '1812 Overture' downloaded!"

page 297

The Tubmans successfully download an entire multimedia MP3 file of Gustav Holst's composition, "The Planets".

page 265

"It's okay. We were just enjoying an MP3 of the Scorpions' 'Rock You Like a Hurricane'."

page 7

"It's not great fidelity, but I'm surprised you can download an MP3 file into an electric pencil sharpener at all."

page 209

"Next time, let me know when you're going to download a 'Red Hot Chili Peppers' MP3 file."

page 39

"Get ready, Mona. I just downloaded 'Mickey' by Starfox."

page 159

Cartoon Information:
Fax: 978-546-7747
E-Mail: richtennant@the5thwave.com
World Wide Web: www.the5thwave.com

Table of Contents

Introduction

*T*his book's not written for digital audio engineers. It's not another tiresome textbook tracing the evolution of musical storage.

Instead, this newly updated book explains how to make MP3 do the fun things you've been hearing about.

What exactly is MP3? Actually, it's a boring algorithm used for compression — a pair of vice grips to squeeze sound into computer files. MP3 technology squeezes song files by 90 percent while preserving their smooth CD-quality sound.

The exciting part lies with what those newly shrunken MP3 files can then do — and I explain it all in this book:

- Convert your CDs into MP3 format and stuff hundreds of songs into your computer. MP3 transforms your computer into a 300-disc CD-changer.

- Tune in to the new Internet radio stations. MP3 files are small enough to be "streamed" through the Internet, letting you hear thousands of radio stations from all over the world. I show you how to find radio stations, create personalized radio stations that match your musical tastes, or broadcast your own radio station across the Internet.

- Portable MP3 players let you listen to tunes while you hit the trails. This book explains how to pick the right player for your specific needs.

- Big-name artists like Tom Petty, Public Enemy, David Bowie, Beastie Boys, Prince, Ice-T, Lyle Lovett, Tom Petty, and others release some of their material in MP3 format, ready to be downloaded from the Internet — this book shows you where to look.

- Tired of today's music? This book turns *you* into a record agent. Thousands of unsigned bands upload MP3 songs to the Internet, hoping you'll lend them an ear. If you like what you hear, the band sells you its CD, often for half the record store price.

- This book contains more than just music. You discover where to find an MP3 file of *The New York Times* front page, updated daily. (A narrator reads the front page while you're eating Krispy Kreme doughnuts or driving to work.) Hear authors such as Dennis Miller, Jack Kerouac, Hunter S. Thompson, Ernest Hemingway, Sylvia Plath, and others read their works or talk about them.

The best thing about MP3? Almost every MP3 file on the Internet is free.

About This Book

This book updates *MP3 For Dummies*, one of the first MP3 books on the market. And like its predecessor, you don't need to read this book cover to cover. Instead, just pick and choose the parts you want to read. When you want to convert your CD collection to MP3 files, for instance, skip ahead to Part III. Read the steps you need, copy the music into your computer, drop the book, and start listening.

Need help grabbing freebie MP3s from the Internet? Chapter 4 contains troubleshooting information for connecting to the Web, configuring your browser, and downloading the goods. Then, when you're ready to annoy the neighbors, turn to Chapter 6 to read how to connect your computer to your home stereo and turn up the bass.

Pick through Chapter 8 for information on tuning into Internet radio stations or broadcasting your own. Head for Chapter 7 for some savvy advice before buying the first MP3 player you spot in an Internet ad.

Or, if your computer isn't beefy enough to handle the heavy demands of MP3 production or playing, flip to Chapter 2 for updated instructions on adding or replacing CD drives, hard drives, and Iomega Jaz drives.

In short, jump from chapter to chapter, picking just the information you need and discarding stuff you'd prefer to tackle later.

What's in This Second Edition?

A lot has happened in the past year or so, and I tell you all about it in this new edition of *MP3 For Dummies*. When the first edition hit the streets, MP3 players were only sold through the Internet. Today, you can find them at Target, alongside the GameBoys. And some of today's home stereo DVD players now play MP3 CDs as well as regular CDs.

The MP3 influence hasn't been only mechanical; lawsuits have shaped MP3's path, bringing changes in copy-protection schemes.

In this edition, I discuss the basics of MP3 that you find in the first edition, and add these new topics:

- Nabbing MP3 files from Napster and Gnutella
- Tweaking MP3 files for the best sound
- Making money from your band's MP3s
- Streaming MP3s from your Web site

✔ Creating, playing, and organizing MP3s with the latest edition of MusicMatch

✔ Understanding copyright laws and protection schemes

✔ Finding today's best MP3 Web sites

How to Use This Book

For best results, jump right into Chapter 1. It explains the basics behind MP3 so that you'll know the latest buzzwords. It's perfect for people who hate reading manuals. By skimming Chapter 1, you can quickly discover what stuff you need to know, and what chapter holds that information.

Chapter 1 also lets you gauge your MP3 knowledge and confirm whether you've been hearing rumors or fact on the Internet and in magazines.

Please Don't Read This!

Many computer books quickly sink into the mire of technical goo. This book wades above the goo level by telling you everything you need to know about MP3 as quickly and as simply as possible. Still, you may want to know what a few of those weird audio technology words mean. Complicated, engineering-level material is marked *Technical Stuff*. Feel free to steer on past it and return when you're in the mood.

And What about You?

Chances are, you're a music lover. You're not necessarily a computer lover, but you know enough to get by. You're fairly new to the terms and concepts surrounding MP3, and you just need something to get you started.

When your computer mumbles something about "proxy servers," and you just want to listen to that hot new band, this book shows you how to break down the barriers and get back to the good stuff.

That's why you need this book — a quick reference allowing you to return to the music.

How This Book Is Organized

Whenever we come home from the grocery store, I love packing the refrigerator. I just get a weird, Tetris-like thrill from trying to fit the tortillas, orange juice, asparagus, and everything else into the shelves and hydrators.

So it's no surprise that I've organized this book into five basic sections, each designed to serve a basic need:

Part I: What's MP3 and How Do I Use It?

Start here for the basics. In Chapter 1, I describe each topic in the book in simple terms. Consider it an expanded Cheat Sheet; head here when you're looking for a few memory-jogging hints.

When you need more information about that topic, you'll find an entire chapter devoted to it elsewhere in the book.

Part II: Downloading and Playing MP3 Files from the Internet

Okay, where *are* all those MP3 songs? Here I show you how to locate the free MP3 songs floating around the Internet (and set up your Internet browser or file-swapping program to ferret them out automatically). Then you discover how to play the songs on your computer or portable MP3 player.

Sick of your computer's tiny speakers? You find out how to connect your computer's sound card to your fancy home stereo — and what to do if that suddenly makes everything sound *worse*.

Big Fun Department: Broadcast your own MP3 Internet radio station for the bopping pleasure of your friends worldwide.

Part III: Creating Your Own MP3 Files

When you're tired of everybody else's MP3s, here's how to make your own — legally — from your own CDs, records, tapes, or even the soundtrack from a TV or VCR.

After you get the MP3-creation bug, and your hard drive begins to fill, this section shows how to store hundreds of songs onto a single CD using a CD-RW (Read/Write) drive.

Part IV: MP3s for the Musician

Do you play guitar in the woods? Do you fiddle around with a home studio or tape recorder? Or are you a band member who's tiring of the bar scene? This part of the book helps musicians create and record compositions and transform the recordings into professional-quality MP3s.

This section also contains interviews with musicians who use MP3 to further their careers. Discover the secrets used by 18-year-old musician Alex Smith to earn nearly $100,000 by releasing his own MP3 tunes on the Internet.

Part V: The Part of Tens

A tradition in *For Dummies* books, The Part of Tens contains information organized into quick-scan lists of factoids. Here you find the ten best places to get MP3 files, ten ways MP3 makes you a better musician, the ten best MP3 programs, ten quick ways to make MP3s do what you want, and other tendrils of information that didn't quite fit anywhere else.

Part VI: Appendixes

Several goodies ride back here. A glossary defines some of the uglier code words used by MP3 aficionados. Plus, you find instructions for all the goodies contained on the CD bound into this book's back cover. The CD contains dozens of MP3 songs, along with all the MP3 software you need to begin making and playing your own MP3s.

Icons Used in This Book

Computer users can't escape icons — little push buttons with pictures. Because this book is a computer book, icons just seem to fall into place. Here's what each icon in this book means so that you can read them or flip past them quickly.

Look here for particularly sound advice. These tips show you how to improve the sound quality of your computer or MP3 player.

This icon makes it easier to find the stuff you're supposed to remember.

Feel free to skip over this one. It marks technical stuff you really don't need to know. But if you want to travel a bit deeper into the MP3 world, you can find some directions plotted out here.

A heavy-duty, non-fading tip hides here. Read this paragraph for a simple way to speed things up, for instance, or boost the sound quality.

You're heading into dangerous ground here. Be extra careful or something quite unpleasant may happen.

This icon directs you to the bonus CD-ROM bundled into the back of this book for all kinds of free goodies.

Where to Go from Here

Open Chapter 1 and give it a quick rundown. It'll either confirm what you know or tell you what areas you need to brush up on. Enjoy!

Part I

What's MP3 and How Do I Use It?

The 5th Wave   By Rich Tennant

"It's okay. We were just enjoying an MP3 of the Scorpions' 'Rock You Like a Hurricane'."

In this part . . .

*I*t took some effort, but "MP3" finally surpassed "sex" as the most requested search term on the Internet. *Rolling Stone* and even cooler magazines talk about MP3 as the next big thing. People yak about it over the Internet and in the corners at cocktail parties. But what exactly is it?

MP3 is simply a boring technology that squishes audio files into less than 10 percent of their size while retaining nearly CD-quality sound. And the size and sound quality are the exciting parts: These tiny hi-fi computer files can be quickly copied and sent over the Internet.

Being new, MP3 confuses many people. Are MP3s really legal? Which are legal and which aren't? How can you tell the difference? Where are the free MP3 songs, and how can you get them? How can you play them? How can you convert your own CDs to MP3 files? If you're a musician, how can you record your songs and convert them to MP3? More importantly, how can a band make money from its MP3 songs?

This section explains all the answers, plus some vital information you didn't know you needed to know. You'll find ways to turn your computer into an MP3 player — and one that sounds as good or better than your home stereo.

Chapter 1

Just Get Me Going!

*I*n this chapter, I examine the bare-bones basics of MP3 — the breakthrough format for squeezing large audio files into one-tenth their normal size. When you're ready for some meatier information, check out Chapter 2 to put the information on your plate.

Dig in.

Joining the Pack of MP3 Users

Technically speaking, zillions of people use MP3 technology today. MP3 tunes are blasted from home stereos, cars, portable players, some cellular phones, and a Casio wristwatch. Here's how people are using MP3 today. You're probably familiar with some of these uses; others may give you some ideas.

Music lovers

The majority of MP3 users love music. Although some MP3 files contain speeches or narrated books, most MP3 contain music. Why?

Because converting music to MP3 makes the following tasks easier:

- ✔ **Collecting and trading songs:** Many MP3 enthusiasts head for the Internet's musical buffet trays known as Napster and Gnutella, which I describe in Chapter 5. Those programs enable visitors to copy MP3 songs from each other's hard drives, although the legality of the process falls in and out of question. In its heyday, Napster offered more than a million songs from today's most popular albums, all up for grabs.

- ✔ **Creating personal radio stations:** MP3 "radio stations" allow people to listen to or create their own radio stations. Anybody with an Internet account can broadcast his or her MP3 collection to listeners anywhere in the world. (Tune in to Chapter 8.)

MusicMatch lets you "personalize" an Internet radio station so it's based on your musical tastes. Type in the name of your favorite artist, and MusicMatch creates a station for playing that artist's music, as well as music from similar musicians you may enjoy. Type **Beatles**, for example, and MusicMatch begins playing Beatles songs, as well as songs from similar artists that you would enjoy. (Much more about MusicMatch in Chapter 11.)

- ✔ **Finding rare songs:** Can't find an old, out-of-print song that's in the public domain? Chances are, someone has converted it to MP3 and uploaded it to the Internet for free downloading. The Internet's under-popularized Newsgroups (Chapter 3) contain a wealth of older MP3 tunes, sorted by decade and genre.

- ✔ **Making Greatest Hits CDs:** The latest batch of inexpensive CD-RW drives read from *and* write to CDs. Software bundled with this book will convert MP3 files back into normal CD files and copy them to a CD for your home or car stereo to play. (I show you how in Chapter 12.)

- ✔ **Organizing songs:** Computers organize huge numbers of songs much better than those tall, black CD racks. No more fiddling with plastic CD cases or home stereo knobs when you want to hear an old favorite. You can double-click that MP3 file's name and hear it play for immediate satisfaction. Plus, a CD usually holds about ten songs. Hard drives hold thousands.

- ✔ **Listening to music on-the-go:** Get out of the way, Sony Discman. Most portable MP3 players don't have any moving parts: That means skateboarders won't hear any sound skips or bumps, even when rail-sliding down the stairs at City Hall. (Chapter 7 covers portable MP3 players.)

- ✔ **Trading bootleg recordings:** Some people make copies of CDs or a band's live show and trade or give them away. If the artist hasn't authorized the distribution of those copies, these CD copiers are currently breaking the law. In fact, so are the people in possession of illegal copied MP3s. More on this bit of ugliness in Chapter 20.

✔ **Finding new bands:** Today's record company agents don't seek musical talent as much as they look for music that *sells*, which leads to waves of newly signed bands with the same sound. Using MP3, undiscovered bands post their songs inexpensively on the Internet, giving the public the first chance to hear new talent. (Bands get their own section later in this chapter, as well as Chapters 13 through 15.)

Musicians

For every band riding the Billboard charts, hundreds of thousands of undiscovered bands still play their Stratocasters in the garage. Most bands can barely afford beer. Without large gobs of money, bands can't distribute their CDs through the music store chains or pay the marketing and advertising costs to expose people to their music. (And who do you have to know to get your tune on a TV show like *Dawson's Creek?*)

MP3 lowers the costs of a chance at success. Any musician with a PC and some microphones can record a song. The computer then creates an MP3 version and uploads the tune to dozens of Internet sites showcasing new talent. MP3.com, one of the leading Web sites carrying MP3 files, offers more than 750,000 songs from 100,000 musicians worldwide.

Many bands — both signed and unsigned — now bypass the record labels and retail chains and use MP3 technology to let millions of people hear their songs, with these potential results:

✔ If listeners like what they hear on a band's MP3, they may buy the band's homemade CD through the mail. Also, MP3.com has a "Payback" system that pays bands based on the amount of activity on their account. (In Chapter 15, I profile some of the most successful money-makers. Chapter 16 explains the convoluted formula MP3.com uses when dishing out the cash.)

✔ The listeners are happy, because they're hearing fresh, new talent that they've discovered themselves. The band's happy because it can compete on merit, not cash.

✔ In fact, everybody's happy except the recording industry and music stores.

Record companies

A few savvy record companies have finally realized that they can embrace MP3 technology instead of battling it. Some labels ask a monthly fee for unlimited downloads from their catalogs. (Check out www.emusic.com in Chapter 16.) Other labels release a few of their artists' tunes in MP3 format and then offer to sell the entire CD through mail order.

The record industry keeps resisting the digital era, however, fearing that it'll lose money. (Maybe record industry executives should talk to the companies who stuff free product samples into our newspapers, magazines, and mailboxes.)

As more record companies view MP3 as a cost-effective marketing tool, you'll hear even more mainstream MP3 songs released legally on the Internet.

Disc jockeys

Your average disc jockey hates toting around turntables, CD players, and boxes of records. Today's ultra-fashionable DJ carries a laptop to work. It's easier to mix MP3 songs on a laptop and pump the results out to the dance floor.

Using MP3, DJs create and store an evening's worth of music on the computer. As the songs play back, the DJ blends them into each other, subtly speeding them up or slowing them down so they play at the same beat. DJs can add special effects and incorporate digital tricks unavailable on the turntable.

- ✔ One of the most popular programs that brings MP3s to the dance floor, Virtual Turntables (www.carrot.prohosting.com), replaces expensive equipment with an on-screen multichannel mixer board. Cyberknobs include fading, backspin, scratching, balance adjustment, and an automatic pitch-matching system.

- ✔ Another popular MP3 DJ program, BPM Studio (www.bpmstudio.com), offers Lite, Home, and Professional versions, increasing the features at every level. The Home version works fine for creating simple mixes. The Professional version offers an elaborate 19-inch control panel that fits into a musician's "rack."

- ✔ Some MP3 DJ programs mechanically overlap songs by a set number of seconds, leaving an evening of boring mixes. OtsJuke DJ (www.otsjuke.com) analyzes the beginnings and ends of songs and varies its mixes accordingly.

- ✔ Visiosonic (www.visiosonic.com) gives away MP3 DJ software with point-and-click control knobs, sliders, and other gizmos that keep DJs and broadcasters happy. Upgrade to more elaborate versions that record your most inspired on-the-fly mixes for later use.

New MP3 disc jockey programs pop up all the time. To find the most current, search for *disc jockey* and *MP3* using one of the search engines that I describe in Chapter 3.

Print media

MP3 files aren't just filled with tunes. Check out Audible.com or Salon.com for the latest spoken word files. At last look, John Grisham offered a narration of his bestseller *The Brethren* for two dollars. For a buck, pick up an MP3 file narrating *The New York Times,* updated daily.

The Audible site also carries MP3-format *audiobooks* with lectures, readings, and business/technology news. (I cover this MP3 format in Chapter 3.)

Comedy lovers

Comedians quickly jumped on the MP3 stage. They're converting sets into MP3 format, distributing them on the Net for free, and hoping that chuckling listeners may laugh their way to the music store and buy their latest CD.

At last look, Audible.com gave away two of Robin Williams's new Internet talk shows — offering a taste at what you'll hear in upcoming shows. The Internet has carried authorized stand-up comedy MP3s from George Carlin, Red Foxx, Maryellen Hooper, and John Pinette (the big guy who gets car-jacked in the last episode of *Seinfeld*).

Students

Other than listening to tunes while running to class (or sitting in class), students use MP3 technology in another important way: Some portable MP3 players also serve as digital tape recorders, letting you record notes or even classroom lectures (if you have the professor's permission, of course).

Taking a literature class? The Audible Web site (www.audible.com) carries poems by Emily Dickinson and study guides to works like *The Great Gatsby.* Audible.com lets you download hundreds of lectures and courses from Harvard and Stanford. Some are free; others require payment.

Studying Martin Luther King Jr. or Winston Churchill? Download their free speeches to hear what they *really* sounded like. You can also find foreign language tutorials to get a flavor of what you're trying to speak.

Understanding the Legalities (And Illegalities) of MP3

The technology behind MP3 is perfectly legal. So are baseball bats, automobiles, and laser pointers. All of these things can be used illegally, however.

Standard disclaimer: Digital music issues are still being tossed around in the courts. But let's start with what's generally assumed to be legal: Downloading MP3 songs from the Internet if the artist has authorized those songs for distribution is completely legal.

Nobody will press charges if you make MP3 copies of your CDs, albums, and soundtracks for your own personal use.

Now, for the illegal parts. Giving away or selling any of the MP3 copies you've made from your CDs, albums, or video sound tracks is illegal. Some Web sites say downloading a bootleg MP3 is okay "if you only keep it 24 hours." That's not true. It's still illegal. Just keep in mind the following points:

✔ In short, MP3 technology *is* legal, and you're encouraged to download, copy, and trade authorized MP3s. *Authorized* means that the MP3 files have been approved for distribution by the artist who created them. (Turn to Chapter 17 for a list of many legitimate Web sites that carry authorized — legal — MP3s.)

✔ Feel free to make your own MP3 copies from your own collection of CDs. You can even copy those MP3 songs onto another CD using your computer's CD-RW drive — as long as you don't give away or sell either the original CD or the copy you've made. If you give away the copy, you must destroy the original, or vice versa.

✔ To be perfectly clear, any time you make unauthorized copies and give them away, sell them, or post them on a Web site, you're breaking the law.

✔ Trading unauthorized MP3 songs means the record company doesn't make any money. Many consumers won't cry over that. But illegal MP3s also take money from the artist who created the work — no matter how little the record company might be paying them.

✔ I cover copyrights, their implications, and the legal clouds surrounding them in Chapter 20.

Finding the Best MP3 Files

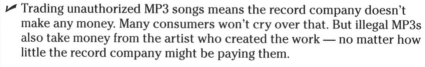

Millions of MP3 files are scattered around the Internet. The key is to know where to look:

- ✔ **Check out the list of Web sites in Chapter 17.** Additionally, Chapter 3 shows you how to locate the Internet's most current MP3 Web sites using search engines. The search engines automatically scour the Internet to locate MP3 sites and songs.

- ✔ **Visit some Internet newsgroups.** These groups are a completely separate world from the Web, yet they provide some of the easiest places to find MP3 files and information — check out Chapter 4 to find out more about newsgroups.

- ✔ **Use FTP (*File Transfer Protocol*) — one of the fastest and most complicated ways to find MP3 files.** You need special software and a detective's cap to figure it all out, but when the switches are set correctly, it's a rocket. I describe FTP in Chapters 3 and 4.

- ✔ **Let file swapping software turn your computer into an MP3-fetching robot (see Chapter 5).** These programs scour the Internet for MP3 files and return a list, ready to be checked out.

Check out the Part of Tens in the back of the book; many Web sites now review authorized MP3s uploaded by bands. By reading the reviews, you can narrow your downloads to the bands you think you'll enjoy the most.

Playing and Creating MP3 Songs

You can listen to MP3 files on your computer, provided it has a sound card and speakers. For the best sound, however, connect the computer's sound card to your home stereo, as I describe in Chapter 6.

Away from home? Portable MP3 players, which I cover in Chapter 7, are the latest toys for taking your music with you. Some PDAs already play MP3s. Most Windows CE palmtops play MP3 files, and the Handspring Visor plays MP3 files through a snap-on module from Good Technology (www.good.com).

By itself, the ever-popular Palm Pilot lacks the muscle required for MP3 playback or storage. Keep your eyes out for PocketPyro (www.pocketpyro.com), however. The company is slowly developing a standalone MP3 player that also clips onto a Palm III, letting you organize song titles through the Palm's screen. Stay tuned.

Creating MP3 files from your own CDs

Creating an MP3 file is a two-step process: ripping and encoding.

> ✔ *Ripping* means placing your musical CD — the latest by Britney Spears, for example — into your computer's CD-ROM drive and telling the software to copy a song or songs into huge files onto your hard drive. (I cover ripping in Chapter 9.)
>
> ✔ *Encoder* software then compresses those huge files (known as WAV files on the PC and AIF files on the MAC) into the much smaller MP3 format, letting you delete the original recording. (Chapter 10 covers this process.)

Some "all-in-one" software, such as MusicMatch, rips and encodes in one step. Just insert the CD, and, after a few minutes, your MP3 files appear on the hard drive.

Creating MP3 files off your records, DVDs, TV, radio, or movie soundtracks

MP3 files aren't always created from CDs, although that's the easiest method. Any recording can be turned into an MP3 file by connecting a few wires from the back of your home stereo's amplifier to your computer's sound card. (In Chapter 9, I describe the process, the adapters you'll need, where to find them, and how to route them.)

Turning your own songs into MP3 files

Elvis Costello put out 12 albums in ten years, but most musicians take a bit longer and have a little more trouble composing, recording, and editing their songs. But when they're finally through creating their masterwork, it's time for the grunt work of turning it into an MP3 file.

Chapter 14 offers tips for musicians on recording and editing their compositions; Chapter 15 explains subtle ways to convert the songs into the highest-quality MP3 files.

Copying MP3 files onto CDs

If your computer has a CD-RW drive, you can free up your hard drive by storing your MP3 files onto CDs, a process that I describe in Chapter 11.

Because songs on a CD that you buy in a record store are stored in a special file format that's much larger than MP3, those CDs usually hold less than a dozen songs. By compressing those songs with MP3 and storing the resulting MP3 files onto a blank CD, you can usually fit hundreds of MP3 files onto a single CD.

Just insert your newly created MP3 disc into your computer, load up your MP3 player, and start listening to the tunes. Remember, though, MP3 is a different format than the one used for standard, "record store" CDs. These MP3 CDs won't play on your normal, home stereo.

The songs found on a CD purchased at a record store are known simply as "audio CDs." These songs are stored in a different format than MP3. They play in both your computer and your home stereo's CD player, but their bloated file format means only 10 or so songs fit onto the CD. A CD with MP3 files plays on your computer, but it won't play on your home stereo's CD player. But MP3's compressed file format lets you store hundreds of songs on the CD.

If you want to listen to MP3 songs in your normal, home stereo's CD player, you must convert the MP3 file back to the normal, "record store" format.

To fix the situation, use software that reads the MP3 file and decompresses it back into the size that home stereos can recognize. Because the music files return to normal size, you can fit only the normal number of songs — 10 or 12 — on the CD. I cover the process in Chapter 12.

What's an MP3 file, anyway?

A German research firm, the Fraunhofer Institute, developed a file-compression technique back in 1991 that squeezes songs to roughly one-tenth the size of a normal audio CD file.

The Motion Picture Experts Group (MPEG) approved the new compression technique as an Official Standard and dubbed it "MPEG-1 Audio Layer 3." Everybody else simply calls it "MP3."

Many Internet users embraced MP3 technology as a quick and convenient way to send music files back and forth through e-mail and Web sites.

Contrary to popular belief, MP3 files don't always contain near CD-quality sound. MP3 technology can squish files with varying degrees of compression. But MPEG-1 Audio Layer 3 defines a specific level of compression that preserves near CD-quality for music files.

The Cheat Sheet at the front of this book compares compression rates and sound quality. The more you compress a sound file, the smaller it becomes, but the worse it sounds. (**Hint:** Most MP3 songs are compressed at 128 Kbps to preserve their high sound quality.)

So, how does MP3 technology work? When sounds are digitized, the computer normally grabs *all* the sound and stores it as numbers. Even if parts of the sound are beyond the range of human hearing, they're digitized and stored anyway. (Your dog may be able to hear them.)

MP3 technology compresses the file by removing any numbers representing sounds beyond the range of human hearing. Technically, MP3 files aren't the same as a CD audio file. Realistically, however, they sound pretty darn close.

How does MP3 differ from other compression formats?

Computerized sound formats vary widely in their size and sound quality.

The tamest, MIDI files, don't contain music or any type of audio. Instead, they contain instructions for musical instruments: which notes to play at what time, and for how long. But when the instruments follow the instructions, they play a song. MIDI files sound wildly different depending on how they're played back. On a cheap sound card, the file may sound like a toy organ. An expensive synthesizer playing the same MIDI song could sound like a ragtime piano with a stand-up bass being slapped in the background. A five-minute song averages about 40K, depending on the detail of instructions.

The largest of the group, WAV files, contain uncompressed sound recordings. They sound the best, but a five-minute song copied from a CD averages around 50MB.

MP3 shrinks that same five-minute song to around 4.5MB, yet preserves the sound quality so that it's nearly indistinguishable from the original.

An older format, MOD, takes loops of compressed sound and repeats them to create songs. You can't record a live performance and store it in MOD format. You just build songs on a computer. Size varies wildly, but a five-minute song rarely consumes more than 40K.

RealAudio earned fame by broadcasting audio over the Internet — a process known as *streaming*. RealAudio's compression system works to enhance fast streaming, not quality, so MP3 almost always sounds much better. RealAudio's contribution to MP3 is RealAudio Jukebox, which converts CDs into MP3 files and organizes the collection.

Microsoft's Windows Media Audio (WMA) format typifies the company's business insight. When Microsoft sees something take off, it either buys it or copies it. In this case, it hauled out its own format, got Mick Fleetwood to say it was cool at Los Angeles' House of Blues, and hoped it would kill MP3. But the format's built-in copyright protection struck a sour note with MP3 fans. Microsoft's latest version of Windows Media Player (Version 6.0 and above) plays both WMA and MP3 formats.

Yamaha, a huge music corporation, created the VQF (Transform-Domain Weighted Interleave Vector Quantization) format that's grown a large fan base. VQF sounds better and creates smaller files than MP3. If your computer struggles with MP3, though, it'll choke on VQF, which requires a faster processor. Both formats are fairly close in sound quality and size, but MP3 is much more widely accepted. Check out www.vqf.com for more information.

Finally, some sets of files end in rar or r00. Although still obscure, this format is rapidly gaining momentum with the video crowd because of its ability to compress gargantuan files. Head to www.rarsoft.com for the full scoop.

Chapter 2

Turning Your Computer into an MP3 Machine

Can your computer keep up with MP3? After all, computers were designed for playing with numbers, not playing back Jimi Hendrix leads.

Compressing guitar riffs into MP3 files takes lots of processing power. Converting those MP3 files back into tunes also takes lots of on-the-fly oomph.

Processor power alone isn't enough. After the MP3 rush consumes you, your MP3 collection will begin clogging your hard drive. Huge hard drives will begin catching your eye at the computer store. Or maybe you'll need Iomega's solution of swappable cartridges: The Iomega Jaz system stuffs around 500 MP3s onto a single cartridge — and you can play back and record songs to and from the cartridge.

Thinking about creating audio CDs with your favorite songs? Then you'll want a CD drive that can write to compact discs as well as read from them.

This chapter serves as both a computer doctor and a mechanic. It helps you examine your computer to see where it needs a little more muscle. Then it provides instructions for bringing it up to snuff, whether that means adding a new CPU, hard drive, CD-ROM drive, an Iomega Jaz drive, or a better sound card.

Actually, this chapter's an accountant, too. Some of these upgrades can be downright expensive, so keep this formula in mind: If your planned upgrades cost more than 60 percent of a new computer's price tag, start looking for deals on a new computer. (It's what you really want, anyway, and it may prove to be more cost effective.)

Computing Muscle Required for MP3

To create or play MP3s well, you need a Pentium or a very fast 486 running Windows 95, Windows 98, Windows Me, Windows NT, or Windows 2000. Then add at least 16MB RAM, a high-quality sound card, and a pair of amplified speakers.

Those of the Macintosh mindset need at least a PowerMac with 6840 or faster processor running OS 7 or later, but a Mac G3 or G4 running OS 9.1 is preferred for more MP3 fiddling.

The less powerful your PC, the longer it takes to create MP3s. Some underpowered PCs strain during playback, adding distracting skips and pops to the music. The least powerful computers can't create MP3s; they can only play them back.

Don't forget to upgrade your Internet connection for the *real* MP3 experience. MP3 files consume several megabytes of disk space. Speedy modems download MP3 files much more quickly, and Internet radio stations sound much better, too. If cable modem service is available in your community, go for it. You'll love it.

- ✔ Although IBM-compatible computers currently rule the MP3 market, they're certainly not the only MP3-compatible computers. Apple fans can create and play MP3s on a PowerMac running System 7 or above. iMacs, too, can make and play MP3s with their PowerPC engine.

- ✔ All Microsoft PocketPCs and some Windows CE palmtops play back MP3 tunes, but neither can create them. Check Chapter 7 for hints on choosing a portable MP3 player.

- ✔ Music-loving programmers have been busy. In addition to the standard, Windows-based MP3 players, programmers have written players for DOS, Macintosh, Amiga, Atari, OS/2, BeOS, FreeBSD, Solaris, Linux, SunOS, IRIX, HP-UX, AIX, and other UNIX platforms.

- ✔ Programmers constantly create new programs for creating and playing MP3 files. The latest ones usually appear on `www.mpeg.org`, listed under MP3 Players.

Do I really need a Pentium III for MP3?

A Pentium III is basically a Pentium II with some extra graphics capability. MP3 players don't have to handle graphics, so there's little reason to worry about upgrading to a Pentium III strictly to play MP3s. A Pentium II works fine, as does a fast Pentium or Pentium Pro.

That's not to say that you should stick with your 486, though. MusicMatch, the handy all-in-one MP3 creation-and-playback software,

recommends a 300 MHz MMX Pentium II or better with at least 64MB RAM. (Don't worry; MusicMatch still runs on a plain ol' Pentium class 200 MHz processor with only 32MB of RAM.)

If you're stuck with a 486 and no spare cash, stick with WinAmp, a freebie MP3 player that's included on this book's CD, along with MusicMatch.

Choosing the Right CPU Upgrade for Your Computer

Upgrading a computer's Central Processing Unit or *CPU* seems easy enough. You remove the case, pull out the old chip, push in a compatible replacement, and screw the case back on. The problem is dealing with the disappointment when you first turn on the computer. Unfortunately, doubling your computer's processing speed rarely makes it run twice as fast.

Your computer's speed depends on many things, including its amount of memory, motherboard speed (known as *bus* speed), and hard drive speed (particularly the amount of free space left on it). Even a slow graphics card can hold back your computer's performance.

Don't be surprised if that new CPU only speeds up your computer by 25 percent. And if that new CPU doesn't increase the speed by at least 100 MHz, the results probably won't even be noticeable enough to warrant the upgrade.

Several companies make upgrades for your CPU; they keep releasing upgrades faster than I can type them into a book. Table 2-1 shows some of the most popular upgrade makers and their Web sites.

Table 2-1		CPU Upgrade Makers
This company . . .	*. . . found here . . .*	*. . . does this*
Evergreen	www.evertech.com	Evergreen's products upgrade a 486, a Pentium III, and just about everything in between. (While there, check out Evergreen's portable MP3/CD player.)
Kingston	www.kingston.com	The world's largest independent memory manufacturer, Kingston also carries an impressive array of inexpensive CPU upgrades.
AMD	www.amd.com	Many companies sell inexpensive "upgrade kits" based on the popular AMD series of CPUs. The AMD Web site keeps a current list of companies selling the kits.
PowerLeap	www.powerleap.com	PowerLeap tackles some of the most difficult upgrades by mounting its replacement chips on a tiny circuit board. Flip the tiny switches on the board to make it compatible with the CPU that you're replacing.

Consider the following when choosing a CPU upgrade:

- ✔ The newer the chip, the more expensive it is to upgrade. That's why it costs less to upgrade a 486 to a Pentium than it does to upgrade a slow Pentium II to a faster Pentium II.

- ✔ Before buying an upgrade chip for your computer, scrutinize the chip's Web site for a list of incompatible systems. The upgrade chips don't work with all computers; some come with programs to determine eligibility.

- ✔ If your computer is more than four years old — or if the chipmaker recommends it — make sure that your computer is running the most current BIOS available before adding the new CPU. The Web site of your computer's manufacturer usually carries a program to update a computer's BIOS. The upgrade chip manufacturer can usually help you here.

When upgrading your computer's CPU, keep in mind the following:

- ✔ **Tools:** One hand, a screwdriver, and the replacement CPU's manual.
- ✔ **Cost:** Anywhere from $75 to $600, depending on the power.

✔ **Stuff to watch out for:** Static electricity can zap a CPU. Tap your computer's case to ground yourself before touching the CPU. If you live in a particularly dry, static-prone area, wear rubber gloves — the kind that doctors and dentists wear these days.

Follow these steps to upgrade your computer's CPU to a faster model.

1. **Check the manual or the upgrade manufacturer's Web site to make sure your upgrade chip is compatible with your computer.**

   Installing an incompatible CPU into your computer can destroy it. Check the manufacturer's guarantees and compatibility list *very* carefully before ordering and installing the chip.

   While you're looking around in the manual and on the Web site, check to see whether you need a BIOS upgrade, as well.

2. **Unplug your computer, and remove the cover.**

   If you live in a dry area with static, buy a *grounding wrist strap* to fasten between your wrist and the computer's case.

   No static problem? Then just touch the case to ground yourself before starting.

3. **Find your computer's Central Processing Unit (CPU) on the motherboard.**

   Your computer's processor is usually the largest black square thing on the motherboard — the large plastic sheet that everything plugs into.

4. **Remove the original processor.**

   Some chips come with a little lever. Pull the lever, and the old processor pops out, ready for replacement. Other chips need to be pried out with a little metal tool. (The cheap tools usually come inside the new CPU's box.)

   A socket with a little lever is called a Zero Insertion Force (ZIF) socket. A lever-less socket is a Low Insertion Force (LIF) socket.

5. **Examine the holes in the socket and the pins in the CPU.**

   Make sure that you're putting the right CPU into the socket. The pins and holes should line up exactly. (Look for a "notch" in the corner of the CPU and socket and match them up.) Check the replacement CPU's instructions; chips requiring a socket with a lever won't work if there's no lever.

6. **Line up the chip's pins over the socket's holes; then gently push the processor into the socket.**

   Don't bend any pins. Please. And don't push too hard; sometimes a motherboard can crack, making you head back to the computer store and frown while buying a new one.

7. **If your new processor came with a cooling fan, install it per the installation instructions.**

   The more powerful your processor, the more it heats up. (Just ask the guy at the airport with a laptop on his lap.) Some upgrade chips need a tiny fan to keep them cool. In fact, some chips come with a fan mounted right on their backs.

8. **Close the socket handle, if necessary, screw the cover back on your computer, plug it in, and see whether it runs more quickly.**

   Hopefully, you'll notice a difference in computer speed, especially when converting CDs to MP3s.

Installing a Card

Whether you're installing a basic-level sound card or a SCSI card controller for an Iomega disk drive, the steps remain the same. And they're surprisingly easy. This section shows how to install a new card, whatever species it may be.

Many multimedia computers come with four speakers, ready to play back Surround Sound. Although four speakers may sound cool for a while, Surround Sound was really designed for DVD players that play back movies recorded with Surround Sound technology. Although it's great for computer games, the technology doesn't really make MP3 songs sound any better.

To install a new card, keep in mind the following:

   ✔ **Tools:** One hand and a screwdriver.

   ✔ **Cost:** Anywhere from $50 to $300 and more.

   ✔ **Stuff to watch out for:** Cards are particularly susceptible to static electricity. Tap your computer's case to ground yourself before touching the card. If you live in a particularly dry, static-prone area, wear rubber gloves — the kind that make cool snapping sounds when you yank them on your fingertips.

Be careful not to bend the cards while installing them. Doing so can damage their circuitry.

Cards are pretty easy to install. They're self-contained little units. For example, they suck electricity right out of that little slot that they plug into. You don't need to plug special power cables into them. (A wire from some CD players connects to some sound cards, however, to route the sound directly to the card.)

Cards come in several different lengths and standards. Be sure that you buy the right type of card for your computer. Usually the choice runs between PCI and ISA cards. (PCI slots are always shorter than ISA slots and usually white; ISA slots are always longer than PCI slots and usually black. Check your computer's manual to be sure.)

Cards are delicate. Handle them only by their edges. Even the oil from your fingers can damage their circuitry.

Also, those innocent silver dots on one side of the card often conceal sharp metal pokers that leave scratches across the back of your hand.

Some cards are longer and fatter than others. You may need to rearrange some of your existing cards to accommodate new cards of different lengths and thicknesses.

To install a card, follow these steps:

1. **Turn off your computer, unplug it, and remove the cover.**

2. **Find the slot that's the right size for your card.**

   See the row of slots along the inside of your computer? Some are already filled with cards. And see the row of slots along the back of your computer, where cables plug into the backs of the cards? Your new card plugs into a slot adjacent to the other cards. A sound card's holes and ports are then accessible from outside the PC.

   Examine the slots closely; then examine the slots along the bottom of your card. Slots vary in size; you need one that will fit your card *exactly.*

   Don't confuse your computer's expansion slots — the ones where the cards plug in — with its much-smaller memory slots, where the RAM chips slide in.

   If you have a lot of room, keep your cards spaced as far apart as possible. Doing so keeps them a little cooler.

3. **Remove the slot's cover.**

   Unused slots usually have a little cover to keep dust from flying in through the back of your computer. With a small screwdriver, remove the screw that holds the cover in place. Don't lose the screw! You need it to secure the card in place.

   Dropped the screw in there "somewhere"? Turn the computer on its side and shake it gently until the screw falls out. You can't leave it inside there, or it may short-circuit something important.

   Removed the dropped screw? Keep it handy, as well as the little cover bracket. You'll want to replace the cover if you ever remove the card.

4. **Push the card into its slot.**

   To spare yourself some possible aggravation, first check your card's manual to see whether you need to flip any of the card's switches or move any of its *jumpers* — little prongs with a movable bar. Then you won't have to take the card back out if it's not working right.

Holding the card by its edges, position it over the slot, as shown in Figure 2-1. The shiny silver edge with the holes in it should face toward the *back* of your computer.

Figure 2-1:
The card's
two tabs
should fit
perfectly
into one of
your
computer's
slots.

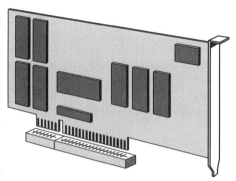

Slots come in several sizes. Modern computers come with PCI (Peripheral Component Interface) slots for the Pentium's Plug and Play technology, and an occasional ISA (Industry Standard Architecture) slot to stay compatible with older cards. PCI slots are shorter; ISA slots are longer. Your card can only fit into one of the slots, so compare the tabs on the card's bottom with the holes in the slots.

Push the card slowly into the slot. You may need to rock it back and forth gently. When it pops in, you can feel it come to rest. Don't force it!

Don't leave any cards resting against any other cards. Doing so can cause electrical problems, and neither the card nor the computer will work.

5. **Secure the card in the slot with the screw.**

   Yep, all those expensive cards are held in place by a single screw. Make sure that you *use* a screw; don't just leave the card sitting there. Cards should be grounded to the computer's case. Without a secure connection, they may not work.

6. **Plug the computer back in, turn it on, and see whether the Windows fancy Plug and Play feature recognizes and installs the card.**

   Windows usually recognizes newly installed cards and sets them up to work correctly.

7. **If everything works, carefully put the cover back on — you're done!**

If the card still doesn't work, you probably have to run the card's installation software. Still doesn't work? Then try the following:

- ✔ Check the manual to make sure that the card's switches and jumpers are set correctly.

- ✔ You may have to run the card's software and restart your computer before it will work. That's because the software puts a driver in one of your computer's special areas. Your computer reads that file only when it's first turned on or when it's restarted.

- ✔ Make sure that the card is seated securely in its slot and screwed in reasonably tight.

- ✔ Make sure that the card is in the right slot and that each of its copper-colored tabs fits firmly into a slot.

- ✔ It can take some fiddling to get a card working right. The key is not to get frustrated.

- ✔ Nine times out of ten, the problem lies with the software. The card is sitting in the slot correctly, but the software is conflicting with some other software or not talking with the card.

- ✔ If the card still doesn't work, root around in its box for the manual. Most manuals list a technical support phone number or Web site that offers help.

Installing a Larger Hard Drive

It happened ever so slowly. But suddenly, your 8GB hard drive has only 500MB of free space. And you still need to convert your new *Trance Factory* CD.

It's no secret why your hard drive suddenly shrunk. MP3 files are huge. Sure, they're compressed files, but that doesn't mean they'll fit on a floppy. The Beatles' *I Am the Walrus* eats up 4MB.

If you're turning your computer into a music player, it's time for a second hard drive. Huge, fast hard drives now cost less than ever. Best yet, most large drives come with much-appreciated installation software to start the drive spinning.

The problem comes when figuring out which type of drive to buy. Over the years, manufacturers have created drives according to more than a dozen different standards. Today, two standards prevail; SCSI and EIDE. Being less expensive, EIDE currently rules the market. Unless you already have a SCSI drive, buy EIDE.

EIDE stands for Enhanced Integrated Device (or Drive) Electronics. Yawn. SCSI stands for Small Computer System Interface.

Also keep in mind the following tips:

✔ When buying a second drive, do yourself a favor and pick up a copy of PowerQuest's PartitionMagic software at the same time. The software makes it easy to install your new hard drive as your C drive, change your existing hard drive to your D drive, and then copy all the information from D to C. (That sounds boring, but it's very handy.)

✔ It takes more hard drive space to create an MP3 than to merely listen to it. Converting an entire CD at once can require 500MB of space or more. Find the largest hard drive you can afford. Then buy one a little bit bigger.

✔ Before installing a second hard drive, do these chores: Back up your hard drive, and use the Windows Control Panel's Add/Remove Programs icon to make a Windows Startup disk. Dig around for your original Windows CD. (You may need the CD's secret password code for installation; it's often on a sticker on the CD case, as well as with your manual.)

Installing or replacing an EIDE hard drive

✔ **Tools you need:** One hand, a screwdriver, and a system disk.

✔ **Cost:** Roughly $100 to $300.

✔ **Stuff to watch out for:** If you're replacing your current hard drive, make sure that you have a Windows system disk on hand. You'll need some of the programs on that disk.

Don't like fiddling around inside computers? Most computer shops will install your new drive for around $50 in labor costs.

When installing a new drive, make it your C: (or *master*) drive. The master drive is the one that the computer looks at first and boots from. The new drive will probably be faster, making Windows run faster, as well. Your old drive then becomes your secondary drive, or *slave*. You need to move a little jumper on the second drive to make that drive work as the slave (see Figure 2-2).

Some hard drives automatically set themselves up for one hard drive if they're set up as the master. You may have to check the drive's manual on this one.

You may need rails to mount your hard drive inside your computer. Some drives come with mounting rails; others don't. If you're replacing an old drive, you can often unscrew its old rails and swipe them. Otherwise, you may need to head back to the store to buy some. (They're usually pretty cheap.)

Okay, what's the complicated stuff?

If your system's more than a few years old, it may need a little pre-installation work. Most computers older than 1994 couldn't handle a hard drive much larger than 500MB. Later, the limits moved up to 2GB, then 8GB. Now, with hard drives even larger, computers face a new set of problems.

Some computers may need both an updated BIOS and a new controller card before they'll handle today's drives. Newer computers may need only an updated BIOS. Sensing problems, some manufacturers bundle installation software with their hard drives, written especially to "fool" the computers into ignoring any bothersome size limits.

So, what do you do? Find out any limits your computer model places on hard drive size. Its manuals or the manufacturer's Web site may have answers. While on the Web site, download a flash BIOS update, if needed. This piece of software updates your computer's BIOS, allowing it to read and write to larger drives.

Finally, to get the most out of an EIDE UltraDMA drive, make sure that your computer has a built-in UltraDMA interface on its motherboard. If it doesn't, buy an UltraDMA controller card (they're less than $50) to squeeze the most performance from your new drive.

The following steps show you how to install a second hard drive or replace your existing drive.

1. Create a System floppy disk.

Insert a blank floppy disk in drive A and open the Control Panel. Choose the Add/Remove Programs icon, click the Startup Disk tab, and choose Create Disk.

Without a System floppy, you may not be able to replace your old hard drive.

2. Make sure that your current hard drive is error-free; then back up its data.

Start by running the Windows ScanDisk program to ensure that your hard drive is error-free. Open My Computer, right-click the drive you want to replace, and choose Properties. Click the Tools tab, and choose the Check Now button. Doing so finds and repairs errors.

Next, back up your hard drive before removing it. You don't want to lose any of your data.

3. Turn off and unplug your computer and remove the case.

Before removing your computer's case, turn it off and unplug it. Then remove the computer's case by removing the screws holding it on.

Figure 2-2:
This hard
drive has
a power
supply
connector, a
ribbon cable
connector,
and a
master/
slave
jumper.

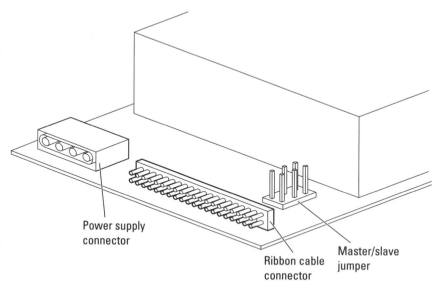

Power supply
connector

Ribbon cable
connector

Master/slave
jumper

4. **If you're replacing your hard drive, remove the cables from the old
   drive; if you're adding a second hard drive, don't remove the cables.**

   If you're adding a second drive, check out the flat ribbon cable connected to the first drive. Do you see a second, unused plug on it? If not,
   head back to the store for a new ribbon cable. It needs to have *two* connectors. (Most already do, luckily.) You second-drive installers can now
   jump ahead to Step 7.

   Hard drives have several cables plugged into them, including the following:

   - **Ribbon cable:** The ribbon cable leads from the hard drive to its
     controller card or the motherboard. The cable pulls straight off the
     drive pretty easily.

   - **Power cable:** The smaller cable is made of four wires that head for
     the power supply. Power cables come in two sizes, as shown in
     Figure 2-3. Like the ribbon cable, the power cable pulls straight off
     the drive's socket; it usually takes a *lot* more pulling, though. Don't
     pull on the wires themselves; pull on the cable's plastic connector.
     Sometimes a gentle back-and-forth jiggle can loosen it.

5. **Remove the mounting screws holding the drive in place.**

   Some drives are held in place by two screws in front. Other drives are
   held in place by screws in their sides. The screws on one side may be
   hidden from view by a particularly long card, or even another drive
   mounted on its side. That means you have to pull out the card or
   remove the obstructing drive just to get at the screws. Such a bother.

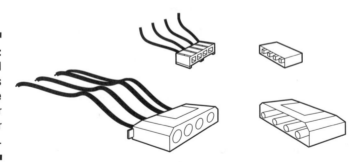

Figure 2-3:
Your hard
drive uses
one of these
two sizes for
the power
cable.

6. **Slide the old drive out of the computer.**

After you remove the old drive's cables and screws, you can slide the old drive out of the computer. Give it a gentle tug. Some drives slide out toward the computer's center; be sure not to gouge your motherboard while pulling out the drive.

Replacing a controller card: Will your new drive need a new controller card? (It will if it's an UltraDMA EIDE drive.) Then pull out your old controller card. Look for the card where all the ribbon cables end up. Found it? Pull all the ribbon cables off, including the ones heading for your floppy drives. See that tiny screw holding the controller card in place? Remove the screw and pull the card straight up out of its slot.

7. **Slide the new drive in where the old one came out.**

Adding a second drive? Slide it into a vacant bay, which usually is next to the first drive. Check your computer's manual; you may be able to mount the drive on its side in a special spot inside your computer.

If you're replacing drives, your new drive should slide in place right where the old one came out. Doesn't fit? If the new drive is smaller than the old one, you need to add rails or mounting brackets to make it fit.

When handling drives, be careful not to damage their exposed circuitry by bumping it into other parts of your computer. Also, be sure to touch your computer's metal case to get rid of any static electricity before picking up your drive.

8. **Add the new controller card if necessary.**

Are you replacing an older drive with an UltraDMA EIDE drive? Then, if the drive can't connect directly to your motherboard, you probably need a new controller card to go with it.

Handling the card by its edges, push it down into the slot where the old controller card sat. Then fasten it down with the screw. (You can find card installation instructions earlier in this chapter.) Check the controller's manual; you need to push ribbon cables onto the controller's connectors for your floppy disks and hard drive.

9. **Attach two cables to the hard drive.**

   Try sliding the drive out a little bit to connect the two cables more easily. (Refer to Figure 2-2 to see where each cable connects to the drive.)

   Ribbon cable: The plug on the ribbon cable should push onto little pins on the end of the drive. The other end of the cable either goes to the controller card or to a socket on the motherboard. (The edge of the cable with the red stripe connects to pin number one.)

   If you're installing a second hard drive, the ribbon cable should have a spare connector on it. (If not, head back to the store.) It doesn't matter which connector goes onto which drive; the computer looks at the drives' master/slave jumpers to figure out which one is drive C.

   Adding a second drive: If this is your second drive, look for its master/slave jumper. Make this second drive the master drive. Again, refer to Figure 2-2 to see the jumpers. The hard drive's manual tells you where to put the jumper. Make your old drive the slave drive.

   EIDE drives usually come configured as master drives. If you're installing just a single EIDE drive in your computer, you usually don't need to mess with any of the jumpers.

   Power supply: The power supply cable fits into the drive's socket only one way. Even so, check the ends to make sure that you're not forcing it in the wrong way. Check out Figure 2-2 to make sure that you've found the right power cable socket.

   Power supply cables come with both large and small connectors. The connectors are supposed to fit only one way, but the small ones often fit either way. The trick? Look for the number 1 somewhere near the drive's little socket. The power supply connector's red wire fastens onto the number 1 prong.

10. **Replace the screws.**

    Cables attached? Master/slave jumper set? Then fasten the drive in place with those little screws. Make sure that they are short screws to prevent damage to the inside of the hard drive.

11. **Replace the cover, plug in the computer, and turn it on.**

    Chances are, your hard drive won't work right off the bat. Hard drives must be prepared before they start to work, unfortunately. Take a deep breath before heading for the next step. Exhale. Now move on; it's time to break in that new hard drive.

Breaking in a new hard drive

Here are the last few hoops you need to jump through before your computer starts speaking to its new hard drive. If the hard drive comes with installation software, rejoice: You may not need to mess with this stuff. Otherwise, here's the scoop:

1. **Set the CMOS.**

   When your computer starts up, it usually says to press a certain key or sequence of keys to enter its Setup program. Enter the Setup program, find the hard drives area, and set both hard drives to "Auto." If your BIOS is new enough, your computer automatically detects the two drives and sets them up correctly.

   Your computer's Setup program is where your computer keeps track of the equipment connected to it. It needs to know what kind of hard drive you installed before you can use it.

   When your computer starts up, four things can happen:

   - Some drives come with installation programs. Run the program, and everything is taken care of. In fact, some programs even copy your old drive's contents onto your second drive.

   - Some drives check the CMOS to see what hard drive your computer expects to find. When you choose Auto, it automatically sets itself up to run properly. Blissfully simple! Move on to Step 2.

   - Other drives let you pick *any* hard drive that's listed in your computer's CMOS table. Choose any drive that's the same capacity (in megabytes) as your new drive, and all will be fine. A bit bothersome, but still workable.

   - The pickiest old drives make you look for information buried in their manuals. Specifically, you need to look for the drive's recommended *cylinders, heads,* and *sectors.* Then you need to plug those numbers into the CMOS *user-defined* area. Yeah, it's a little complicated, and only needed by old-fashioned computers. But if you're lucky, one of the first three options works.

2. **Partition the drive.**

   Partitioning a drive completely wipes out any information stored on it.

   After you finish setting the CMOS, you need to *partition* your new drive. Many drives come with a program for partitioning your new hard drive. Partitioning the drive divides it into chunks, assigning a letter to each chunk. You can divide your master drive into C and D, for example, assigning E to your slave drive.

   PowerQuest PartitionMagic software, shown in Figure 2-4, lets you change your partitions later on — even if you've already installed Windows and other programs — so don't worry if you want to rearrange your partitions later.

3. **Format the drive.**

   The Disc wizard or drive installation program bundled with most new EIDE drives automatically handles this as part of the installation process.

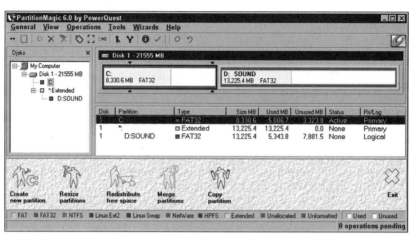

Figure 2-4: PowerQuest Partition-Magic software makes it easier to partition hard drives — even when they already contain information.

Formatting a disk completely wipes out any information stored on it.

4. Copy your information to the new drive.

If you replaced your drive, reinstall Windows and use the backup program to copy your old drive's information to the new drive.

If your new drive is now C and your old drive is D, use PowerQuest's PartitionMagic to copy everything over. (The Windows plain old "Copy" command can't handle this kind of thing.)

Installing a New Compact Disc Drive

Most CD drives created after 1998 let you make MP3s from your CDs. But to create your own CDs with your favorite MP3s, you need a CD drive that reads *and* writes to a CD.

- ✔ **Tools:** One hand and a screwdriver.
- ✔ **Cost:** Anywhere from $50 to $300.
- ✔ **Stuff to watch out for:** Compact disc drives come in two types: *internal* and *external.* The external ones are little boxes that take up room on your desk. The internal ones slide into the front of your computer like a floppy disk. Both internal and external drives are usually either EIDE or SCSI.

When you install an internal CD or CD-R drive, both types of drives come with a card that plugs into one of your computer's slots, although some EIDE CD drives plug straight into the motherboard. You had better pop the cover and make sure that you have an empty slot before doing anything else.

To install an internal CD or CD-R drive:

1. **Turn off your computer, unplug it, and remove its case.**

2. **Plug the CD drive's card into one of your available slots and screw it down.**

   Card installation gets its due earlier in this chapter.

3. **Slide the CD drive into the front of your computer.**

   You need a vacant drive bay, which is an opening where your disk drives normally live. The drive should slide in through the front.

4. **Connect the cables.**

   First, connect the cable between the CD drive and the card you installed in Step 2. It should fit only one way.

   Next, rummage around the tentacles of wires leading from your power supply until you find a spare power connector and plug it into your CD drive. CD drives usually use the small-sized connector shown in Figure 2-2.

   Finally, connect the thin audio cable from the drive to the tiny CD Input pins marked on your system's sound card. Nothing marked "CD Input"? Try "Line Input" pins, or a different type of Input pins.

5. **Screw the drive in place.**

   Although some drives screw in from the sides, most fasten with two screws along the front.

6. **Replace your computer's cover, plug the computer in, and turn it on.**

   When Windows boots up, it may recognize the new CD drive and automatically install it for you. If so, you're finished! If not, move to Step 7.

7. **Run the CD drive software.**

   The software should take over the rest of the installation chores and show you how to make your own CDs. (Chapter 12 covers that, as well.)

Some CD drives use SCSI ports and cards. If you don't have a SCSI card in your computer, stick with an EIDE CD drive.

If you already have a SCSI card in your computer, things can get either better or worse. Here's why:

   ✔ **The Good News:** SCSI ports can chain a handful of other SCSI devices, which means that you can connect your new CD drive into the chain. For example, if your hard drive connects to a SCSI card, you don't need the CD drive's card. Just add the CD drive into the hard drive's SCSI cable, saving time and, more importantly, a slot.

✔ **The Bad News:** Different brands of SCSI ports aren't always compatible with each other. Sometimes they work in a chain; sometimes they don't. Before investing in SCSI devices, call the manufacturers to be sure that the devices can all get along.

Choosing and Using an Iomega Disk

The Iomega dada-sounding Zip, Jaz, and Clik drives are plastic disks that hold from 100MB to 2GB of information. Because they're relatively cheap and convenient, they've become the closet shoeboxes of MP3 storage.

Clik drives hold 40MB and fit into cameras and portable MP3 players like the HipZip. (See Chapter 7.) Zip drives cost less, but they hold only 250MB. The speedy Jaz drives shown in Figure 2-5 hold 2GB, making them the CD-burner's dream. A 2GB drive holds roughly 500 MP3s, or about 50 CDs, give or take a handful.

And Jaz drives are speedy. You can play songs directly from the Jaz drive. You can even record songs onto them. ("Record the baby through a microphone," brags Iomega on its Web site.)

Figure 2-5:
The latest Jaz drives hold 2GB of storage or about 500 MP3 songs apiece.

They're also expensive. But because so many people use them, they've become an industry standard.

A Jaz drive comes with very detailed installation instructions, so these steps just give you an idea of what to expect:

1. **Check your SCSI connection.**

   A Jaz drive requires a SCSI or USB connection. You can link it to an existing SCSI card in your computer or, lacking that, install a SCSI card for the drive. (Buy Iomega's brand of SCSI drive; it's specifically designed for the quickest file transfers.) The USB version is even easier to install; just run the cord between the Jaz drive and your computer's USB port.

2. **Turn off the computer, unplug the power cord, and remove the computer's cover.**

3. **Slide the Jaz drive into an empty drive bay.**

   You may need to screw some mounting brackets onto the drive, one on each side, or the drive won't slide in correctly. (Don't screw the drive into the bay yet.)

4. **Connect a power supply cable.**

5. **Connect the SCSI cable.**

   If you already have an existing SCSI card, connect the closest connector from the wide, flat SCSI cable onto the Jaz drive. (It fits only one way.) Or, if you had to install your own SCSI card, connect the cable from the card to the Jaz drive.

   The SCSI cable has two connectors, one for your Jaz drive and the other for future devices. Attach the packaged plug to the empty port, or the drive probably won't work.

6. **Screw the Jaz drive into the drive bay.**

7. **Check your connections, and replace the computer cover.**

8. **Plug in your computer, turn it on, and insert the Jaz disk.**

9. **Insert the installation CD into your drive and run the installation program.**

   Your Jaz drive shows up as a new drive letter, waiting for you to copy information to it. Jaz drives aren't cheap, but they're fast and convenient. Let's hope somebody lets you mount a car MP3 player in the dash that takes Jaz drives. Choose from 50 CDs to match the traffic.

Part II

Downloading and Playing MP3 Files from the Internet

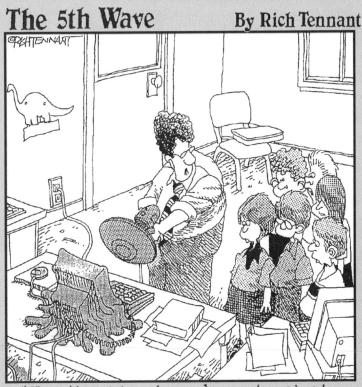

The 5th Wave   By Rich Tennant

"Next time, let me know when you're going to download a 'Red Hot Chili Peppers' MP3 file."

In this part . . .

This book's first chapter contains a crash course of MP3 information — the type of stuff for people who don't have time to read entire books. The second chapter shows how to soup up your computer so that it's ready to create, play, and store MP3 files.

Now it's time for the meatier stuff. This part of the book explains how to locate free MP3 files on the Internet, download them, and play them on your computer. Plus, it takes a look at the portable MP3 players that let you listen to your favorite songs while kick-boxing, parachuting, mountain climbing, or simply sitting in front of your computer.

Best yet, this part of the book shows how to share your MP3 collection with the world: You can join the cutting-edge crowd who have set up their own MP3 radio stations on their computers to broadcast tunes over the Internet.

Chapter 3

Finding the Best Free MP3 Files

· ·

· ·

*T*he Internet is stuffed with hundreds of thousands of MP3 files. Unfortunately, it's also stuffed with millions of other types of files. How can you separate the wheat from the chaff?

Forgetting the breakfast cereal metaphors, where are all these darn MP3 files hiding? This chapter explains how to unleash the Internet's built-in tools to ferret them out. The next chapters show you how to download them after you locate them. (Don't forget to check out Chapter 5 for the scoop on technologies like Gnutella and Napster, the hotly contested free music sources under attack from the record industry.)

Finding Web Sites with Free MP3s

Never tried Pleasantville Mountain Shampoo? If you had a free sample in a little plastic pack — and you were out of regular shampoo — you just might give it a try.

How about those "trial" magazine offers, where you get a free issue or two? If you hate it, you write "cancel" on the invoice, and mail it back. But if you like it, you pay the bill and keep the subscription.

That's the reason thousands of bands upload MP3 songs to the Internet. Download the MP3 song with your Web browser and give it a listen. If the song's awful, dump it or give it to a friend. If you like it, however, the band will sell you a CD full of its new songs — at a price much less than what you find in a music store.

The biggest and best MP3 site, MP3.com, offers hundreds of thousands of free MP3s for downloading. Bands from all over the world upload their songs, as you can see in Figure 3-1. Choose an artist or type of music, and MP3.com (www.mp3.com) shows you its offerings, ready for you to sample.

The success of MP3.com led to many copycat sites. Many Web sites offer similar services, as shown in Table 3-1. (Chapter 17 describes these sites in more detail, as well as several more MP3 sites worth a good browse.)

Table 3-1		Sites with Free and Legal MP3 Music
Site	*Location*	*Description*
MP3.com	www.MP3.com	Try this huge site first. More than a million people visit this site daily to sample tunes from Acid Jazz to Zydeco, uploaded by bands from Afghanistan to Zimbabwe. (You'll also find freebies from artists as diverse as Madonna and Charlie Parker.) Visitors have downloaded millions of songs, and the site grows daily. Contains lots of up-to-date MP3 news, hardware, software, and links to other areas.
RollingStone	www.rollingstone.com	Although too corporate to embrace MP3 quickly, this age-old music magazine's Web site now offers mainstream MP3 releases and radio stations. The site's "Garage Band" radio station would be fantastic, for example, if only Rolling Stone left out the annoying commercials. ("Our business model is predicated on ad revenue," reports the *Stone*.)
RioPort	www.rioport.com	Created especially for Diamond's Rio series of portable MP3 players, this site features authorized MP3s of all genres.

Site	Location	Description
Listen.com	www.listen.com	The staff at San Francisco-based Listen.com has one of the best jobs I've seen. All day, they kick back with headphones and listen to their favorite types of music posted across the Web. They describe each tune and post its Web link. (A handy resource, it lists big-name artists as well as newbies, posted in MP3 and other formats.)
MusicMatch	www.musicmatch.com	MusicMatch, the all-purpose software for playing with MP3s, features downloadable MP3s on its site. Click the Get Music tab to see where the tunes are hidden. (The site's MP3 radio stations, which I describe in Chapters 8 and 11, are where things get really exciting.)
MP3 Box	mp3.box.sk	A fine MP3 resource from the Slovak Republic, MP3 Box offers news, searches, links, and lots of general MP3 and music information.

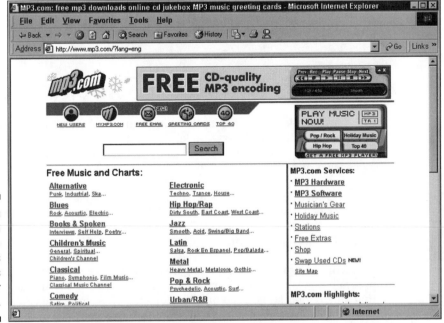

Figure 3-1:
MP3.com offers free MP3 songs from bands all over the world.

Keep in mind the following when perusing MP3 sites:

✔ Sites in Table 3-1 carry *legal* MP3s. The artists have authorized the song's distribution for promotional purposes. By downloading the song and playing it — or even giving it to friends — you're not violating any copyrights. (Don't try to sell it, though.)

✔ Other sites aren't as discriminating. Sites like Napster (Chapter 5) carry unauthorized MP3s of songs and entire albums. Some sites carry a mix of legal and illegal files. Telling whether a song is posted legally or not is difficult, especially because the Grateful Dead, Billy Idol, Tom Petty, and several other artists have authorized some MP3 releases.

If you spot at least one illegal song on a Web site, chances are that site carries a lot of other illegally copied songs, too.

✔ Most Web sites let you download songs right from their pages; some offer links to other sites with free MP3s. Click the link — usually the underlined word — and your Web browser takes you to that site.

✔ When you find a great Web site that meets your needs, *bookmark* it with your browser so that you can easily find it again: Press Ctrl+D, and the site's name appears under Favorites in Internet Express or Bookmarks in Netscape Navigator.

✔ To find the best new songs, visit an MP3 site and find the charts. Check out MP3.com's Top 40 chart, for instance, to hear that day's most popular songs. (MP3.com also features the Weekly Bottom 40 for kicks.)

✔ Many Web sites carry links to *search engines* — programs that search the entire Internet, looking for MP3 songs or other files, for that matter). I discuss search engines in the next section.

Finding MP3s with Web Search Engines

Ever had trouble finding a misplaced book in your house? The problem increases in a library. Unless you know exactly where to look, you would never stumble upon the book you're after. That's why libraries have card catalogs and computer search systems.

The Internet's search systems are called *search engines,* and dozens of them can offer help when you search for MP3 files. Each search engine works in a slightly different way, so you often need to try two or three search engines before finding your favorite file.

My favorite all-purpose search engine is Google at www.google.com. The program quickly scrutinizes more than a billion Web sites and displays any that match your subject. If you're looking for MP3s from the Grateful Dead, for example, type **"Grateful Dead"** MP3 into the Google Search box. You should enter it exactly as I show in Figure 3-2.

The words *Grateful Dead* should be in quotation marks so that the computer knows to search only for those words when they appear together. The word *MP3* tells the search engine to find only those Grateful Dead sites containing the word *MP3*.

Figure 3-2:
Put quotation marks around the words *"Grateful Dead"* and add the word *MP3*, just like this.

Click the site's Google Search button to see your matches. The results will look something like Figure 3-3.

Figure 3-3:
Here, the Google search engine dug through millions of sites, displaying only those that carry Grateful Dead MP3s.

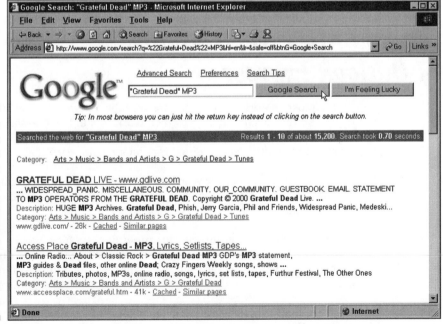

Scroll down the description list until you find a site that looks promising. Click the site's name — it's underlined, and Google pulls that site onto your screen.

✔ As opposed to most bands, the Grateful Dead doesn't mind if you upload or download the band's MP3 songs. You can collect them, trade them, or even make your own CDs from them. You just can't sell them or try to make money from them. (That includes selling advertisements on a Web page that distributes them.)

✔ Google remains a good bet for finding MP3s on Web pages. It can find both official and unofficial Web sites dealing with bands. Try searching for your favorite artist; then add the words *official* and *MP3*. Today, many bands give away promotional MP3s on their official site (try Courtney Love's site, www.hole.com, for instance).

✔ Feeling confident that Google will find your request fairly easily? Instead of clicking the "Google Search" button, click the "I'm Feeling Lucky" button to see the single site that most closely matches your request.

✔ Lycos, at mp3.lycos.com, caused a stir with its indiscriminate searching through the Internet for MP3 files — both legal and illegal. However, it's often inaccurate because most of its searches come from unverified FTP sites, which I explain a little later in this chapter.

✔ AudioFind.com (www.audiofind.com) contains an advanced MP3 search engine that pulls up a wide variety of MP3s.

Finding MP3 Newsgroups in Outlook Express

One of the most esoteric — and the most reliable — ways to find MP3 files is through the Internet's *newsgroups,* which work sort of like messages on a bathroom wall. One person writes something, another person writes a response, and a multithreaded conversation soon appears.

Those conversations appear in a special section of the Internet called newsgroups. And instead of merely posting words, many people post files on newsgroups to share them with other users.

Although dedicated newsgroup-viewing programs, such as Agent (www.forteinc.com), make it easy to find and download newsgroup files, Outlook Express, which comes built in to Windows, also finds and download MP3 files.

Although Outlook Express isn't nearly as efficient as Agent, it's on nearly everybody's PC, so I cover it here.

Wacky Web site error messages

MP3 sites change constantly. Sometimes the record industry shuts down a site for carrying illegal MP3s. Other times, a site's owner can't afford to pay his ISP and abandons the site. Even the successful sites have problems when their content grows larger than what their ISP allows. Here are some of the most common error messages you'll encounter when browsing MP3 sites.

File Not Found (or 404 Not Found): This means the site's Web address has either been entered wrong or the site has moved to a new address. Either way, your Web browser couldn't find the requested file. First, double-check how you've spelled the address. If that doesn't work, chop the address down to its base level. For instance, if `www.mp3.com/wierd` gives you that error, type in its *root*, `www.mp3.com`, and search for the "wierd" site from that point.

401 Unauthorized: The Web address is correct, but for some reason the Web site's owner has placed a restriction on the page. (The owner might be charging for access, for instance.) It's worth another try later before giving up.

403 Forbidden: You've reached the site, but you're trying to do something on the page that the site's owner doesn't allow.

500 Server Error: This general-purpose message means something's gone wrong with the Web site's server. Try again; it might just be a temporary problem.

501 Not Implemented: The Web address tells the server to do something that hasn't been set up. Try again later.

Connection Refused: You've reached the right Web address, but so have many, many other users. In fact, the server can't handle that number of servers, so it's leaving you out. Keep trying every few minutes (or try again very late at night).

Unable to Locate Host: The Web address you've entered points to a server that's incorrect or has changed. Again, check your spelling.

Unable to Contact Host: You've typed in the right Web address, but the Web site's server isn't responding. This is probably a temporary problem; try again in a few hours.

These steps tell Outlook Express to find MP3 files on the newsgroups. (Chapter 4 shows you how to download the files you find interesting.)

1. **Open Outlook Express.**

2. **Choose Tools from the menu bar along the top of the window and select Newsgroups from the drop-down menu.**

   If something goes wrong up to this point, head for the sidebar "But what if Outlook Express doesn't list *newsgroups*?" elsewhere in this chapter. You need to set up your browser so that it includes News.

3. **Click the Reset List button.**

   This collects the most current list of newsgroup topics — usually more than 30,000 of them. It's an aggravatingly slow process, especially on a dial-up modem, but you only have to do it once. (From now on, just click the New tab to see any newsgroups added since you last reset the list.)

4. **Type** MP3 **into the box labeled** Display newsgroups which contain.

   A list of all the newsgroups containing MP3 appears, as shown in Figure 3-4.

Figure 3-4:
Outlook
Express
accesses
the
Internet's
freebie
news-
groups, a
treasure of
MP3 files
sorted by
era or
genre.

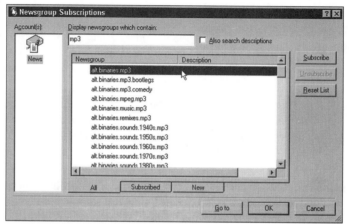

5. **Select the newsgroups you would like to subscribe to, click the Subscribe button, and click the OK button.**

To subscribe to more than one newsgroup, hold down Ctrl while clicking their names. To subscribe to *all* of them, click the first one on the list. Then, while holding down the Shift key, click the last name on the list. Wham! Windows selects them all.

- ✔ Newsgroups with the word *binaries* in the title contain files — in this case, MP3 files. Newsgroups without the word *binaries* in the title usually serve as bulletin boards where visitors exchange messages about MP3s.

- ✔ Newsgroup users upload binary files by dicing them into pieces and spreading the contents through the newsgroup. (Chapter 4 shows you how to download those parts and put them back together into a single song.)

- ✔ Your best bet for finding the most MP3s is the alt.binaries.sounds.mp3 newsgroup.

✔ Newsgroups carry *lots* of MP3 information posted by music lovers. Feel free to spend some time on the MP3 information groups to read the latest about MP3 players, utilities, and other MP3-related news.

✔ In addition to searching for MP3s, search for names of bands. Some newsgroups are dedicated to a single band.

✔ Newsgroups contain some of the best and some of the worst of the Web. Scientists, technicians, and hobbyists use newsgroups as a place to gather and swap information. But pornographers and bootleggers also use them — be wary if you're easily offended.

Finding MP3 Files on FTP Sites

Your computer communicates with the Internet in several very different ways. You're probably the most familiar with the way computers locate and display Web sites. Web sites use addresses known as *URLs* to let computers hold conversations. For instance, typing **www.mp3.com** tells your Internet browser to talk to the Internet in the method required for finding and displaying Web sites.

The letters *http* stand for *hypertext transfer protocol,* which is a method of placing fancy pushbuttons around a Web site's information. Visitors click the site's buttons to navigate the Web site, download files, or visit other sites.

Another method of Internet communication is called FTP (File Transfer Protocol), and it's used strictly for transferring files. People dump files onto a site with no easy-to-use front end. These sites have addresses that start with the letters *ftp,* usually followed by an obscure string of numbers and words like this: ftp://123.123.123.123:21.

Some FTP sites require passwords for entrance; others offer *anonymous* access, meaning the public can waltz right in without leaving a name or typing a password. After entering, you can usually download anything you see.

The person running the FTP site can shut it down at any time; some smaller sites go up and down according to the owner's sleep schedules.

✔ FTP sites are often called *servers.*

✔ To find and download files from FTP sites, you need special software. Windows doesn't come with anything quite up to the task.

✔ You can often find FTP sites with your Internet browser. In fact, sometimes a Web site only offers downloads using FTP — the browser refuses to download the file properly. (See Chapter 4.)

✔ Chapter 4 explains what software to use for searching and downloading files from FTP sites.

> ✔ Some dedicated search programs scan the Internet for MP3 files on FTP sites. MP3Fiend (`www.mp3fiend.com`) for example, employs several search engines to search for a desired MP3 file. It lists the FTP address for each site containing your request and then tries to log on to each FTP site to make sure that it's up, running, and willing to let you log on and download the file. When the program turns up a valid address, head to Chapter 4 for information on how to download specific files from an FTP address.

Finding "Spoken Word" MP3s

Although MP3 files contain sound, they don't always contain music. Some of the most fun MP3 files contain spoken words: a person reading *The New York Times,* for example, or a stand-up comedian's routines.

You can also find entire books being read, all stored in a string of MP3 files. Finding them is fairly easy; the best spoken word MP3s live at these sites:

> ✔ Audible.com carries only narrated MP3 files. You can find newspapers, magazines, study guides, college lectures, bestsellers, and other goodies. Audible.com sells most of its files, though, and they're encoded with a copy-protection scheme. Its Web site explains the process in more details.

> ✔ Don't forget to drop by Salon Audio at `www.salon.com/audio`. It took over MP3Lit a while back and carries the epitome of literary hip — Dylan Thomas, Jack Kerouac, J.R.R. Tolkien, T.S. Eliot, Dennis Miller — all reading from their own works. Check out Edgar Allen Poe's "The Raven," read by Basil, uh, Rathbone.

> ✔ MP3.com carries hundreds of free narrated MP3 files without copy protection. Look under the site's Books & Spoken section to find interviews, poetry, self-help, spiritual, and audio books, and similar files.

What Are All Those Other Sound Formats?

Although MP3 is the most widely used format for storing music online, it's not the only one. The recording industry — worried that people are downloading MP3s instead of buying records — is coming up with new formats that can't be copied as easily.

But what if Outlook Express doesn't list *newsgroups*?

Outlook Express doesn't automatically know that newsgroups exist, you must tell the program about them. In short, you must set up an Outlook Express newsgroup account — similar to the mail account you use to send and receive your e-mail. Here's how it's done:

1. **Choose Tools from the menu along the top of Outlook Express and choose Accounts from the drop-down menu.**

2. **Select the News tab, click the Add button, and choose News from the pop-up window.**

3. **Type in the name you'd like to be known as on the group.**

   Use your own name or an alias like *PeeledPotato*; then click the Next button.

4. **Type your e-mail address and click the Next button.**

   Unfortunately, some mean people send evil robot programs to scoop e-mail addresses off the Internet. These people then sell the list of addresses to senders of Internet junk mail, known as *spam*. Many newsgroup users type in a fake address to avoid receiving spam.

5. **Type the word** News **into the News (NNTP) server box and click the Next button.**

   If you're running a network with a proxy server, you might need to type something else in here. Check with the person who set up your network.

6. **Click the Finish button.**

   You've now created an Outlook Express account to store your newsgroup messages and files. Click the Close button and head back to the steps in the section "Finding MP3 Newsgroups on the Internet" to begin mining the newsgroups' riches.

Audible.com, for example, shown in Figure 3-5, stores the bulk of its "spoken word" files in a format incompatible with MP3. The site sells its own portable player, the Audible MobilePlayer, for playing its files on the go. (That player doesn't support MP3, either. Audible.com promised to convert the bulk of its files to MP3 format, but the site hasn't set a deadline.)

LiquidAudio (`www.liquidaudio.com`), a distributor of commercial music, also uses its own format known as "Liquid Tracks." After purchasing a song or CD from the site, shown in Figure 3-6, you download the Liquid Tracks from the Web site. You can only play Liquid Tracks from LiquidAudio's own software player, and the format places restrictions on how the songs can be copied to a CD. Plus, Liquid Tracks won't play back on many MP3 players.

The LiquidAudio proprietary player, however, can play back MP3 files, along with its own Liquid Tracks.

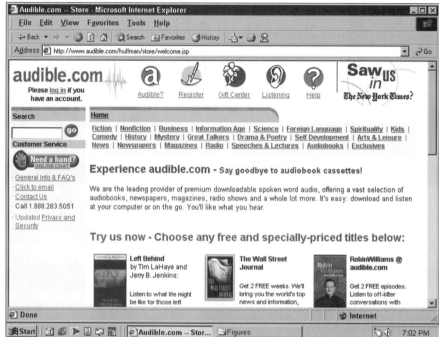

Figure 3-5:
Audible.com
carries the
bulk of its
files in a
copy-
protected
format that
requires its
own special
software.

Figure 3-6:
LiquidAudio
(www.
liquidau
dio.com)
sells
songs by
mainstream
artists in a
copy-
protected
format that
requires its
own player.

Several software packages allow users to take *any* sounds currently being played from their sound card — including LiquidAudio songs — and convert them into MP3 or WAV files. Search `www.google.com` for a WinAmp *plugin* that does this, or head for `www.highcriteria.com` and check out its Total Recorder software. After being converted to MP3 or WAV format, even copy-protected songs can be played on portable MP3 players or stored on CD with a wider variety of CD-ROM drives.

A2b music at `www.a2bmusic.com` uses the a2b format from AT&T Labs to sell music. After you purchase and download a song onto your computer from its site, shown in Figure 3-7, it won't play on any other computers; it must be played through its own proprietary player on your computer. And some of the free, sample songs expire after a set time. Groovy parts: Downloaded songs come with cover art, lyrics, and links to the band's Web site. Unfortunately, the proprietary player doesn't play back MP3 files along with a2b music files.

Check out the last part of Chapter 1 for information on still more audio formats, like WAV, MIDI, RealAudio, MOD, VQF, and others.

Figure 3-7:
A2b music, like LiquidAudio, also sells copy-protected songs by mainstream artists that require special software for playback.

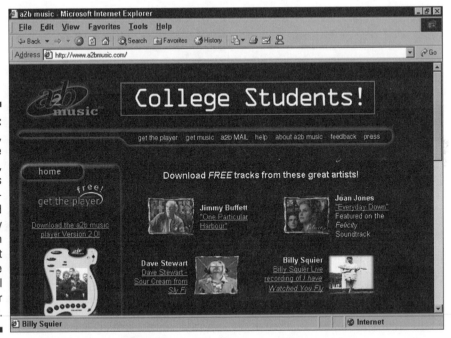

Chapter 4

Downloading MP3 Files from the Internet

C hapter 3 shows you how to locate the millions of MP3 files stuffed into the crevices of the Internet. This chapter shows you how to copy those files from the Internet to your hard drive.

Sometimes the process is simple: Just right-click the MP3 file's name, and tell your Web browser where to store the file. Other times, you may run into the abysmally elaborate procedures used by fans of FTP sites and newsgroups.

No matter which method you choose, this chapter shows you how to grab your favorites from the Internet's huge bank of MP3 files.

Don't forget to schedule a little time for your downloads, though. Even though MP3 files are one-tenth their original size, they're still pretty huge. Start the downloads, hit the sack, and listen in the morning.

Downloading MP3 Files with a Web Browser

Internet Explorer, Netscape Navigator, and just about any other Web browser can download MP3 files to your hard drive quickly and easily. Because Internet Explorer comes free with Windows 98, I cover that here.

When you spot a cool MP3 file while browsing the Internet, follow these steps to copy it onto your computer. In fact, follow these steps whenever you download *anything* onto your hard drive, including MP3 players and other utilities.

Contrary to some Internet rumors, you can't get a virus from an MP3 file. (At least no dastardly person has figured out how to write one *yet*.) However, MP3 *utilities,* like any other programs, may contain a virus. Check *any* downloaded programs with a virus checker before running them on your computer, and be especially wary of files that come attached to your e-mail.

1. **Load Internet Explorer or Netscape Navigator and head to the desired Web page.**

   Type the Web site's address into your browser's address box, and press the Enter key.

2. **Locate the MP3 file.**

   Web sites display their downloadable MP3 files in a variety of ways. Some sites take a stark approach, displaying files by their names, date, and size, as shown in Figure 4-1.

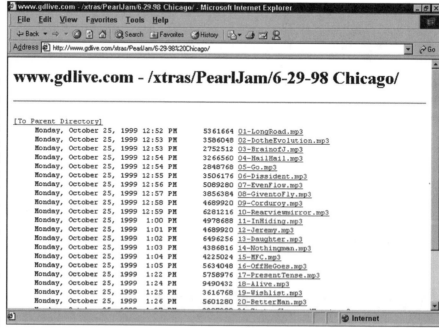

Figure 4-1:
Some Web sites arrange their MP3 files in an unpretentious list, displaying the MP3's creation date, the song's name, and its file size.

Other times, the file's name sits in the Web site itself, like in Figure 4-2.

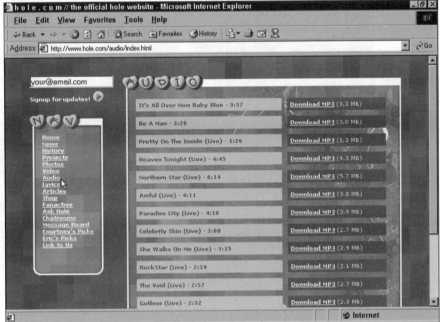

Figure 4-2:
Courtney
Love's Web
site (www.
hole.com),
like others,
lists MP3
files of her
concerts on
a fancier,
more
traditional
Web page.

3. **Right-click the MP3 file link.**

   A *link* is a Web page "push-button" that makes something happen. In Figure 4-2, for instance, the link is a push-button for downloading a particular file. Links are almost always underlined or in a different color. In this case, when you right-click the words <u>Download MP3</u> next to the desired song — Awful (Live), for instance — your browser tosses out a window similar to the one shown in Figure 4-3, asking you for further instructions.

4. **Choose Save Target <u>A</u>s from the pop-up menu.**

   Choosing the Save Target <u>A</u>s option (refer to Figure 4-3) lets you save the chosen file to your hard drive. (Using Netscape? Then choose the Save Link As option.)

5. **When your browser asks how to save the incoming file, as shown in Figure 4-4, create an MP3 folder (or use an MP3 folder that already exists), open that folder, and click <u>S</u>ave.**

   To create a new folder, click the little exploding folder icon in the upper-right corner of the Save As box. A new folder appears, just waiting to be named. Name it something that describes its contents — **MP3**, for example — and click <u>S</u>ave. The song downloads from the Web site into the folder you selected.

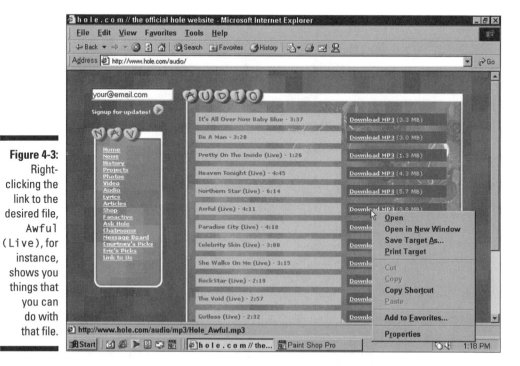

Figure 4-3:
Right-clicking the link to the desired file, Awful (Live), for instance, shows you things that you can do with that file.

Figure 4-4:
Either create a new folder to store your incoming MP3 file or store the file in an existing MP3 folder.

The file begins to copy onto your computer. Always helpful, your browser gauges the file's progress in a window like what you see in Figure 4-5, showing connection speed and the remaining download time.

The Web site often determines connection speed, not your modem. If the site has lots of traffic, downloads take longer, and your modem may receive information at only one-quarter of its potential speed.

Figure 4-5:
Here,
Internet
Explorer
downloads
a song at
81.4KB per
second and
says that
the file
will finish
download-
ing in 23
more
seconds.

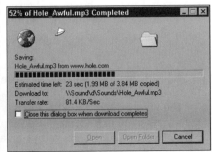

6. **Click OK after the program finishes downloading.**

   When you finish downloading the file, open the folder where you saved
   it. From there, you're ready to play it using MusicMatch, Winamp, or any
   other MP3 player. (I describe several of them in Chapter 6.)

   ✔ As soon as you download a file, think about how to organize it on your
   hard drive. Create a new folder for each new CD or album, for instance,
   and store all the MP3 files for that CD or album in that folder. Then
   organize those folders by genre: Jazz, Blues, Rock, Rap, Opera, and
   so on. Finally, store those categories in a folder named MP3.

   ✔ If a page seems to be crawling onto your screen, click your browser's
   Stop button and try loading the page again. Sometimes that gives your
   connection a kick and speeds up the connection.

   ✔ You store MP3 files on CDs in two different ways: You can either store the
   files on a CD and play them on your computer, or you can convert the
   MP3 files to a different format and store them on a CD that works in your
   home stereo. Chapter 12 holds the briefing papers on both methods.

Troubleshooting with Your Internet Browser

Face it — Internet browsers often freak out. When you follow the downloading
steps provided in the preceding section and your file doesn't appear on your
hard drive, it's time to start tweaking. This section lists some of the problems
that you'll eventually encounter and offers a solution or two.

Instead of an MP3 file, I get an HTML file

This one's easy to spot. You right-click an MP3 file and choose the browser's Save As command. Your song appears in the box shown in Figure 4-4, but it ends with the letters `htm` or `html` instead of MP3. Your song's file name looks like `Crying_Carrots.htm`, for example.

Or sometimes the file's name is garbage, like `CACV4P4V`, and Internet Explorer attempts to save the file as an HTML document, as shown in Figure 4-6. Either way, stop by clicking the Cancel button. Your browser jumped the gun, and the site wasn't ready to hand over the file. Instead, the site wants you to left-click that file's name, which opens a new page of information — usually material about the song or band. The desired MP3 file is generally available for downloading on that second page. Give it another try.

Figure 4-6:
If Internet
Explorer
attempts to
save the file
as an HTML
document,
click Cancel
and *left-*
click the file,
instead of
right-
clicking.

My file says, "Server returned extended information"

Sometimes your MP3 file download ends in a puff of ugly smoke. Instead of downloading the file, the browser comes up with bizarre reprimands like these:

- ✔ Server returned extended information.
- ✔ The password was not allowed.
- ✔ The login request was denied.

These clues mean that the Web page doesn't like to allow downloads through a mere Web browser. Instead, the Web page is set up as an FTP site — a unique file transfer system that I describe later in this chapter. You need a special program to download these files, which I also describe later in this chapter.

My file says, "A connection with the server could not be established"

This one means your file is linked to a Web page that has closed its doors. The site may be shut down temporarily while its Webmaster is picking up pizza, or perhaps the site's Internet Service Provider shut it down for offering bootleg files.

There's no way of knowing whether the site will return to life or not. Keep trying every once in a while, and then give up. There are plenty of other sites out there.

Downloading MP3 Files from MP3.com

MP3.com in San Diego offers the largest selection of authorized MP3s from bands around the world. The site makes it easy to download songs and to give them a quick listen before bothering to download the entire file.

Best yet, almost all the songs are free. If you like the band, you're free to order its CD and listen to the entire batch of songs.

When you visit the MP3.com Web page (www.mp3.com) and spot an interesting-looking MP3, the page looks like Figure 4-7.

The page offers several options, depending on where you click:

- **Listen to all tracks:** Choose Lo Fi Play if you have a dial-up connection, choose Hi Fi Play if you have a Cable or faster modem. MP3.com then creates a sort of personalized Internet radio station that plays all the songs uploaded by that artist.

- **Add all tracks:** This adds all the artist's songs to MP3.com's My.MP3.com service — check out the sidebar "Okay, what's My.MP3.com?" a bit later in this chapter.

- **Lo Fi Play:** Clicking this option immediately plays the song through your computer's speakers using your MP3 player. The file isn't saved, just played in a low fidelity mode.

✔ **Hi Fi Play:** The same as Lo Fi Play, but for people with speedy cable, DSL, or T1 Internet connections. The songs sound *much* better — just like you were playing the MP3 file from your hard drive.

✔ **Download:** Right-clicking this option brings up a box, shown in Figure 4-4, that lets you choose the incoming file's location on your hard drive. After you choose a spot, MP3.com begins sending the file to its destination. The site usually offers a fast connection that takes full advantage of your modem's speed.

✔ **Add to My.MP3.com:** This option stores the file's name on MP3.com, allowing convenient access from any sound card-equipped computer connected to the Internet.

✔ **E-mail Track to a Friend:** Click here to send the song's link to a friend. Your friend can then click the link to hear the song, or visit the site to download it himself. Beware, though — choosing this option automatically signs you up for the My.MP3.com service that I describe in the sidebar.

✔ **Song Lyrics:** This button, it's no surprise, lets you read what that vocalist's crooning.

On your first visit to MP3, you must fill out a short form that asks for your e-mail address, country, and zip code before any of the buttons will work. The site remembers the information so that you don't have to bother with it more than once.

Figure 4-7: Depending on where you click, MP3.com lets you listen to a song, save it to your computer, read the lyrics, e-mail it to a friend, or save it in the "My.MP3. com" service.

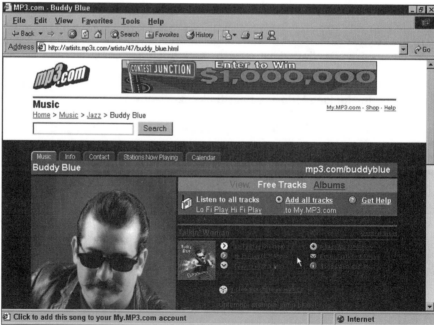

Don't have MP3 player software? Chapter 6 evaluates the best on the market and explains the way-cool players included free on this book's CD.

The Microsoft Windows Media Player plays MP3 files, but not the version originally shipped with the first version of Windows 98. If Media Player has trouble playing MP3 files, go to the Microsoft Web site at `www.microsoft.com` and click the downloads section to grab the latest version of Media Player.

Windows Media Player merely *plays* files from the Internet — it doesn't always save them to your hard drive. If you click a Web site's MP3 file and Windows Media Player pops up right away to play it (as it often does in the default setup), you're not saving the file as it plays. Windows Media Player is merely playing it. If you want to hear the MP3 song more than once, click the Cancel button and choose the Save option, instead.

Okay, Windows Media Player *does* save the file when you left-click the download button. But where? Quite often, it's sitting in your C drive's Temporary Internet Files folder. Other times, Media Player renames the file with random letters and numbers before storing it. Can't find it? Check the dates of the MP3 files in that temporary folder and find the newest one. Rename the file to `song.mp3` and see if Windows Media Player plays the right song again. If so, you've found it; rename it to the correct title and breathe a sigh of relief.

If Winamp begins playing a song when you click MP3.com's Play button, you're not saving the song, either. Earlier versions of Winamp did this, but not the current one. (To find earlier versions of Winamp, head for `www.mp3.nl`. At last look, that site carried nearly every version of Winamp released.)

If your browser doesn't play MP3 songs when you click the Play button, perhaps you need to choose an MP3 player. Chapter 6 helps you determine which MP3 Player Windows will automatically call into action when necessary.

Internet Newsgroups

Chapter 3 shows you how to log on to the Internet's newsgroups section and find the MP3 newsgroups from the 30,000 other categories. But a look at the files in the MP3 newsgroups reveals something rather unsettling. The MP3 files are usually broken into small pieces — a single recording often comes spread out into 15 to 20 pieces.

Why? First, most Internet Service Providers frown on their users trying to post large files onto the Internet's newsgroups. And some servers balk at postings larger than one-half of a megabyte (500K). Because MP3 files are rather large, breaking them up and posting the pieces is an easy solution to size restrictions.

Okay, what's My.MP3.com?

Today, a person's music collection usually stays stuck in one place: next to the home stereo or stored on the computer's hard drive. So, MP3.com came up with a novel idea: Because MP3 songs are so easy to move around, why not set up a system where music lovers can access their music collections from *any* computer?

So, MP3.com bought thousands of commercial CDs, converted them to MP3s, and stored them on its huge servers. Users then stick their CD into their home computer for a few seconds — just long enough for MP3.com to verify the CD's title. MP3.com then places the MP3 versions of that CD's songs into the user's new account, called a *My.MP3.com* account.

Users loved being able to hear their CD collection anywhere. The record labels hated it, calling it a blatant act of copyright infringement. After several legal squabbles, the judges agreed with the record companies. After paying around $170 million in legal costs and settlement fees, MP3.com finally made friends with the five big labels. The labels promptly licensed their content to MP3.com, and the My.MP3.com service began anew.

To sign up, click the My.MP3.com button at the top of the MP3.com Web page, fill out the forms, and start listening. And be prepared for the charges MP3.com will eventually tack on.

Newsgroup users download each piece of the binary file and link them back together to form the original file. Some specialized newsgroup reader programs do this automatically, as do some e-mail readers.

This section shows you how to grab each piece of a newsgroup's binary file and glue them back together with Outlook Express, a program bundled with Windows. You can download and recombine any type of binary file in Outlook Express by following these steps:

1. **Click the newsgroup you want to use (or, as they call it, *subscribe* to).**

   Figure 4-8 shows how Outlook Express is subscribed to the alt.binaries.sounds.mp3 newsgroup. In the figure, it contains 12,811 files, which appear on the right side of the screen. Remember, though, that the newsgroup doesn't contain 12,811 actual songs — those files are split-up pieces of MP3 files.

2. **Locate the file that you want to download.**

   To see your favorite artists more easily when posted in newsgroups, click the Subject bar above the listings. That arranges the listings in alphabetical order, so all the artists' MP3s are listed together.

   Click on the scroll bars to browse through the files manually. When you find something posted by someone you like, move ahead to Step 3.

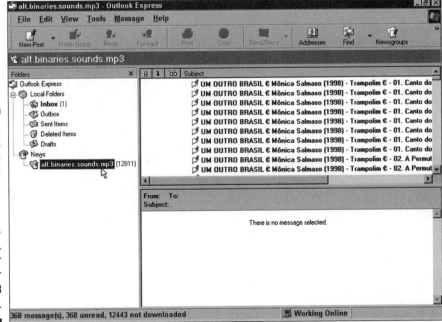

Figure 4-8:
Outlook
Express is
subscribed
to the alt.
binaries.
sounds.
mp3
newsgroup,
a popular
spot for
posted MP3
files.

Don't feel like browsing? Then click Edit from the Outlook Express main menu and choose Find from the drop-down menu. Finally, choose Message in this Folder from the menu that squirts out the side. Type the name of your favorite artist in the Look for box, and click Find Next. Outlook Express searches the listings for files bearing that artist's name.

3. **Look for information about the desired file.**

Merely point at the desired file — don't click — and an information screen pops up, as shown in Figure 4-9. Here, somebody has posted a song from a Grateful Dead live show. The song is titled *Turn On Your Lovelight.* The numbers (020/148) mean that the file is spread across 148 posts, and you've found the 20th post. To grab that particular MP3, you need to grab all 148 posts and combine them. Although that sounds like a daunting task, it's not as difficult as it sounds.

Some postings start with the number zero rather than one. If the preceding song had a post starting with (000/148), that first file would contain text about the post, usually describing the song, artist, and information about the recording. Although the information is helpful, it isn't necessary because you don't have to combine that posting with the others in order to hear the song.

4. **Select all the postings comprising the file.**

To find all the posts for a song, be sure to click the Subject bar above the list of file names, as I describe in Step 2's tip. Wham! Outlook Express lines up all the files by their names.

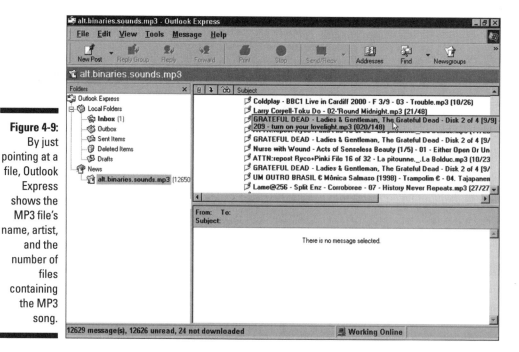

Figure 4-9:
By just pointing at a file, Outlook Express shows the MP3 file's name, artist, and the number of files containing the MP3 song.

Now, click the first file in the sequence (001/148, for example) and then press and hold down the Shift key while you click the last file in the sequence (148/148, for example). Outlook Express highlights all the files in the sequence, as shown in Figure 4-10.

5. Right-click the highlighted files and choose Combine and Decode.

A window appears (see Figure 4-11), asking you to drag the messages into numerical order.

6. Arrange the selected files in numerical order.

When the Order for decoding window pops up, look at the numbers in parentheses at the end of each file's name. Make sure that all the file's numbers are lined up correctly. You might need to click some that are out of order and click the Move Up or Move Down buttons until everything's right. (You can drag and drop them into the correct order, if you prefer.)

If some of the file numbers are missing, leaving an incomplete sequence, stop, sigh, and give up. Missing numbers mean that some of the file's parts were lost in the upload and didn't make it through to the newsgroups. If you continue to decode that MP3 file, the song will have missing portions.

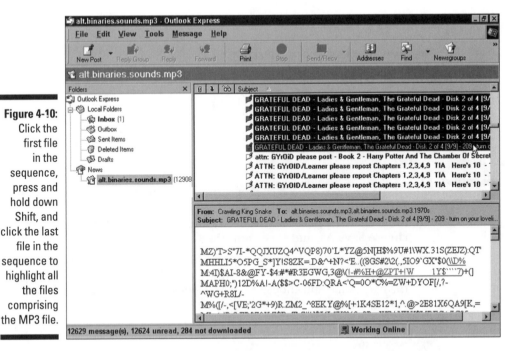

Figure 4-10:
Click the
first file
in the
sequence,
press and
hold down
Shift, and
click the last
file in the
sequence to
highlight all
the files
comprising
the MP3 file.

Some people mess up a file name's numbers when posting. For example, they might post the first file as 1/35 instead of 01/35, and the second as 2/35 instead of 02/35. Big deal? Actually, it is. When the computer sorts files numerically, it starts with 1/35, then jumps to 11/35, 12/35, and so on. If the first nine posts don't have a zero in front of their number, they're out of order, and you have to move them into their correct numerical order before combining them.

7. Press OK.

Outlook Express downloads, sorts, and squishes together all the file pieces, as shown in Figure 4-12. When it's through combining the pieces, Outlook Express lists the file as an "attachment" to a message.

Figure 4-11:
Check that
files are
listed in
numerical
order so
the pieces
go back
together
properly.

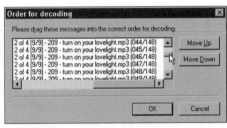

Figure 4-12:
Outlook
Express
downloads
all the file's
pieces and
combines
them into
a single
MP3 file.

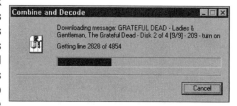

8. **Right-click the name of this newly combined file in the Attach box, choose Save As, and save your file.**

The combined file shown in Figure 4-13 isn't officially downloaded until you save it. So either choose Save As from the File menu, or right-click the file's name and choose Save As. Choose a location for the file, and save it there.

Figure 4-13:
Be sure to
save the
attached
file — it's
not saved to
your hard
drive yet,
even when
Outlook
Express
displays it
like this.

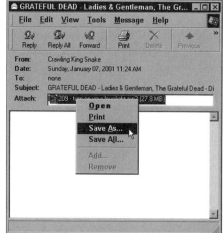

✔ Please don't forget Step 8. The file looks as if Outlook Express downloaded and saved the file, but the file's not actually saved to your hard drive. If you close that piece of e-mail without saving it, it's gone. (You can download it again, so you've lost nothing but time.)

✔ Although Outlook Express can handle newsgroup chores, it's certainly no skilled technician. Several third-party programs specialize in newsgroups, whether organizing messages or downloading and reassembling binary files with a single click. I prefer Free Agent (`www.forteinc.com/agent/index.htm`). Mac users can choose from several newsgroup programs available at `www.macorchard.com/`. (Look for them under the "Usenet" category.)

✔ Want a more detailed explanation of MP3 newsgroups? Head to `www.mp3-faq.org` for extraordinarily detailed advice on requesting, creating, posting, retrieving, and playing MP3s.

✔ Why bother with the complicated world of newsgroups when places like Napster or Gnutella (which I cover in Chapter 5) are around? Because newsgroups often carry songs that Napster doesn't — especially older songs that aren't as popular with Napster's younger audience.

✔ You can sample a song on a newsgroup before completely downloading it. Just download the first few pieces of a song, put them in numerical order, and save the result. Winamp or many other MP3 players play only the short portion of the song you've downloaded.

Downloading MP3 Files from America Online

America Online users aren't shut out of the fun. If you use America Online, you can download files from Web sites with your Internet browser using the same steps that I describe in the section "Downloading MP3 Files with a Web Browser," earlier in this chapter.

To retrieve binary files from newsgroups, use America Online's Filegrabber utility to download the files and put them back together. Here's a brief rundown:

1. **Log on to America Online, type the keyword** newsgroup, **and press Enter.**

   The Internet Newsgroups window appears.

2. **Click the Search All Newsgroups button.**

3. **Search for words describing your interests.**

   Type **dead** for Grateful Dead, for example, and press Enter. When the Search box reveals all newsgroups mentioning the word *dead,* double-click the desired newsgroup. In this case, double-click `alt.binaries.gdead` to find the binary files containing MP3 songs.

4. **When the box appears, click Subscribe to newsgroup** `alt.binaries.gdead`.

   AOL subscribes you to the `alt.binaries.gdead` newsgroup — or whatever newsgroup you searched for in Step 3.

   5. **Click the Preferences button and select the box marked Show only Complete Binary Files which AOL Can Automatically Download and Decode.**

   Clicking that box makes AOL take a look at the newsgroup, decide what files it recognizes, and display those files.

   6. **Click the Save button to save your preferences.**

   7. **Double-click any one of the listed pieces of a particular song.**

   Binary files are stored in pieces, as I describe in the section "Internet Newsgroups." When you double-click any piece of the song, a box appears. If the box contains a button saying Download File, you're in luck. If it doesn't say that, America Online won't automatically download the file. Move on to another one.

   8. **Click the Download File button.**

   9. **Save the incoming file in a folder on your hard drive.**

   Choose a folder on your hard drive and click <u>S</u>ave to begin the download.

   10. **Play the file with an MP3 player.**

If all goes well, following these steps brings MP3 files to your hard drive. However, America Online isn't the most reliable nor the easiest-to-use source for MP3 files. Here are some problems you may run into:

   ✔ If you don't see the words `Download File` in Step 7, you can't download the file automatically. Also, don't choose the Download Message button, or the file won't download correctly.

   ✔ America Online's software sometimes won't recognize all parts of a particularly large posting. If you simply *must* have that file, you can manually download each individual piece of the file and then use a third-party program to combine and decode them.

   ✔ When first installed, America Online automatically blocks binary downloads as part of its Parental Control feature. (Some binary files contain naughty pictures.) Whoever holds the master account for AOL needs to head for the Parental Control area and uncheck the Block Binary Downloads box.

   ✔ Still confused? Don't worry, America Online makes it extremely difficult to download files from newsgroups. For more detailed advice, head for `http://members.aol.com/Rgordon202/faqpt3.html`. Bob Gordon covers the subject in explicit detail.

   ✔ Rich Barker, this book's technical editor, offers another way to grab MP3s from America Online: Type in the keyword "File Search", click the Shareware section, click the Music and Sound category, and type the name of the band or artist in the search. Or, just type in the keyword "mp3" for AOL's own music downloads and links to some of the big sites.

Downloading MP3 Files from an FTP Site

Sooner or later, you'll come across a site listed by an odd string of letters and numbers rather than the typical Web address. These sites are known as *FTP* (File Transfer Protocol) sites.

In Chapter 3, I explain how some people use a file transfer system called FTP to distribute files across the Internet. Instead of using their Internet browser to move the files around, they use specialized FTP programs to grab the files and copy them to their computer.

Windows Me comes with an archaic FTP program, but you'll definitely want a third-party FTP program to handle the chores. CuteFTP (`www.cuteftp.com`) fits the bill nicely for PCs, and Fetch (`http://fetchsoftworks.com`) works well for the Mac.

Before telling a program to download an FTP file that you've found on the Net, dissect the vitals of the FTP address. An FTP site with the address `ftp://123.123.123.123 l:dead p:head`, for example, reveals this information:

- ✔ The letters `ftp` at the beginning of the string indicate that it's an FTP site. (Web sites usually have the letters `www` in front of them.)
- ✔ The FTP site's address is `123.123.123.123`. Your computer uses that address to locate the computer holding the files.
- ✔ The login word for the site is the word `dead`. (See the letter `l` for *login* before the word *dead*?) The login is similar to the user name.
- ✔ The password is the word `head`. (See the letter `p` for *password* before the word *head*?)

Sometimes that same site might be listed as `ftp://dead:head@123.123.123.123`. All the information is the same, but the login and password are listed up front, with the login listed first.

Here's how to download a file from an FTP site using CuteFTP:

1. Install and load CuteFTP.

Download CuteFTP from `www.cuteftp.com` and run the installation program. You can use the program for free for 30 days. After that, some of its features stop working, and you must then purchase the program.

2. Open the program, click FTP from the top menu, and choose Quick Connect from the drop-down menu.

The Quick Connect window appears, as shown in Figure 4-14. Pressing Ctrl+C also brings up the Quick Connect window.

Figure 4-14:
Fill in the
FTP site
address, the
login, and
the
password.

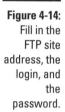

3. **In the Quick Connect window, fill in the FTP site address (in the Host Address box), the login (in the User ID box), and the password; then click the OK button.**

   Suppose that you're looking for Grateful Dead tunes on the site `ftp://dead:head@24.2.55.166`. Figure 4-14 shows the CuteFTP window filled out with that information. When you click OK, CuteFTP automatically logs on to the FTP site using the login name and password that you entered.

4. **Use the browse buttons along the program's top to place your incoming folder on CuteFTP's left side, and the song's folder on the right.**

   Each side of CuteFTP works like a mini-Explorer window. Move up or down the folders until your hard drive's MP3 folder appears on the left side of the CuteFTP window and the FTP site's song's folder appears on the right.

5. **Drag and drop the MP3 songs into your hard drive's folder.**

   Point at the song you want and, while holding down the right mouse button, point at the left-hand window featuring the directory on your hard drive. Figure 4-15 shows the action. Let go of the mouse button to "drop" the file.

6. **Click Yes when CuteFTP asks whether you're sure you want to download the file.**

   CuteFTP begins copying the file from the FTP site onto your hard drive.

7. **Close CuteFTP to disconnect.**

   You should find your song in the folder in which you placed it.

To simplify the process of grabbing FTP files, load CuteFTP in the background. When your Web browser displays an FTP link to an MP3 file, right-click the file and select Copy Link Address from the menu that appears. CuteFTP automatically starts downloading that file in the background. (CuteFTP automatically begins downloading whenever a URL or FTP address appears on the Clipboard.)

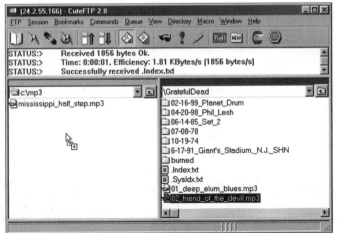

Figure 4-15:
Drag and
drop your
desired file
from the
FTP site's
window to
the folder in
your own
window.

Troubleshooting Your FTP Downloads

Of course, nothing always works perfectly in the computer world. Here's how to deal with FTP foul-ups, the strange vocabulary of its users, and odd error messages that inevitably appear.

The site wants me to click banners for passwords!

The owners of Web pages make money when people click their site's advertisements, called *banners*. That's why many sites ask you to click an advertisement and use a word in the banner's first sentence as the FTP password. It's a moneymaker.

What's a leech site?

Sites that let people download all the files they want are called *leech* sites. The people who eagerly scoop up all the MP3 files are called *leechers*, naturally. As people begin to hoard their MP3s, offering them only for trade, leech sites become increasingly rare.

What's a ratio site?

To discourage leechers from copying all their files and running, some Webmasters require visitors to upload a file before downloading any. A one-to-five ratio means visitors can download five files for each one they upload. Most ratio sites contain bootleg MP3 files.

On some sites, a one-to-five ratio means you can download 5MB of songs for every 1MB of songs you upload.

My Internet Service Provider cuts off my connection before the download's finished!

While a file pours into your computer through an FTP site, your Internet Service Provider sometimes thinks you've lost interest, and tries to shut down your connection midstream.

Click CuteFTP's Keep Alive box in the Advanced Options area and CuteFTP sends a special command every 90 seconds that tickles your ISP connection into staying alive.

What's a reliability indicator?

Many search engines seek out and identify FTP sites carrying MP3 files. However, some of these sites aren't open 24 hours; others have shut down since the search engine found them. Many search engines use a database of FTP sites that's only updated once a week — a dead site then stays listed for a full week before being removed.

Some search engines such as Lycos.com (www.lycos.com) give sites a reliability rating based on how often they're up and running. The higher the rating, the better chances of finding the MP3 file aboard.

The more often that an MP3 search engine double-checks its list of active sites, the more reliable its lists will be. That's why MP3Fiend (www.mp3fiend.com) is often the most accurate. First, it searches all the FTP sites for your requested MP3 file, and then it immediately verifies all its findings to see whether any of them are up and running.

The site says "Too many users" when I try to connect

FTP sites can't let everybody connect at the same time, so many limit their wares to 25 simultaneous users or less. If the site's busy, you must wait it out.

Instead of punching the button yourself every few minutes, CuteFTP has a "redial" feature that automatically tries to reconnect until it gets through.

Speeding Up Your MP3 Downloads

Downloads from Web sites, newsgroups, and FTP sites have one thing in common: They can take a long time to finish. A single MP3 file seems to average 5MB; some live Grateful Dead shows can be 20MB or more.

Here are some tips to speed up the download process:

- ✔ **Upgrade to the newest version of your browser.** It might not do the trick, but it often helps.

- ✔ **Buy a faster modem.** If you're using a telephone line, get a 56K or faster modem. If a cable modem is available in your area, spring for it — it can download an MP3 file in less than a minute. Call the phone company or some of the larger Internet Service Providers to check on DSL lines. Look into satellite links. *Speed* is the key word here.

- ✔ **Download one song at a time.** Although it's tempting to download bunches of songs simultaneously, download them one at a time. They download faster that way. Plus, if your connection cuts off somehow, you'll already have several songs in your basket. If you download seven songs simultaneously and you're cut off, you'll end up with portions of seven songs.

- ✔ **Don't download during the day.** Instead, browse the Web during off-peak hours, such as early mornings or late evenings.

Chapter 5

Swapping or Swiping: Napster, Napigator, Gnutella, BearShare, and Aimster

● ●

In This Chapter

▶ Getting the scoop on Napster

▶ Searching for songs

▶ Downloading songs

▶ Discovering some Napster tips and tricks

▶ Switching servers with Napigator

▶ Understanding Gnutella

▶ Putting BearShare to work

▶ Getting to know Aimster

● ●

Some folks revel in the promise of MP3 file-swapping technologies like Napster and Gnutella, calling them the most effective music marketing tools of all time. That's because the programs let music lovers download songs from the Internet for free. When music searchers discover songs from new artists they really like, they can buy the CD versions for better quality music and better packaging.

Other folks revile Napster and Gnutella, calling them ugly thievery, pure and simple. By stealing free music through the Internet, these folks theorize, users will no longer buy music. That not only robs musicians, but also slows down the entire music industry, cutting out jobs for recording engineers, instrument manufacturers, employees at Tower Records, and blue-haired musicians looking for jobs at Guitar Center.

The truth probably lies somewhere in between these two opinions, and the courts will be deciding where to draw the line for quite some time. Some record companies fight to condemn digital music swapping, whereas other record companies embrace it.

In the meantime, this chapter describes the Internet's file-swapping areas, such as Napster, Gnutella, BearShare, and Aimster, that are sending music into a new era.

Understanding Napster

The Internet uses various technologies for moving information across the Internet. Whenever you send e-mail, access a Web site, or download a file, you're using a different type of Internet technology or *protocol* to perform each job. Napster (www.napster.com) is just another Internet protocol for swapping information through the Internet.

Napster's protocol is very specialized, however. Its creator designed the Napster protocol specifically for swapping MP3 files directly between two people's personal computers.

How does the Napster technology work? Well, a piece of software called a Napster *client* runs on your personal computer. The most popular client is simply called "Napster," because that's the software created by 18-year-old Shawn Fanning, who invented the whole Napster technology. (The company is called Napster, Inc.)

After you install Napster's software and connect to the Internet, you type the name of an artist or song — Desi Arnaz, for example — and click the Napster Find It! button. In a few seconds, you'll be staring at a list of Desi Arnaz MP3 songs all ready for downloading (see Figure 5-1).

Where do all these songs come from? Well, although the Napster software squirts out a list of MP3 songs available for downloading, those songs aren't stored in any central location. Instead, Napster uses dozens of servers — powerful computers — to store the *locations* of those MP3 files. The songs themselves stay on the hard drives of Napster users around the world.

When somebody tells their Napster program to search for a song, the program checks a server to see which currently connected Napster users have that song stored on their hard drives. Then the Napster program provides the list that you see in Figure 5-1. When the user chooses a song from the list and clicks the Get Selected Files button, Napster connects that user's computer to the computer holding the song. To complete the process, Napster copies the selected song to the other computer as fast as modem conditions allow.

Although the numbers vary as users log on and off, more than 5,000 users are often online simultaneously, sharing more than a million songs. That makes it fairly easy to find the most popular tunes — as well as some of the rare ones you can't find anywhere else.

Figure 5-1:
Here,
Napster lists
all the files
by Cuban
big-band
artist Desi
Arnaz.

Napster v2.0 BETA 9								

File View Actions Help

🔄 Home   💬 Chat   📁 My Files   🔍 Search   📋 Hot List   ⇄ Transfer   Discover   ◄ ►   Shop for music at **CDNOW**

Artist: Desi Arnaz   Find It!

Title: Advanced >>

Filename	Filesize	Bitrate	Freq	Length	User	Connection	Ping	
Music\Desi Arnaz & His Orchestra - Forever Darling.mp3	2,624,405	128	44100	2:46	Starz2	Cable	247	
Music\Desi Arnaz & Lucille Ball - California, Here I Come.mp3	960,052	128	44100	1:04	DRMN...	Unknown	316	
Music\Desi Arnaz & Lucille Ball - We'll Build A Bungalow.mp3	3,869,884	128	44100	4:02	dmarco81	56K	343	
Music\Desi Arnaz - I Love Lucy.mp3	1,798,606	128	44100	1:55	dmarco81	56K	343	
Music\Desi Arnaz - We're Having A Baby (My Baby And Me) (I Love Lucy).m...	1,478,784	128	44100	1:36	dmarco81	56K	343	
Music\Desi Arnaz & Lucille Ball - California, Here I Come.mp3	960,052	128	44100	1:04	dmarco81	56K	343	
wma\Desi Arnaz - Babalu.wma	1,670,771	64	44100	3:25	rhmcvey	T3	357	
wma\Desi Arnaz-Cuban Pete.wma	1,550,071	64	44100	3:10	rhmcvey	T3	357	
Desi Arnaz-Cuban Pete.mp3	3,055,100	128	44100	3:12	rhmcvey	T3	357	
Desi Arnaz - Babalu.mp3	3,284,992	128	44100	3:26	rhmcvey	T3	357	
Music\TV Theme - Desi Arnaz - I Love Lucy.mp3	1,798,606	128	44100	1:55	IDontS...	33.6	371	
Music\Desi Arnaz - I'm On My Way To Cuba.mp3	1,626,697	128	44100	1:45	bvonn	Cable	412	
Music\Desi Arnaz & His Orchestra - Babalu.mp3	3,081,741	128	44100	3:14	bvonn	Cable	412	
Music\Desi Arnaz - Cuban Pete.mp3	3,059,712	128	44100	3:12	bvonn	Cable	412	
Music\Desi Arnaz & His Orchestra - Cuban Cabby.mp3	3,045,250	128	44100	3:11	bvonn	Cable	412	
Music\Arnaz, Desi - Cuban Pete.mp3	3,055,100	128	44100	3:12	zmster	56K	481	
Music\Desi Arnaz - Babalu.mp3	3,081,741	128	44100	3:12	goddes...	T3	494	
Music\Desi Arnaz - There's A Brand New Baby At Our House.mp3	1,319,207	64	22050	2:47	carl0987	56K	508	
Music\Desi Arnaz-Straw Hat Song.mp3	2,697,745	128	44100	2:50	carl0987	56K	508	
Music\Desi Arnaz - Babalu (stereo).mp3	3,081,741	128	44100	3:14	carl0987	56K	508	
Music\Desi Arnaz - Mi Vida (Made For Each Other).mp3	2,372,150	96	44100	3:19	carl0987	56K	508	
Music\Desi Arnaz - Cuban Cabby.mp3	3,080,192	128	44100	3:09	carl0987	56K	508	
Music\Desi Arnaz-Brazil.mp3	2,601,889	128	44100	2:44	carl0987	56K	508	
Music\Desi Arnaz - Morning Light.mp3	2,288,744	128	44100	2:25	carl0987	56K	508	
Music\Desi Arnaz - quizas, quizas, quizas.mp3	2,064,323	96	44100	2:53	carl0987	56K	508	

Returned 100 results.

Get Selected Files   Add Selected User to Hot List

Online (rottensquash): Sharing 1 files.   **Currently 7,556 users sharing 1,287,831 files (5,494 gigs)**

✔ Don't enjoy waiting about five minutes for the 2MB Napster program to download with your 56K modem? Then Napster might not be your game. MP3s usually consume at least 4MB, meaning they'll take about ten minutes or more to download. (Download times vary wildly according to server speeds and phone line conditions.)

✔ Napster users consider file sharing as proper etiquette. If nobody shares files, there won't be any MP3 files to download. In fact, some users check the upload/download ratios of downloaders. If they're not sharing anything, they're considered *leeches or leechers,* and the people with the files cut off their downloads.

✔ Napster is just a *protocol* — a way to transfer information across the Internet. The Napster software isn't the only software that works with Napster technology. Dozens of Napster *clones* — other clients using the Napster protocol — can also access servers created by Napster, Inc. In fact, many people have put up their own servers for Napster clients to access. (See the section "Serving Yourself with Napigator," later in this chapter, for more information.)

✔ To find out more about Napster, head to the official source. Click Help at the top of the Napster screen, and you're transported to the official Napster Web page where you can read a fairly comprehensive explanation of what's going on. For unofficial answers, head to www.deja.com and search for the word **Napster**.

The legalities of Napster

Napster, Inc. has been twisting and turning through several legal battles. Napster compares itself to a "messenger service" that lets people send information back and forth between their own personal computers. Because Napster has no control over the information that's being sent, it's not responsible if people use its service to break existing copyright laws when giving away music.

The record companies disagree, however, and say that Napster is merely "taking music which isn't theirs and giving it away." The judges agreed, but under certain conditions.

For instance, Napster can be used legally, so the record companies can't just shut it down. Instead, the record companies must provide Napster with a list of copyrighted songs that shouldn't be listed as available for trade.

Napster must then "filter" out the artists and titles of songs provided by the record companies. However, like other copy-protection schemes, Napster's filters have already been circumvented by determined users. Some users simply rename their songs by using a form of Pig Latin. The "Beatles – Yesterday" song, for instance, becomes posted as "eatlesB – esterdayY".

Napster's legal battles change daily. To keep track of it all, head to `http://dailynews.yahoo.com/` and type **Napster** in the Search News box. Click Search to find the latest Napster news.

Finding and Downloading Songs on Napster

It's easy to find favorite songs using Napster. Downloading really isn't much of a problem, either. Napster usually finds dozens — even hundreds — of copies of the songs you're after.

The key is to refine the process to create the fastest downloads of the best quality songs. The following steps explain just how to do that using the official Napster software, although most Napster clones work similarly.

1. Load Napster.

Choose Napster from your Start menu. (Unless you specifically installed it somewhere else, it should be listed under Programs.) The program leaps to the screen.

2. Click the Search button and type your search term.

At the top of the program's screen, the Search button brings up the Napster Search window, shown in Figure 5-2. Although Napster claims to search only by Artist and Title, it looks for much more.

Napster searches for *any* words in the name of the artist or song title. It also looks inside the song's *ID tag* — an area built into an MP3 file that holds information about the song. It checks the MP3 song's file name, as well as the name of the folder where it's stored on the user's hard drive.

So, pretend you're using an Internet search engine such as Yahoo! or Alta Vista, and you want to narrow down the search as much as possible. Type the artist's last name and part of the song's title to see what Napster delivers. It usually comes up with too many songs, so keep refining your search until you find what you're after.

Many Napster users are terrible spellers, especially when trying to avoid Napster's copy-protection filters. Plus, after a song is misspelled once, it's often downloaded by other Napster users. That spreads the misspelling all over the Internet. So, try misspelling the name a few different ways to see what comes up. Try searching for a few key words in the lyrics, too. Also, keep track of the current schemes used to bypass Napster's filters. Songs titles are often misspelled intentionally.

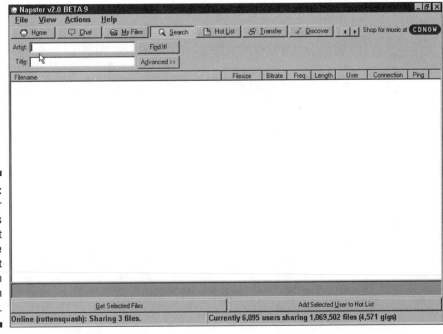

Figure 5-2:
Napster
searches
just about
everywhere
to find what
you type in
the Search
window.

Napster added a helpful search feature in the latest versions of its software. If you want to see all the songs by The Carrot Fibers except for their hit, Creamed Corn, type **carrot fibers –corn**. Napster searches for all the songs by The Carrot Fibers that don't contain the word corn. It's a great way to search for *other* songs recorded by bands that are one-hit wonders.

3. Decide which songs to download.

Here's where the tricky part comes in. When returning a list of songs, Napster doesn't just display the name of the artist and title, it displays information about the connection. Table 5-1 explains the meaning of the search information provided by Napster and offers some ways to use this information in determining what to download.

Table 5-1	Napster Search Information	
This	*Means This*	*So Do This*
File size	The size of the file	Look for songs with the same file size, which usually means they contain a complete version of the song.
Bitrate	The song's encoding rate	Higher numbers mean better quality sound, but larger files. Stick with 128.
Freq	The song's quality	Look for 44100 to ensure near CD-quality recordings.
Length	The length of the song	Look for songs of the same length — those usually contain a complete version.
User	The name of the person with the song	Right-click the name and click View User information to see how many songs that user is currently uploading/down loading — the busier the user, the slower the user.
Connection	The person's reported modem speed	Look for slow connections because they often disguise faster ones.
Ping	The amount of time it takes for a signal to reach from your computer to the other computer and return	Faster ping speeds mean closer computers, which somethimes mean faster transfer rates.

When Napster displays the list of songs — both legitimate and illegally posted ones — it sorts them by *ping* speed; it also displays the connection speed (see Figure 5-3). Computers with low ping numbers are close to you on the Internet. Logically, a low ping number and a fast connection speed should mean fast downloads, but that's not always the case.

What's a proxy, anyway?

Sooner or later, you'll come across a program that asks if you're using a "proxy server." Huh? Here's the scoop:

Just as traffic lights manage the flow of cars on the streets, a proxy server is a computerized manager that supervises the data flow between a computer application — your Internet browser, for instance — and a larger server or a group of servers, like the Internet.

But a proxy server does much more than that. It examines the information moving back and forth between the two. If the proxy server can handle the request itself, it goes for it, saving time. If it can't, it sends the request on to the real server for processing.

Here's an example to make this less confusing. America Online uses proxy servers for two main reasons. If one user calls up a popular Web site,

the proxy server remembers that page. Then if another user somewhere else quickly calls up the same page, the proxy server merely shuffles that same page over to the other America Online user. Because America Online doesn't need to connect to that Web site again, it saves time, and everybody's happy.

Because proxy servers watch the data that moves back and forth between computers, they perform another important task: They work as filters. Big corporations, for instance, might set up a proxy server to keep employees from visiting eBay when they should be working. Universities, too, have been known to use proxy servers to block out Napster and other file swappers so students don't hog all the bandwidth, slowing down the networks — or accumulating lawsuits.

Figure 5-3:
A search for the Dave Matthews Band turned up legitimate as well as illegally posted songs.

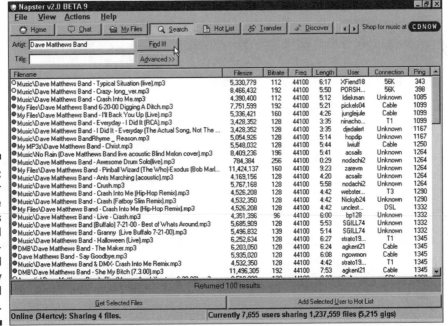

In fact, you should never make download speed your sole factor in choosing a song. Your first factor should be finding a song that's complete and encoded without skips or glitches.

The best way to find those songs is to search by song length. So, click the Length bar at the top of the Length column to sort the songs by their duration. When you find a bunch of songs with the same title and the same length, those files probably contain the complete song, not just a portion of it. A second or two off is okay, but avoid anything more than that.

Now it's time to download that complete song.

4. **Double-click the desired song.**

   When the file has downloaded completely, its status changes to Finished. You're through.

✔ Am I telling you how to do something illegal? Not in the steps I've shown here. The Dave Matthews Band posted the song *I Did It* on Napster to promote an upcoming album.

✔ All this stuff isn't as complicated as it sounds. You don't have to sort files by their song lengths. You can just search for a song, double-click it when it appears on the Search list, and wait for it to appear on your hard drive. However, following the previous steps leads to the quickest and highest quality downloads.

✔ Check out the following tips and tricks section for more tips on grabbing the best quality songs from Napster in the least amount of time.

What's Napster's Hot List?

The deeper you dig into Napster, the more you find. For instance, sometimes you'll find a user whose name keeps turning up during your searches. This user obviously has similar tastes in music. Wouldn't it be nice if you could peek at his or her hard drive? With the Hot List, you can.

When you find a user with similar tastes — or simply with a fast connection — right-click the song and choose Add to Hot List from the pop-up menu that appears. Next, click the Hot List button along the top of Napster. A window appears on the left that lists the user name that you've just added.

Double-click the user name (or, in earlier versions, right-click the user name and choose Browse Files), and Napster displays all the files that this user has posted for sharing. Chances are, you'll find some other songs you like, ready for plucking.

Tips and Tricks for Napster Picks

The more you use Napster or its clones, the more you realize all the little tricks involved in finding the best songs in the least possible time. Here's a list to keep by the desk when Napstering:

- ✔ Try searching for the word **Rare**. Many people use Napster to post songs you simply can't find in the record stores.

- ✔ Get a cable modem if at all possible. It makes the difference between downloads that last a half hour or several minutes.

- ✔ It's better to download files a few at a time using fast rates than to download zillions at slow rates. Many people only use Napster to grab a song or two and then disconnect. If your files weren't completely downloaded from them in that time, you'll be stuck with only part of the songs.

- ✔ Napster displays only 100 songs for each search. When searching for lesser-known songs from very popular bands, be as specific as possible in your Title field. Otherwise, the band's best-selling songs will fill up the 100-song space, pushing the lesser-known songs off the edge.

- ✔ Stick with songs encoded at a bitrate of 128. Anything lower sounds awful. Anything higher translates into a bigger file that sounds just a little bit better. If sound quality is that important to you, just buy the CD. The latest version of Napster makes it easy: Just click on the CD Now button.

- ✔ Napster's version 9 lets you exclude terms when searching. Searching for the word **Turnip**, for example, will find both *The Bitter Turnips* and *Turnip Salad*. If you don't want to see *The Bitter Turnips*, type **turnips - salad** in the Artists box.

- ✔ Don't use any punctuation in band names or song titles. Plus, search for whole words, not parts of words. Napster won't find Matthews if you lazily type in **Mat**.

- ✔ Napster has lots of different servers. If you can't find what you want, choose Disconnect from the File menu. Wait a minute or two and then choose Connect. That might connect you with a different Napster server — and a whole new set of songs to search. Or, even better, use Napigator, which I describe in its own section later in this chapter.

- ✔ *Always* check song lengths before choosing the one to download. Sometimes songs are cut off during downloads, yet people still keep them in their collection. Unfortunately, those truncated songs end up being passed around Napster like chain letters. Look for songs with nearly identical lengths, and then choose the one with the fastest download rate.

- ✔ Be sure to use the Hot List, which I describe in the sidebar "What's Napster's Hot List?" (elsewhere in this chapter) — it's a great way to find your favorite songs quickly.

✔ Don't assume that you need to download from the fast cable, DSL, T1, or T3 modems for a speedy transfer. Very few people have 14.4 or 28.8 modems these days, and the ones who do are usually disguising the fact that they have lightning fast modems. (And if it turns out that they do have slow modems, which is leading to a slow transfer, right-click the transferring song and choose Delete/Abort Transfer to stop the incoming file.)

✔ If you're using one of those "other" computers or operating systems, head to www.pzcommunications.com or http://opennap.sourceforge.net for a list of more than 100 Napster clones. Last look showed similar MP3 fetchers for the Amiga, Linux, Beos and other operating systems.

✔ Stuck with a slow modem? Then choose your downloads late at night, and let them download while you sleep. Be sure to check them out the next morning to make sure that you received complete versions. (Delete them if they aren't complete so that you aren't passing around truncated or glitchy songs.)

✔ Napster sends music as fast as your modem allows, regardless of the modem speed you choose here. The speed you choose here appears next to your user name when somebody finds a desirable song on your computer. That's why aggressively sneaky Napster users with fast cable modems or T1 lines often lie about their speed, choosing "Don't Know" or "14.4." That tricks users into skipping these "slow" computers, leaving these sneaky Napster users with more bandwidth for their own downloads.

✔ Don't share the same folder that Napster uses to store your incoming MP3 files. Create a different folder for sharing, and then move your downloaded MP3 files into that shared folder only when you're sure that the downloads contain complete songs, without skips or other problems.

Serving Yourself with Napigator

Napigator doesn't really use Napster technology, and it's not a file-swapping program. But it's an incredibly powerful Napster enhancer that deserves mention.

The Internet holds dozens of servers run by Napster, Inc. Unrelated companies and private citizens place their own servers up, as well. But when your Napster software connects to the Internet, it arbitrarily selects one official Napster server, and you're stuck with it. You can only search through that particular server's indexes to find your favorite songs.

Napigator, shown in Figure 5-4, doesn't tolerate this rudeness. Instead, it lists *all* of the currently running servers that use Napster technology. The program delivers statistics on each server, displaying the number of files and users, the connection speed, port numbers, IP addresses, and even more technical information.

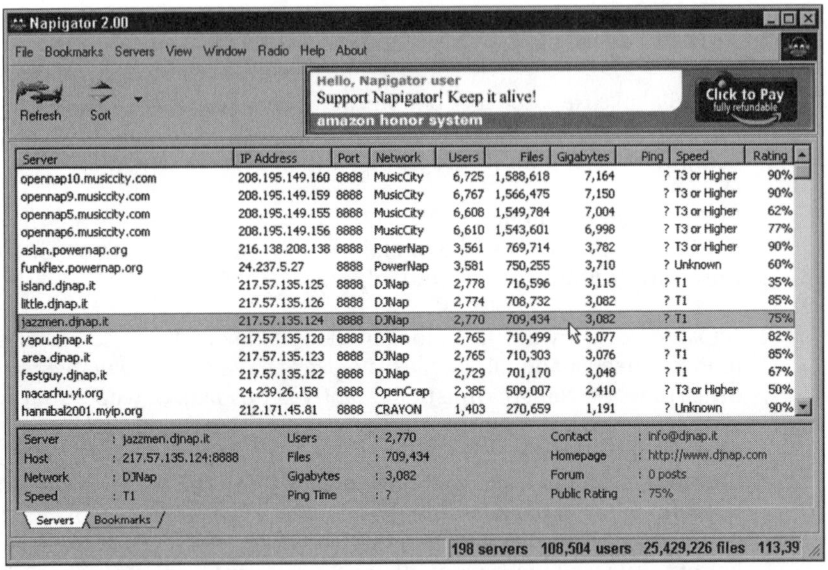
Napigator 2.00
File Bookmarks Servers View Window Radio Help About
Refresh Sort
Hello, Napigator user
Support Napigator! Keep it alive!
amazon honor system
Click to Pay
fully refundable
Server | IP Address | Port | Network | Users | Files | Gigabytes | Ping | Speed | Rating
opennap10.musiccity.com 208.195.149.160 8888 MusicCity 6,725 1,588,618 7,164 ? T3 or Higher 90%
opennap9.musiccity.com 208.195.149.159 8888 MusicCity 6,767 1,566,475 7,150 ? T3 or Higher 90%
opennap5.musiccity.com 208.195.149.155 8888 MusicCity 6,608 1,549,784 7,004 ? T3 or Higher 62%
opennap6.musiccity.com 208.195.149.156 8888 MusicCity 6,610 1,543,601 6,998 ? T3 or Higher 77%
aslan.powernap.org 216.138.208.138 8888 PowerNap 3,561 769,714 3,782 ? T3 or Higher 90%
funkflex.powernap.org 24.237.5.27 8888 PowerNap 3,581 750,255 3,710 ? Unknown 60%
island.djnap.it 217.57.135.125 8888 DJNap 2,778 716,596 3,115 ? T1 35%
little.djnap.it 217.57.135.126 8888 DJNap 2,774 708,732 3,082 ? T1 85%
jazzmen.djnap.it 217.57.135.124 8888 DJNap 2,770 709,434 3,082 ? T1 75%
yapu.djnap.it 217.57.135.120 8888 DJNap 2,765 710,499 3,077 ? T1 82%
area.djnap.it 217.57.135.123 8888 DJNap 2,765 710,303 3,076 ? T1 85%
fastguy.djnap.it 217.57.135.122 8888 DJNap 2,729 701,170 3,048 ? T1 67%
macachu.yi.org 24.239.26.158 8888 OpenCrap 2,385 509,007 2,410 ? T3 or Higher 50%
hannibal2001.myip.org 212.171.45.81 8888 CRAYON 1,403 270,659 1,191 ? Unknown 90%
Server : jazzmen.djnap.it
Host : 217.57.135.124:8888
Network : DJNap
Speed : T1
Users : 2,770
Files : 709,434
Gigabytes : 3,082
Ping Time : ?
Contact : info@djnap.it
Homepage : http://www.djnap.com
Forum : 0 posts
Public Rating : 75%
Servers Bookmarks
198 servers 108,504 users 25,429,226 files 113,39

Figure 5-4: Napigator lets you choose which of Napster's many servers to search through.

Spot a server that looks promising? Double-click its name, and Napigator loads your Napster client, which then tries to connect to the server. If all goes well, Napster connects, and you begin searching for favorites. If the server's too crowded, Napster says it can't connect, and you try a different server.

Why bother with Napigator? Well, you and your friends can all meet on a particular server at a particular time to swap MP3 files from your hard drives. Or, you can choose servers specializing in particular types of music. Or, perhaps your currently connected server doesn't have the songs you're seeking.

Some people even create their own servers that use Napster technology. If you're interested in creating your own server, using different Napster clients, or even using different file-sharing protocols, check out OpenNap (`http://opennap.sourceforge.net/`). A second-generation of Napster, OpenNap allows the sharing of *any* types of files. (Yes, the movie industry is worried.)

Official Napster software works only on Windows or the Macintosh. If you're using a different type of computer or operating system — or if you'd like to try a different Napster client — check out the Ultimate Resource Site `www.ultimateresourcesite.com`. It lists dozens of file-sharing programs similar to the official Napster.

Whispering Across Gnutella

Gnutella, like Napster, lets people share files across the Internet. And, like Napster, Gnutella isn't a program; it's yet another technology, or *protocol*, for computers to communicate amongst themselves.

While Napster is limited to MP3 files, Gnutella users share anything on their hard drives that they'd like to make public: MP3 files, videos, documents, or the entire contents of selected folders.

Napster works by keeping close track of its users. It collects user names, modem speeds, and all the files the users have made available for sharing. In order to work, Napster must constantly keeps lists of who's sharing what.

Gnutella, by contrast, simply concentrates on transmitting information. It doesn't need a central storehouse of users and the files they've shared. Everything takes place on the fly.

For example, say you're looking for a document on the genetics of detached ear lobes. When you log onto a Gnutella-based program to search for that information, the program asks the most closely networked computers for your request. Plus, it asks those computers — if they don't have the information — to pass your request to computers closest to them on the network.

As computers begin asking each other for the information, your request spreads like ripples on water. Finally, if a computer happens to be sharing your requested information, the computer sends the information to the computer that requested it. That computer, in turn, sends the information to the computer that requested it. And so on, and so on, until eventually the information returns to you.

To prevent the request from growing exponentially and clogging the network, every user is limited to a group of about 10,000 other computers. And because that group constantly changes, it's difficult for anybody to track the person asking the question, the person with the answer, or the question itself.

As the group changes, so does the pool of information, meaning you'll find different things at different times. And, because no direct path connects two computers, Gnutella is much slower than Napster.

It's a novel concept, and it brings up some novel questions:

> ✔ **What if nobody in my network area has the information I want?** It's entirely possible. And you'll be out of luck — at that particular moment. But as the information pool keeps changing, so will your odds of finding what you're after. Try again a few minutes later.

✔ **What if people start trading illegal things — copyrighted music or software, for instance?** Then those people are doing something illegal, just as some people send illegal things through the U.S. Postal Service. But that doesn't make the post office a criminal, it's just the conduit. Similarly, Gnutella is just a conduit for funneling information. It's not responsible for the actions of its users.

✔ **Can Gnutella be sued and shut down, just like Napster?** Not exactly. Napster depends on its own bank of servers to track the information and who it's flowing between. Gnutella is a free-flowing protocol where hundreds — thousands — of computers talk among themselves. If Napster loses its servers, it no longer works. Because Gnutella has no servers, it's much more difficult — if not impossible — to shut down. Gnutella is like a bunch of people in a crowded room, whispering information among themselves. Napster, Inc. is like a telephone service, where people talk through the phones. When the phones are removed, the service disappears.

✔ **Where can I find more information about Gnutella and other file-sharing programs?** Try www.zeropaid.com and www.bearshare.net. They both carry downloads of the latest file-sharing programs, explain how to set them up, and provide forums where users help each other out.

Where did Gnutella come from?

Early in the MP3 game, a hip group of Arizona programmers named "Nullsoft" (www.nullsoft.com) created Winamp, a powerful MP3 player that quickly attracted zillions of dedicated followers. (Winamp is on the CD in the back of the book.)

Led by wunderkind Justin Frankel, the group followed up with another winner, SHOUTcast, a program that let anybody listen to or run an Internet radio station from a home computer. (I cover it in Chapter 8.)

Frankel and his group impressed not only MP3 users with Winamp, but America Online execs, who waved enough cash in front of the young men to convince them that being an America Online subsidiary wasn't all that bad.

A few weeks later, however, as record labels began attacking Napster, a "pre-release" version of Gnutella appeared on the Nullsoft Web site. Like Napster, Gnutella allowed users to share files. Unlike Napster, however, the file sharing couldn't be traced as easily, making it more difficult to shut down.

America Online, in the midst of merging with Time Warner (which owns Warner Music — a charter member of Napster's nemesis, the Recording Industry Association of America), immediately condemned the project, and Nullsoft pulled Gnutella from the Web site. It was too late, however. Nullsoft had not only posted the software, but its source code, which had been downloaded by dozens of other programmers.

Other programmers picked up the axe to create dozens of Gnutella-based programs to run on different computers and operating systems. Should Napster disappear, either by lawsuit, excessive surcharges, or lack of users, Gnutella's waiting.

Taking Care of BearShare

Gnutella lacks the "point, click, and grab" simplicity of Napster. But BearShare's quickly making Gnutella just as easy to use as Napster. Adding easy-to-use buttons and a user-friendly Help menu, BearShare (www. bearshare.net) makes Gnutella nearly as easy to use as Napster.

Nonetheless, the program starts its installation with a warning screen, begging users to read the documentation before running the program.

Take the advice of BearShare and read its documentation. You'll thank yourself later. If you change a setting while installing the program, you could let anybody download any file on your computer. Specifically, read the sections about firewalls. Just as with Napster, you should have a firewall running on your computer when connecting to any file-swapping service. I recommend ZoneAlarm at www.zonealarm.com.

Here's a quick primer on finding files through BearShare.

1. **Load BearShare.**

   When you first load BearShare, the program finds other computers logged on using Gnutella. It weeds out the ones that are too busy or have logged off until it comes up with a few strong connections, as shown in Figure 5-5.

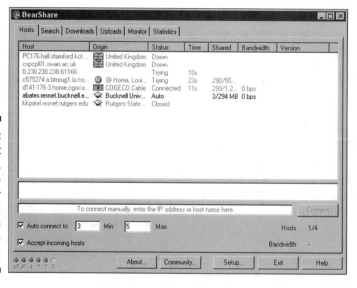

Figure 5-5:
When first loaded, BearShare searches for a few strong connections to swap information.

When it's found a few initial connections, or *hosts,* you're ready to start searching.

2. **Click the Search tab, type the name of a song or artist, and then click Start.**

   Actually, BearShare uses Gnutella to search for any type of file, not just MP3s. When you click Start, BearShare begins its search by asking your immediate hosts for the file. Chances are, they won't have the requested information. However, they'll quickly pass your request along and the search intensifies.

   BearShare begins spitting out the results of your search, as shown in Figure 5-6.

3. **Right-click a song and choose Download.**

   BearShare begins downloading the song onto your own hard drive. Remember, though, no direct connection lies between your computer and the computer with the song, as was the case in Napster. Instead, the desired song "hops" from computer to computer as it downloads onto your hard drive.

Depending on the number of hops, the service is often slower than Napster. But because nobody's in charge of the whole thing, the service is much more difficult to shut down.

> ✔ Although Gnutella, as a whole, can't be sued out of existence, Gnutella users can still be traced individually. Some industry gurus speculate that the record industry could file lawsuits against a few individual Gnutella users to make them examples, hoping the "fear factor" will keep people from using the service.

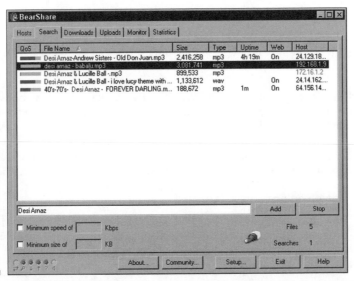

Figure 5-6: Using Gnutella, BearShare starts spreading the word of your desired file among other connected computers.

✔ To download files the quickest, look at the QoS listing in the far left of the BearShare Search tab. See the little green bars? The bars containing the most green are the fastest connections. Click on the word QoS until a little downward pointing arrow appears. That sorts the files according to their download speed.

✔ After you've started downloading files, stop searching for more. That only consumes unnecessary bandwidth and slows your download.

✔ Some bozo's already written a worm that preys on Gnutella users. Luckily, it's easy to thwart. First, it's a program that ends in EXE. Unless you change its settings, BearShare automatically filters out programs from showing up as downloads. Second, the worm is an easily recognizable 8,192 bytes in size. Third, the worm automatically renames itself to what you're searching for. So, if you search for "Harpo" and a Gnutella program returns a file named "Harpo" that's only 8,192 bytes in size, don't grab it.

✔ BearShare plays it safe by only allowing other users access to a Sharing folder and a Download folder within your BearShare folder. Unless you change the settings, they can't access other parts of your computer.

✔ BearShare also filters the files being shared on the network. Unless you change the settings, you won't be able to see any shared files ending in DOC, DOT, EXE, VBS, or XLS. Those are potentially dangerous files that could contain viruses or worms.

✔ You'll find plenty of help in the BearShare Help system, as well as the forum on its Web site (www.bearshare.net).

Aiming for MP3s with Aimster

Officially, Aimster has nothing to do with America Online, nor that online service's Buddy System. But it works similarly. By "piggy-backing" on the America Online Instant Messaging (AIM) service, it allows users to "swap" files with people on their buddy lists.

Or, if they're particularly friendly, Aimster users can call everybody a buddy, letting any user search through and download any information they've placed in their list of shared files list.

The program's easy to use, promises "plug-ins" to work with messaging services from other companies, and it works fairly simply.

1. Download and install Aimster.

Download Aimster from its Web site at www.aimster.com and install the program. Aimster hops onto the screen, as shown in Figure 5-7.

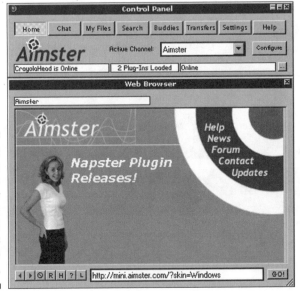

Figure 5-7:
Aimster lets
people
share any
files with
specified
individuals
or the entire
service.

As with any file-sharing program, be sure to install a firewall onto your computer to prevent unauthorized access from unscrupulous individuals. My favorite is ZoneAlarm (www.zonealarm.com).

Always leave the Aimster Control Panel window on-screen. The main window, the Aimster Control Panel lets you open other parts of the program by clicking the buttons along its top.

2. **Click the Search button, type the name of your desired file, and click Search.**

   Click the Search button along the top of the Aimster Control Panel window, and type the name of your desired file in the Search For box — Desi Arnaz, for instance. Click the Search button, and Aimster begins searching for your term.

   Right now, you don't have to worry about not having chosen any "buddies." When Aimster installs itself, the program automatically sets itself up so that any Aimster user may search through your shared files.

3. **Click the name of the desired file and click the Download button.**

   As shown in Figure 5-8, Aimster has located several matching songs. Click the name of the one you want, and then click the Download button to begin downloading the file.

Figure 5-8:
Choose your
desired file
and click
Download.

Finding and downloading files on Aimster is as easy as Steps 1-2-3. But if you're interested in the mechanics of Aimster, here are a few more tips:

✔ When Aimster is installed, the program allows any Aimster user to access the files you've designated for sharing. That lets people find files simply by using the previous steps. If you'd prefer to share files only with *specific* people, turn that feature off. Click the Aimster Control Panel's Settings button and remove the check mark from the box marked Allow Guest Access to My Files.

✔ To share files only with certain people, use the Aimster Buddy List: Click the Aimster Control Panel's Buddies button to bring up the Buddy List window. To add another Aimster user to your list, right-click Aimster Buddies, and then choose Add Buddies from the pop-up window. Type the Buddy's name to give that person access to your files. (Follow similar steps to add AOL Buddies to your list.)

✔ Be very careful when choosing what files to share on Aimster. Click the My Files button on Aimster's Control Panel window to see the files you're currently sharing. (Click the Full Path button to see where they're stored.) If you ever add another folder or directory to be shared, Aimster shares *every file in that folder* or directory. It's much safer to move individual files into a few shared folders than to add new folders for sharing.

✔ Here's an easy way to browse files of other people: Click the Aimster
Control Panel's Chat button, and click the Join Chat button from the
Chat Manager window that pops up. When the Aimster Chat Room List
appears, click a Chat Room with a lot of Users, and click the Join
button. Finally, click a Buddy's name from the right side of the window
and click the Browse button. That lets you browse through that buddy's
files — if she's left these files accessible for Guest Access.

✔ Aimster uses Gnutella and Napster protocols, and it automatically adds
your AOL buddies to its own buddy list. Additional plug-ins are on their
way for adding Microsoft Networking.

Chapter 6

Playing MP3 Files on Your Computer and Home Stereo

● ●

In This Chapter

▶ Using Winamp

▶ Customizing Winamp

▶ Using other MP3 players

▶ Changing the Windows default MP3 player

▶ Connecting your computer to your home stereo

● ●

*B*y now, your computer is stuffed with MP3 songs. It's time to sit back, pop open a Pellegrino, and give your music a good listen. But what MP3 software works best to play them all? Choosing between home stereos at a music store is easy; you walk in a room, and the salesperson flips the buttons.

But who has time to try out all the MP3 software out there?

This chapter describes the major contenders, focuses on one of the most popular, and wraps things up with tips on wringing out the best possible sound: hooking your computer up to your home stereo.

Using the Winamp MP3 Player

Hundreds of MP3 players float around the Internet, but one player has broken rank as the clear leader among the hip crowd: Winamp. Shown in Figure 6-1, Winamp (www.winamp.com) stuffs an incredible amount of power into a relatively small package, earning it more than 25 million downloads in the past two years.

Figure 6-1:
Although it can't create MP3s, Winamp has powerful and custom- izable features that make it a favorite player among music fans.

Winamp has plenty of chops, playing MP3, CDs, MIDI, WAV, and even WMA — the format used for Microsoft Windows Media Audio files. Winamp doesn't cater to copy protection schemes, it's free to download, and it doesn't float any advertisements across its screen.

The program's built-in ten-band equalizer adjusts the sound; a minibrowser pops up Web pages when necessary. Winamp tunes in Internet broadcasts from MP3 radio stations around the world. More than 150 special software enhancements called *plug-ins* allow fiddling with the sound — eliminating a singer's voice, for example, storing the files in different formats, or adding 3-D sound effects.

Goofier plug-ins create animated dancers, oozing lava lamps, and light shows to squirm across the screen. More than 20,000 utilities called *skins* decorate the look of Winamp, making it as fashionable as you prefer. Savvy users create their own skins, and upload them for sharing.

Recently purchased by the investment-savvy America Online, Winamp continues to grow in speed, power, and fan base. (You'll find a copy of Winamp, along with some of its most interesting plug-ins and skins, on the CD bound into the back of this book.)

This section shows you how to wring the best sound quality from Winamp. Mac users should check out the Macintosh version of MusicMatch (Chapter 11) or SoundJam (www.soundjam.com).

Winamp is an MP3 *player* only — it doesn't burn MP3s onto CDs nor can you use it to create MP3s from music CDs. For an all-in-one player/encoder/burner, check out MusicMatch, which I discuss in Chapter 11 and have included on the CD.

Installing and running Winamp

Compared to many programs, Winamp is a breeze to install. Use either the version included on this book's CD or download the latest version at www. winamp.com. (The programmers issue new versions almost monthly.)

Winamp comes in several versions. Unless you're pressed for hard drive space, download the Full version. It supports the Microsoft WMA format and Mjuice Audio media files, and it also includes a cool visualization package for putting swirlies and dancers on-screen. Besides, the Winamp installer lets you choose what parts to install, so you can change your mind at the last minute.

Click the Web page's Download button, as shown in Figure 6-2. Your computer will grab a copy of the latest version of Winamp and place it onto your hard drive.

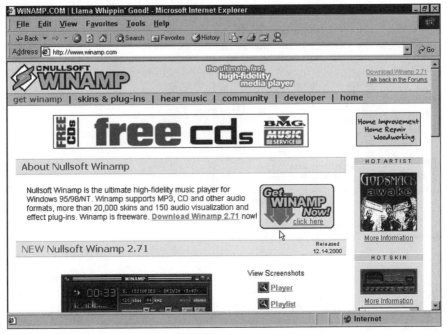

Figure 6-2: Click the Download button on www.winamp.com to download the program's latest version.

Follow these instructions to install your copy of Winamp, whether you downloaded its installation program from the Internet or copied it from the CD in the back of this book:

1. **Double-click the Winamp installation program's name, and read the standard legalese.**

2. **Click Next when you finish reading the License Agreement.**

3. Choose what parts of Winamp you'd like to install and click Next.

Chances are, you'll want the full version so that you get all the goodies. If not, choose between Standard, Lite, Minimal, or Custom, depending on your computer's space needs. (If you choose Custom, you can pick and choose.)

If you don't choose Full, be sure to choose Support for Writing WAV Files. This feature lets Winamp convert MP3 files into WAV files. CD-burning programs can then copy those songs onto a CD so that you can play them in any standard CD player.

4. Choose where to install Winamp and click Next.

Winamp asks to install itself into your Program Files folder with your other programs. Unless this offends you, click Next; Winamp scoots itself onto your hard drive and then asks how it should act.

5. Choose your settings and click Next.

As shown in Figure 6-3, leave all the boxes checked. You want Winamp to play your CDs and other sounds, and you want its icons easily accessible. If you don't want a box checked, though, click in the little box above the llama to remove the check mark.

Figure 6-3:
Hold your
mouse
pointer over
any of the
settings to
see what
they mean.

Be sure to choose whether you connect to the Internet through a network (cable modem users should check here) or through the phone lines. A working Internet connection lets Winamp identify songs from inserted CDs to ensure that you're using the latest version.

Don't know what some of those settings mean? Hold your mouse pointer over the head scratchers and an explanation appears to the right.

6. Visit the Winamp Walkthrough if you're a new user.

Winamp calls up its Web page for a demo of its many features, as shown in Figure 6-4.

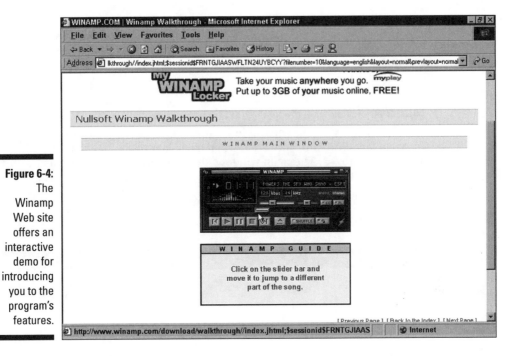

Figure 6-4:
The Winamp Web site offers an interactive demo for introducing you to the program's features.

7. Click the Run Winamp button.

Winamp appears on-screen (refer to Figure 6-1), ready to play your CDs, MP3s, and just about anything else relating to sound.

Here are some points about Winamp to keep in mind:

✔ Winamp is absolutely free, with no "pop-up" ads. It used to be *shareware*, meaning that if you liked it enough to keep it, you were morally obliged to send its creators $10 for their efforts. But now, Winamp is freeware.

✔ Winamp resembles a wall where other people hang their signs. Winamp is the framework, and users write software to add features — plug-ins and skins — to Winamp.

✔ Not too proud to embrace this grassroots group support, Winamp's Web page offers a wealth of add-on programs, plug-ins, and skins. You'll also find documentation, the most current version, and forums for online discussion.

✔ Like a wine club, the Winamp community often praises the virtues of past versions. Some versions run better on certain computers or sport different features. To sample past vintages, head for Winamp Heaven at www.winampheaven.com where you'll find about 100 versions for download, dating back to computing's Precambrian days of April 21, 1997.

✔ Once installed, Winamp includes four parts for pushing and pulling it into different configurations. The next four sections cover those parts. (To start running Winamp, choose its icon from your Start menu, Desktop, or the Quick Launch toolbar — that row of little icons by your Start button.)

Adjusting Winamp's main controls

Winamp consists of four separable windows, but it keeps most of them under wraps. In fact, Winamp works fine when shrunken to the pencil-thin waif shown in Figure 6-5. The main window, shown in Figure 6-6, serves as the control panel for the others; it works like the front panel of a CD player.

Figure 6-5:
Winamp's minimalist window.

Toggle Windowshade Mode

Sliding bar changes current position

Visual song display   Toggle size

Double-click to close program

Song title

Bring up Equalizer or Playlist

Stop | Eject

Pause | Random play

Play | Continuous

Figure 6-6:
Winamp's basic control window.

Back one song   Forward one song

Right-click for options

Nullsoft Winamp...

Play
View file info   Alt+3
Bookmarks

✔ Main Window   Alt+W
Playlist Editor   Alt+E
Equalizer   Alt+G
Minibrowser   Alt+T

Options
Playback
Visualization
Skins

Exit

Anybody with a CD player is already familiar with the controls for moving from song to song or skipping parts of songs. Some of the other controls aren't as apparent. Here are a few to remember (check out the dissected parts in Figure 6-6 for reference):

✔ To toggle Winamp between full size or miniscule, click the word WINAMP on the bar along the program's top. (Check it out, because you'll end up using that feature a lot.)

✔ Slide the bottom-most bar in the Winamp section back and forth to skip forward or backward within the song. The second longest bar, right above it, changes volume. (It also turns from cool green to fiery orange as the volume increases.) The smallest bar adjusts the sound's positioning between the two speakers. It's lime green when the balance is right.

✔ In Figure 6-6, you can tell that Winamp is currently playing back music in stereo because the Stereo button is lit up; some older songs or live recordings light up the adjacent Mono button.

✔ The song in Figure 6-6 was recorded at 128 Kbps and 44 kHz. That's the standard sampling rate for MP3s, making them sound nearly as good as a CD.

✔ Click the tiny EQ and PL buttons to bring up the Equalizer and Playlist windows, respectively. I cover them next.

Adjusting the equalizer

Winamp's equalizer adjusts the volume of various frequencies in a song, making it sound better according to your physical location, your mood, or the song's particular sound. Tweak the controls yourself, moving the bars up or down to increase or decrease the volume in certain ways. Slide up the bars on the left end to increase the bass, for example; move down the bars on the right to decrease the treble.

Click the Presets button to load custom-made sound settings, as shown in Figure 6-7. Choose the Jazz setting, close your eyes, and the band sounds as if it were playing in a smoky jazz club. Another setting puts that same band in a church or stadium.

✔ If the Equalizer isn't working, turn it on by clicking the EQ button in the upper-left corner. (It lights up when turned on.)

✔ The ten-band equalizer controls frequency ranges from 60 Hz to 16 kHz.

✔ Don't be impatient when switching from different preset frequency settings. It takes a few seconds for the changes to be heard in the song.

✔ A Preamp bar on the left side increases or decreases the sound's volume before it reaches the equalizer, which not only affects the overall sound, but the overall volume.

✔ When playing through your computer's speakers, the sound may not change much — no matter how much you tweak the equalizer. When you hook up your computer to your stereo, as shown later in this chapter, you'll hear more subtleties in the sound.

Figure 6-7:
Click the EQ
button and
then the
PRESETS
button to
see
equalizer
settings for
different
moods.

Creating playlists

Want to hear the blues all night? Or a mixture of your Miles Davis and Night Ranger MP3s? Winamp lets you create customized MP3 playlists for playback randomly, in alphabetical order, or in any order you choose.

Creating a playlist is easy enough; click the PL button to bring up Winamp's Playlist window. Then drag and drop the files you want to play into the Playlist window, as shown in Figure 6-8. As the songs drop into the window, their names and lengths appear.

Figure 6-8:
Drag and
drop sound
files into
Winamp's
Playlist
window to
place them
in the
playback
queue.

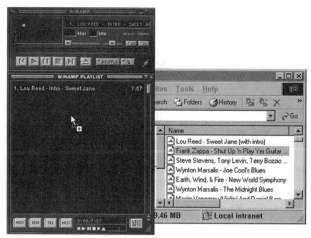

Not into dragging and dropping? Each of the buttons along the bottom of the Winamp window help manage your playlist. Click the Add button, for example, to reveal the Add Dir button. Clicking the Add Dir button reveals a standard Windows file browser box. Choose the directory where you store your MP3 files, and click Open to add them to the Playlist.

✔ After you load files into Winamp, click the Misc button to sort them alphabetically.

✔ To save a playlist, hold your mouse button down on the List Opts button in the playlist's bottom-right corner. A menu pops up. Without releasing the mouse button, slide the mouse pointer up to the pop-up menu's Save List option. Release the mouse button, and a window pops up in which you type the file's name.

✔ To load a playlist, repeat the process above, but slide the mouse pointer up to the Load List option, and then choose your playlist.

✔ As opposed to MP3 files, a Winamp playlist file merely contains text. Each line consists of a file's name, its path on the computer, and the artist's name and song listed on the ID tag. Winamp uses the playlist as a map when pulling files from different directories. Playlist files end with an M3U extension; MP3s end with an MP3 extension.

✔ The Misc button allows for sorting the list, creating an HTML version of the list, and other goodies. Feel free to experiment.

✔ To select all the songs loaded on Winamp's current playlist, double-click the Sel button. Hit Del or click the Rem button, and Winamp removes all those songs from the playlist. It doesn't erase any files, it just removes the songs from the current list.

✔ Click the Sel button once, and a menu appears. Choose Sel Zero from that menu, and Winamp *deselects* any songs you've currently selected. (But it leaves the songs on the playlist.) Choose Inv Sel from the Sel menu, and Winamp deselects any songs you've currently selected, and instead selects the songs you hadn't selected. Yes, you have to play with these playlist buttons a few times before you'll figure them out completely. Just remember that they never delete any files, they just alter your playlist.

Using the minibrowser

Winamp's minibrowser is a tiny Internet browser — a little window for grunt-level Web chores. Hold down Alt and press T to bring up the Minibrowser window, as shown in Figure 6-9. From there, a single click leads you to the Winamp Web site to grab skins, plug-ins, and other goodies. Another click brings up an online store for MP3-inspired CD purchases.

Be sure to check out SHOUTcast Radio, Nullsoft's collection of Internet Radio Stations. (I cover SHOUTcast Radio in Chapter 8.) A list appears, showing the hour's most popular Internet radio stations. Click something interesting, and you'll join the others listening through Winamp to hear an MP3 Internet radio station.

Figure 6-9:
Winamp includes a minibrowser for those without a "real" browser.

Customizing Winamp with add-ons

Although Winamp works great "out of the box," its users have made it even better by creating thousands of add-ons — from decorative *skins* to plug-ins for altering an MP3 sound. This section shows you how to find and install Winamp skins, plug-ins, and MP3 utilities.

Adding skins

Skins are just that — wraparounds for Winamp's face, giving it a new look. Figures 6-10 through 6-18 show a few of the thousands of available skins.

Figure 6-10:
The Mediterraneo skin.

Figure 6-11:
The Britney Paradise skin.

Figure 6-12:
The "42"
skin.

Figure 6-13:
The PAC-
AMP skin.

Figure 6-14:
The New
Beetle skin.

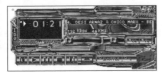

Figure 6-15:
The Dark
Chrome, 2nd
Edition skin.

Figure 6-16:
The Silence
skin.

Figure 6-17:
The "Zelda:
A Link to the
Past" skin.

Figure 6-18:
The Surgical
Steel skin.

Where's Winamp's Easter Egg?

Computer history buffs point back to the late '70s for the origins of "Easter Eggs." Back then, savvy players of Atari's 2600 game console discovered a secret room with the programmer's initials hidden in the Adventure game cartridge.

Just as painters sign their paintings, programmers often place their own digital signature onto their work. Dubbed an *Easter Egg*, it requires you to enter a predetermined sequence of keystrokes in a precise order before it reveals itself.

After Winamp is installed and loaded, it plays back its "trademark" logo sound. (The one about the llama.) When you enter the following keystrokes, the logo appears across the top of Winamp, on its title bar:

1. **Open Winamp.**

2. **In this order, press the letters N, U, and L.**

3. **Press the Esc key.**

4. **Press the letter L.**

5. **Press the Esc key again.**

6. **Press the letters S, O, F, and T.**

Winamp's logo appears on the title bar. Special keystrokes in older versions revealed the age of Winamp programmer Justin — calculated to the second — as well as a picture of him and his cat.

When configured for Internet access, Winamp automatically lets you check out the latest in skins. Found some eye-pleasers? Follow these steps to wrap them around your copy of Winamp:

1. **Right-click the lightning bolt in the bottom-right corner of the Winamp main window — the window with the play control buttons.**

2. **On the menu that appears, click Skins and choose <<Get more skins!>>.**

   Your Internet browser appears, and opens the Winamp site to the Skins page.

3. **Pick and choose from the available skins, and download the file directly into Winamp's Skins folder. Winamp automatically begins wearing the skin.**

   • To load a different skin, right-click the lightning bolt again, choose Skins, and a window pops up to reveal all your installed skins. Click a skin's name, and Winamp quickly slips it on.

   • Want Winamp's normal, default skin? Then choose <Base Skin> from the list of skins.

   • Skins come in a wide variety of themes, including Anime, Cars, Futuristic, Games, Music, People, Retro, Sports, TV, and a bunch of others.

   • When adding things to Winamp, start with skins. They're an easy way to introduce yourself to the program's fun. Just remember to choose <Base Skin> to return to normal if something looks too wild.

Using plug-ins

Skins merely change how Winamp looks. Plug-ins change what Winamp does and how it sounds. Check out Table 6-1 for a description of Winamp's built-in battalion of plug-ins.

Table 6-1 only describes the plug-ins that come built-in to the full version of Winamp. Winamp's Web site carries hundreds of additional plug-ins written and submitted by users to perform different and often more esoteric functions.

Table 6-1	Which Plug-in Does What?
Plug-in Type	*Function*
Input	Handles the player's guts: Decoding MP3s, WMAs, Mjuice, Audiosoft, VOC (the old Soundblaster format), CDs, MIDI, and MOD. Users add their own plug-ins for different formats and fun.
Output	Converts your songs into other file formats: WAV, WMA, Microsoft DirectSound (allowing you to hear music while a game is using your sound card, for instance), or files ready to copy onto a "home stereo" format CD.
Visualization	Three-dimensional graphics that dance to the sound's groove are visualizations, as shown in Figure 6-19. They're meant for people who don't have to pretend they're working on their computers. The program's full version includes a customizable cool light display editor; custom-built plug-ins live at the Web site.
DSP/Effect	Digital Sound Processors that add reverb, chorus, strip the singer's voice, or tweak the audio in other ways.
General Purpose	Various. Anything that doesn't fit into other categories appears here. DJ tools, cross-fading mixers, 3-D sound controllers, equalizers, song looper, alarm clocks, and other Winamp-influenced bursts of creativity.

Here are a few things to remember about plug-ins:

✔ For years, only well-heeled "hi-fi" enthusiasts could afford to collect the latest equipment, always testing their sound with the latest gadget. Winamp lets users play with more gadgets than they have time for. And for the most part, everything's free.

✔ To load an effect, right-click the lightning-bolt symbol in the bottom-right corner of the Winamp window, choose Select Preferences from the Options menu, and click the desired category of plug-in. Choose a plug-in from within that category, and click the Start, Stop, or Configure button to stir things up.

✔ You can configure most plug-ins to your taste. Highlight your plug-in and click the Configure button. The About button reveals the plug-in version number and author.

All-in-One MP3 Players and Encoders

Winamp wins hands down at playing MP3s, but several other players have a little more functionality than Winamp. They *create* MP3 files as well as play them back. In fact, all-in-one software is fancy enough to warrant its own coverage in Chapter 11. Here's a quick preview of what you can find there:

✔ **MusicMatch Jukebox (**www.musicmatch.com**):** Plays, organizes, and creates MP3s — for free. (Best yet, it's on the CD in the back of this book.) An extra $19.95 gets the professional version, which rips CDs into MP3s much faster, creates CDs up to 12 times faster, creates CD covers, and other goodies.

✔ **RealPlayer Jukebox:** Plays MP3s and creates low-quality MP3s from your CDs. The full-featured version creates standard-quality MP3s for an extra $29.95, but the software doesn't do much more than MusicMatch. RealPlayer Jukebox has also gained a reputation among users as *spyware,* setting itself up by default during installation to send information to the company about how the program's being used.

Figure 6-19:
Although most visualizations are wild light displays, WildTangent released a holiday visualization of a woman in a Santa costume dancing to the beat.

The Other MP3 Players

Hundreds of programs play MP3 files. If you're not enamored with Winamp, head to www.askmp3.com, click the word MP3 along the top, and head to the MP3 Players section. You'll find plenty of players to sample for just about every variety of operating system.

Here's a brief look at two of the more popular MP3 players you may run across. They don't create MP3s, they just play them back.

Windows Media Player

When Microsoft entered the MP3 player race, the corporate giant simply added MP3-playback capabilities into the sound arsenal of Windows Media Player. The result, shown in Figure 6-20, still doesn't record, but it plays MP3s and a wide variety of other audio and video formats.

Figure 6-20:
The versions
of Windows
Media
Player
released
with
Windows 98,
Second
Edition, and
Windows
Me play
MP3 files.

Microsoft also whipped up a new music compression format to compete with MP3. Dubbed WMA or *Windows Media Audio* by Microsoft creative titans, the new version is half the size of MP3 files, reducing download time.

The WMA format is incompatible with MP3, however, and sometimes you can't freely copy it because it contains a rights-management system for copyright holders.

The version of Media Player bundled with Windows 95 or Windows 98 sometimes can't play MP3s. If so, you need to download a newer version of Media Player. (The free program is available at www.microsoft.com — head for the Downloads section.)

- ✔ Media Player is a convenient, albeit awkward, freebie, but it isn't nearly as configurable as Winamp or MusicMatch.

- ✔ To find your version of Media Player, choose Programs from the Start button, click Accessories, and then choose Entertainment. (Windows 95 users should choose Multimedia instead of Entertainment to find Media Player.)

- ✔ Owners of portable MP3 players sometimes use WMA format because the files are usually half the size of an MP3 file. That's because MP3 must generally be formatted at 128 Kbps for near-CD quality sound, whereas WMA sounds nearly the same when formatted at 64 Kbps. That makes them half the size, so twice as many can be stuffed onto a portable MP3 player. Not all players handle the WMA format, however, so check first.

- ✔ Microsoft may be a late starter in the MP3 race, but it started late with Internet browsers, too. After a few years, it hammered the competition into the ground.

Sonique

Sonique (www.sonique.com) breathes cool. Figure 6-21 shows one configuration of the interface; other faceplates blink and swirl like Las Vegas neon. Sonique is coming on strong behind Winamp. The program attracts skins, features an equalizer, uses playlists, and, best of all, sounds great.

Figure 6-21:
This free program changes shapes, supports skins and plug-ins, handles Internet radio, and plays MP3s as well as other programs.

Sonique plays them all, including MP3 files, Microsoft Windows Media files, music CDs, and other formats. Check it out for kicks, and see if you don't get hooked. Beware, though. Sonique uses a rather bizarre user interface. Instead of Winamp's buttons and menus, Sonique uses an odd collection of knobs and widgets that take some time to figure out.

Changing Your Default MP3 Player

MP3 players have big egos. As soon as you install one, it assumes that you want it to automatically play all your sound files, including MP3s, CDs, and any other piece of sound on your hard drive.

And that's the problem. What if you don't like this newcomer and want to switch back to your old player? If you're lucky, it's as easy as clicking a button.

For example, to reassign MP3-playing rights to Winamp, follow these steps:

1. **Right-click the little lightning bolt to bring up the Options menu; then choose Preferences.**

2. **Choose File Types and click the Select All button.**

   You might need to double-click the word Setup in the Winamp Preferences window to make the File Types option appears.

   When you click the Select all button, Winamp highlights all the file types it supports.

   To ensure that you don't lose Winamp as your default player in the future, click to place a check in the box marked Register Types On Winamp Start.

3. **Click Close, and Winamp grabs back its abilities.**

Most MP3 players come with a similar method for reassigning their MP3-playing rights. If you spot it, use it — it's much simpler than the Windows method.

If your player doesn't offer a way to assign MP3 files, or if something goes wrong, the next two sections explain the manual way to tell your computer what program to use for playing MP3s.

Changing your current MP3 player in Windows Me

Windows Me makes it easy to change which programs are supposed to open which files. Follow these steps to make the appropriate program handle the action when you click an MP3 file:

1. **Open Control Panel and choose Folder Options.**

2. **Choose the File Types tab.**

   Windows Me shows a list of all the file extensions that it recognizes. MP3 files end in the letters MP3, so those are the ones to change.

3. **Scroll down the list until you see MP3 listed under Extensions.**

   The window should look like Figure 6-22.

Figure 6-22: Choose MP3 from the Extensions column to change which program will open your MP3 files.

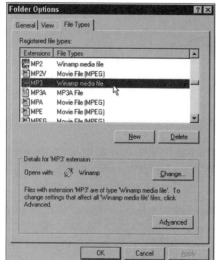

4. **Click the Change button.**

5. **Scroll down the list of programs until you see the MP3 player you'd like to assign to your MP3 files.**

6. **Click the OK button and then click Close.**

   Windows Me now calls up your newly assigned program whenever you open a MP3 file.

Changing your current MP3 player in Windows 98

Being a little older, Windows 98 is a little clunkier when it comes to changing the program that opens your MP3 files. When you click an MP3 file, if the wrong MP3 player opens your file, you need to follow two procedures. First, you need to disable your current MP3 player; then you must assign the MP3 files to the proper MP3 player. The following two sections show you how to do these two tasks.

Disabling your current MP3 player

First, you need to disable your current default MP3 player by following these instructions. (If you've never installed an MP3 player, jump ahead to the next set of steps.)

1. **Open Windows Explorer.**

   This is Explorer the *file* browser, not Internet Explorer the *Web* browser. On your desktop, right-click the My Computer icon, and choose Explore from the pop-up menu.

2. **Choose Folder Options from the View menu.**

   Folder Options lies at the bottom of the menu.

3. **Click the File Types tab.**

4. **Find your current MP3 player in the list.**

   Look for the words MP3 file (used by Windows Media Player) or Winamp media file (used by Winamp). Your existing player may say something different. You know you've found the right one when you see the words MP3 listed after the word Extension in the window's File Type Details area, as shown in Figure 6-23.

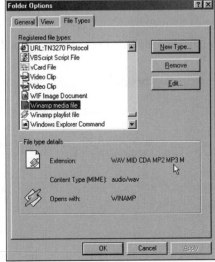

Figure 6-23:
Your current default MP3 player has MP3 listed as the extension in the File Type Details area.

5. **Click your MP3 player in the Registered File Types list, and then click the Remove button.**

   The words Winamp media file have been clicked in Figure 6-23, for example, and are ready to be removed with the Remove button.

Don't stop now! At this point, Windows doesn't know what program opens your MP3 files. When you try to open one, Windows will be confused.

Assigning an MP3 player to your MP3 files

Sometimes, the wrong MP3 player pops into action when you double-click an MP3 file or play it from an MP3 Web site such as www.MP3.com.

Windows gives you two ways to assign a different MP3 player for your MP3 files. Try the simple method first; if that doesn't work, dig a little deeper with the second solution.

The simple way to change default MP3 players

Follow these six steps to change the MP3 player that plays your MP3 files:

1. **Click once on any MP3 file.**

   Just a single click — just enough to select it, but not to start playing it.

2. **Hold down the Shift key and right-click the same MP3 file.**

3. **When the menu pops up, choose Open with.**

4. **When the list of programs pops up, choose Winamp, Sonique, or any other MP3 player.**

   Click the program's name to choose it.

5. **Check the box that says Always Use This Program to Open This Type of File.**

6. **Click the OK button to save your changes.**

Now, whenever you click an MP3 file, your newly selected MP3 player should pop into action to play it.

The more difficult way to change default MP3 players

If the first method didn't let you change the MP3 player that automatically plays your MP3 files, try these steps. They're more complicated, but sometimes that's what it takes.

1. **Open Windows Explorer.**

   This is Explorer the *file* browser, not Internet Explorer the *Web* browser.

   Right-click the Start button and choose Explore from the menu.

2. **Click View and choose Folder Options.**

   Folder Options lies at the bottom of the menu.

3. **Select the File Types tab.**

4. **Click the New Type button.**

   The Add New File Type appears.

5. **Type** MP3 file **in the Description of Type box.**

6. **Type** .mp3 **in the Associated Extension box.**

   Don't forget to put the period before mp3.

7. **Type** audio/mpeg **in the Content Type (MIME) box.**

8. **Click the New button beneath the empty Actions box.**

   A window labeled New Action appears.

9. **Type** open **in the Action box.**

10. **Type "C:\Program Files\Winamp\WINAMP.EXE" "%1" in the Application Used to Perform Action box.**

The preceding example installs Winamp as your default MP3 player. To install a different player, substitute that program's name and location for the words `"C:\Program Files\Winamp\WINAMP.EXE"` in Step 10. Be sure to add the `"%1"`, complete with quotation marks, or it won't work.

If you experiment with several different MP3 players, each player tries to set itself up as the default player. Following these two procedures lets you pick the player that should automatically jump up and begin playing MP3 files.

When you first listen to an MP3 file being played back from MP3.com, a box appears. Select the option that says Open This File from Its Current Location. Then uncheck the option that says Always Ask before Opening This Type of File.

Connecting Your Computer to Your Home Stereo

The speakers connected to many computers sound like squawking menus at drive-up fast-food joints. To improve the sound, ditch the tinny speakers and connect your computer to your home stereo.

Run the right-sized wires between the right places, as I describe later, to turn your computer into a 300-disc CD player.

> ✔ **Tools you need:** A Y-cable (a ⅛-inch stereo plug with two RCA phono plugs, usually red and green; see Figure 6-24) and an extension cable long enough to connect your computer and stereo.

> ✔ **Cost:** About $5 to $10, if the sound card didn't already come with the correct cable.

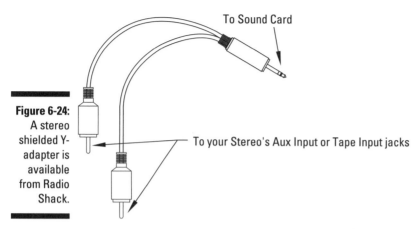

To Sound Card

To your Stereo's Aux Input or Tape Input jacks

Keep the volume turned down on the stereo and also on the sound card while connecting the cables — you don't want to pop anything.

1. **Turn down the volume on your stereo and sound card.**

   Turn down the stereo's volume knob, usually pretty easy to find.

   If you can't find your sound card's volume knob — which is either some-where on the back of the card or through its software program — simply turn off your computer (after saving any open files, of course).

2. **Find the correct cable.**

   You need a shielded Y-adapter cable, shown in Figure 6-24. This cable has a stereo ⅛-inch plug on one end and two RCA phono plugs on the other end. You can find the cable at Radio Shack. (The six-foot cord is part number 42-2481; the three-footer is number 42-2475.) Other elec-tronics stores and some computer stores carry the cord, as well.

   The package of a stereo Y-adapter cable calls it a male stereo ⅛-inch plug to two male RCA plugs. That sounds confusing, but that's often what the package says.

   The best sound card manufacturers throw the cord in for free; others make you head to Radio Shack. If your computer and stereo aren't very close together, pick up a 12-foot stereo cable (part number 42-2356). A 20-foot stereo cable (part number 42-2462) provides even more room. If your computer and stereo are more than 20 feet away, ask the Radio Shack salesperson how to buy the right cable and plugs to make your own extension cable.

3. **Plug the ⅛-inch stereo plug into your sound card's speaker jack.**

   Hopefully your sound card has all its little jacks labeled so that you know which little hole does what. If it doesn't, you have to open the card's manual. Then run the extension cord between your computer and your stereo system.

If you have a carpet, push the cord into the crack between the carpet and the edge of the wall. Use the right tool for the job: A spoon handle works well. No carpet? Buy a rug. But don't leave the cord lying across the floor. If somebody trips over it, they'll pull out the plug, and the music will stop.

4. **Plug the cable's two RCA phono plugs into the stereo's Aux Input or Tape Input jacks.**

   Check the back of your stereo for some unused input jacks; you should see several pairs of stubby little metal heads. Use the Aux Input or the Tape Input jacks — whichever isn't being used.

   One jack of the pair is probably red or labeled "Right" — push the cord's red plug into that jack. The other jack is probably black, white, or green — this jack is for your other plug, no matter what color it is.

   Don't plug your sound card's output into your home stereo's Phono Input jack. Your stereo doesn't expect such a strong signal from that jack. (If you throw caution to the wind and plug the cord in there anyway, keep the card's volume *very* low.)

5. **Turn on the stereo and switch it to Tape Input or Aux Input.**

   Turn the stereo's input select switch to the jack you've used, either Tape Input or Aux Input.

6. **Play an MP3 file on the sound card and adjust the volume.**

   Gradually turn up the volume on your stereo and sound card. If everything is hooked up right, the sound should start filling the room.

   If the sound doesn't start filling the room, make sure that the stereo is turned to Aux Input or Tape Input — or whatever input jack you plugged the sound card into. If the stereo isn't turned to the correct input switch, your sound card won't come through. (Oh, is the stereo plugged in and turned on?)

   Your home stereo isn't always a friend. It reveals the shortcomings of a cheapie sound card, for instance, as well as an MP3 encoder that's not quite pulling its weight.

Chapter 7

Choosing and Using MP3 Players

● ●

In This Chapter

▶ Choosing an MP3 player

▶ Understanding storage devices

▶ Choosing portable players

▶ Choosing home players

▶ Listening to MP3 files in your car

▶ Considering your needs

● ●

*W*hen Diamond Multimedia released its Rio portable MP3 player in 1999 — the first portable MP3 player in the United States — the record companies quickly filed suit. This new-fangled device was illegal, they claimed, and violated copyright laws. To the relief of MP3 fans, the record companies lost the case.

Diamond faces new problems today: The Rio line's been hit with legions of competitors. A few years ago, only a few small imports released players. Today, big names like Sony, Panasonic, Toshiba, Iomega, Nike, and even Intel have released portable MP3 players. The Microsoft PocketPC and the Handspring Visor can play MP3 files, as well.

The home stereo market's opened up, too. Some of the latest CD/DVD players handle CDs stuffed with hundreds of MP3 songs.

Which MP3 player is best? Is it finally time to buy one? Or are they still yet another toy for people with too much money? This chapter helps you decide.

No matter which portable player you purchase, splurge on a new set of headphones. Check out a stereo shop for some lightweight sports headphones. The cheap little ones shipped with most players almost always stink.

Deciding on a Storage System

Keep one key element in mind when choosing an MP3 player: How many tunes can it hold?

See, MP3 technology squishes songs to less than 10 percent of their normal size, but that's still a huge amount of space. Songs average about 4MB of space apiece. That means storage capacity is the key factor to consider when shopping for a portable MP3 player.

Unfortunately, nobody's come up with a standard storage medium for portable MP3 players. Most of today's portable players use one of seven types: CompactFlash, SmartMedia, or MultiMedia cards; Sony Memory Sticks; CDs; hard drives; or Iomega's PocketZip cartridges.

If you graduate from one MP3 player to another, the new one might use different storage, rendering all your old storage cards useless.

The next sections examine the pros and cons of each type of storage system, and the last section explains how to choose one that's right for you.

When looking at storage systems, remember that one minute of music consumes about 1MB of MP3 storage space. That means a 32MB card holds roughly a little more than half an hour of music.

CompactFlash

If you've seen a laptop, you've probably seen a PC card — those business-card-sized thingies that slide into the laptop's side to add more storage, a modem, or other fun accessories.

Cut a standard PC card in half down the middle, and it won't work anymore. But the two remnants will each be about the size of a CompactFlash card, as shown in Figure 7-1. Popular with many portable MP3 players, digital cameras, and other gadgetry, CompactFlash cards store information without requiring a battery. Best yet, CompactFlash cards have no moving parts, making them great for joggers and stunt drivers.

CompactFlash cards come in sizes from 4MB to the recently announced 1GB. The most popular sizes for MP3 players are from 32MB to 128MB. In fact, the best MP3 players toss in a CompactFlash card in the box. (Read the box's fine print closely.)

Figure 7-1:
A 192MB
Compact-
Flash card.

Here are some pros and cons about CompactFlash cards:

✔ CompactFlash cards are sturdy. Encased in plastic, they can survive a ten-foot drop. (Your MP3 player might not, but you can still salvage the CompactFlash card.) Under average use, the card will last more than 100 years without losing data.

✔ Although CompactFlash cards are a bit larger than SmartMedia or MultiMedia cards (which I discuss next), they hold more information, and they're often slightly less expensive.

✔ CompactFlash cards certainly aren't cheap, though. At last look, a 32MB card cost around $80, a 64MB cost about $120, and a 128MB card cost $190. Shortly after introduction, Simple Technology's 512MB card carried a price tag of $1,599.

✔ SanDisk began cranking out CompactFlash cards in late 1995, giving the technology a big head start compared to other types of tiny storage devices.

✔ To transfer information quickly between a CompactFlash card and your computer, check out some of the PC-card adapters. Slide the CompactFlash card into the end of the PC card, slide the PC card into a PC-card slot like the ones on a laptop, and you have immediate access to the CompactFlash data. A slightly less speedy alternative is to buy a card reader that plugs into one of your PC's ports.

✔ Head for the CompactFlash Association at `www.compactflash.org` for all the information you could ever want to know about CompactFlash cards. Even more information comes from the card's creators: SanDisk (`www.sandisk.com`), **Kingston** (`www.kingston.com`), or Simple Technology (`www.simpletech.com`).

IBM's Microdrive

IBM invented the hard disk drive and sold the first one in 1956. Now it has pulled out a magnifying glass to shrink a hard drive. *Really* shrink it. IBM's Microdrive, shown in Figure 7-2, fits into a CompactFlash card.

The Microdrive's whirling platter is the size of a large coin, and the whole thing weighs less than an AA battery. Yet it stores many hours of near CD-quality audio.

Figure 7-2:
The IBM
Microdrive.

Microdrive is a registered trademark of IBM.

It's no panacea for your MP3 storage needs, however (even if that word rolls merrily off your tongue at high-tension social gatherings):

- ✔ Whirling hard drives consume much more electricity than solid-state memory cards. Don't count on powering the thing very long — if at all — with a single AA battery, like those used by many of today's MP3 players. Microdrives are also more fragile and subject to possible skipping.

- ✔ Like any CompactFlash card, Microdrives aren't cheap. Count on spending about $275 for the 340MB card and $500 for the 1GB card. That's cheaper than a regular CompactFlash card, but it still might cost more than your player.

- ✔ The Microdrive is a Type II CompactFlash card, meaning it's slightly thicker than some of the other, Type I cards. Better make sure that your player can use it before shelling out the bucks. (Most players can use them.)

- ✔ For more information about IBM Microdrive products, race to www.ibm.com.

SmartMedia

The postage stamp-sized cards are relatively easy to find because digital camera owners have snapped them up for years. Toshiba created the Solid State Floppy Disc Card (SSFDC) that's now, thankfully, referred to as a plain ol' SmartMedia card (see Figure 7-3).

Figure 7-3:
A
SmartMedia
card.

Smaller than a CompactFlash card and only as thick as thin cardboard, SmartMedia cards result in smaller MP3 players.

So what's the big problem with SmartMedia cards? Make that two problems. First, they're still expensive, costing around $60 for a 32MB card and more than $100 for a 64MB card. The other problem? It's rare to find a card larger than 64MB. Everybody seems to favor the higher-capacity CompactFlash cards, so these cards might be on their way out. Bummer. I still have a bunch of them.

SmartMedia cards come in two voltages: 3.3 volts and 5 volts. Hardly any device uses the 5-volt card anymore. (Turn the card with its shiny side up; the voltage is stamped on that side. Also, the 3.3-volt card has a notch on its right side; the 5-volt card has a notch on the left side.)

The old Rio PMP300 uses a *proprietary* SmartMedia format for copyright protection. After you format the cards for your MP3 player, you can't use them in your digital camera or other portable MP3 players unless those devices can reformat their cards. Luckily, Simple Technology offers beta software called RioDiag.exe at its Web site (`www.simpletech.com/support`) to reformat the card back to standard format.

MultiMedia

The designers of the CompactFlash recently came up with the MultiMedia card — a postage stamp-sized card created to compete with the SmartMedia card (see Figure 7-4). It's one of the tiniest storage devices available.

However, it's never taken off the way it was supposed to, and its lack of acceptance mirrors the SmartMedia cards. Costing about the same price as the other expensive cards, it's certainly no bargain. Plus, it's difficult, if not impossible, to find in sizes larger than 64MB.

In short, CompactFlash has quite a head start on both SmartMedia and MultiMedia cards. But plenty of MultiMedia card enthusiasts hang out at `www.mmca.org`.

CDs

CDs seem like a natural storage solution. MP3 files are huge, and CDs hold huge amounts of data. Once you leave off the extended Grateful Dead jams, a single CD can often hold 200 or more MP3 songs.

Figure 7-4:
MultiMedia
cards.

For years, though, only *computers* could play MP3 CDs. Home stereos require their CDs to store music in a different format that allows only between 10 and 12 songs per disc.

But that's changing, albeit slowly. Sony is creating a Walkman that plays MP3 CDs, and several other companies are also jumping on this bandwagon (see Figure 7-5).

Some people will scream in delight when receiving one of these as a birthday present. Others will say, "Wellllll." That's because a CD player is still a CD player, even if it's finally able to play MP3 files. It's too big to drop into a shirt pocket. Plus, it will be susceptible to motion, making it a second-tier option for the athletic crowd.

It also takes a relatively long time to burn a CD with your favorite songs. And all those moving parts can cause problems: hinges break, CDs scratch, and some players are persnickety about how the MP3s are stored on the disc.

But hey, these new players are cheap, coming out at around $100 apiece. CDs are about the cheapest storage medium around, costing less than a buck for about 200 songs. Adding the two prices together makes this one of the cheapest solutions around — if you can put up with the awkwardness of a CD.

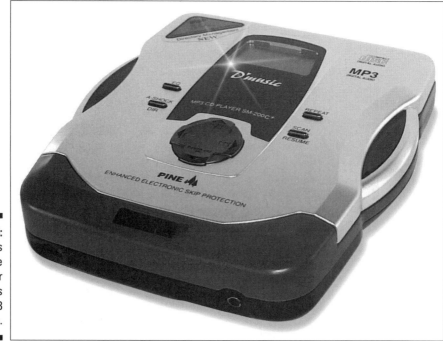

Figure 7-5:
This
portable
MP3 player
reads CDs
with MP3
files.

Hard drives

Everything about computers has grown smaller through the years, and hard drives are no exception. That's why serious MP3 aficionados are waiting for a player with a tiny hard drive that's big enough to hold their entire collection.

Those players are starting to arrive. Creative Labs, an early innovator in MP3 players, sells a player with a 6GB hard drive. The Nomad Jukebox, shown in Figure 7-6, is a little hefty, weighing in at nearly a pound.

But 6GB holds about 150 CDs or about 100 hours of music. You can listen to tunes 24 hours a day for four days and never hear the same song twice.

Other hard-drive-based systems, such as the Archos Jukebox 6000, are appearing at cheaper prices than Creative Labs, so let the price wars begin. (The batteries on my Archos Jukebox 6000 last more than 6 hours between charges.)

Some people have upgraded the Archos Jukebox 6000 from its 6GB hard drive to a 20GB hard drive. Apparently it uses a Fujitsu hard drive designed for laptops. For more information, head to MP3.com, find the Archos listed under the MP3 Hardware category, and check out what its users are posting on the product forum.

Figure 7-6:
Portable
MP3 players
with hard
drives hold
100 hours or
more of
music.

Iomega's PocketZip

Iomega is certainly no stranger to storage systems, having introduced the Zip drive and taken off from there. Its entry into the portable MP3 player market comes with the PocketZip disk, and the HipZip player that plays them.

PocketZip disks, shown with the HipZip in Figure 7-7, hold 40MB of MP3s. That's not quite enough for an entire CD, unfortunately, unless the songs are converted to the Microsoft WMA format. But the HipZip comes bundled with two disks, and that's plenty of room for a CD.

The HipZip system's best feature is the cost: Each 40MB PocketZip disk costs only $10 when bought in a ten-pack. That's a heck of a lot cheaper than most other formats. The second generation of HipZips, slated for store shelves during the 2001 holiday season, uses 100MB disks that cost $10. No word yet on how that will affect the cost of 40MB disks.

Although the PocketZip disk uses moving parts, it seems surprisingly stable. In fact, the HipZip's case includes a clip so that you can wear it on your jogging shorts.

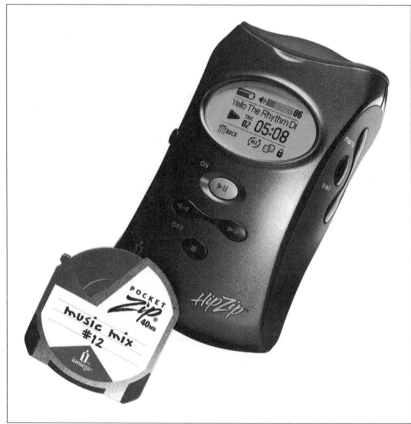

Figure 7-7:
The Iomega
HipZip and
PocketZip
disk.

At only $10 per disk, it's easy to stock up on a bunch of the little critters, stick 'em in a zip-lock baggie, and toss them into the glove compartment. If you lose one, you're out only $10.

The HipZip might not be the best solution, but it's looking better than some of the other players that suck up expensive CompactFlash or SmartMedia cards.

Sony Memory Sticks

Companies have two ways to make money on portable MP3 players. They can sell the player, or they can make a player that uses a new breed of card and sell both the player and the card.

That's what Iomega did with its HipZip. And that's what Sony did with its Memory Stick, shown in Figure 7-8.

Figure 7-8:
The Sony
Memory
Stick.

Sony is using its Memory Stick for a good portion of its product line, from cameras to recorders to MP3 players. It's a sturdy little beast, with a good design — it's hard to touch the metal contacts, so that keeps them clean and free of dust.

Unfortunately, very few — if any — other MP3 players can use Memory Sticks. If you buy them, they'll work only on Sony products. I bit the bullet and bought a 64MB Memory Stick for my Sony PC-5 camcorder. But I was sure upset that the camera couldn't use my collection of SmartMedia cards or my growing collection of CompactFlash cards.

So, which storage format is best?

When deciding which storage format is right for you, start with cost. Table 7-1 explains the cost per megabyte of storage of each of the types that I discuss in the previous sections. Remember, each megabyte equals about one minute of a song.

Table 7-1	Dollars per Megabyte		
Storage Type	*Common Size*	*Cost*	*Cost per MB*
CompactFlash	64MB	$100	$1.50
Microdrive	340MB	$250	$.74
SmartMedia	64MB	$100	$1.50
MultiMedia	64MB	$100	$1.50
PocketZip	100MB	$10	$.10
CD	640MB	$1	$0.001
Hard drive	1024MB	$400	$.39
Memory Stick	64MB	$100	$1.50

If you're trying to save money in storage costs, it's obvious that MP3 CD players are the cheapest way to go. Because you're only paying about a penny per minute of song storage, you can buy a bunch of blank CDs, fill 'em up with your MP3 collection, and be done with it. But there's more to consider than just storage costs:

- ✔ First, the cost-effective CD player might be the one for you, but only if you don't mind the awkward size.

- ✔ If you're clumsy and afraid of losing something expensive, go for the HipZip or a CD player. You won't be out a bundle when you leave a card at the bar.

- ✔ If you need something smaller, the CompactFlash, SmartMedia, or Multimedia card or the Memory Stick might be the thing. They're all relatively expensive, however — especially if you're prone to losing things. But they're also more convenient than some of the other systems when it comes to transferring songs back and forth.

- ✔ A Microdrive stores songs for half the price of the CompactFlash and similar cards, but it draws more power and is subject to rattles. Plus, if you lose one of those expensive little things, you'll be crying for weeks.

- ✔ Today's best bet — if you don't mind carrying around a slightly larger device — is a hard drive player. With 6GB of storage, it might hold your entire music collection, letting you take it with you wherever you go. Plug the gadget into your home or car stereo and you won't have to think about buying a dedicated home MP3 player. And at only $.39 per megabyte, it's quite a value. (I love my Archos 6000 Jukebox from www.archos.com.)

- ✔ If you have a digital camera or other device that already uses one of these formats, think about buying a portable MP3 player that uses the same format. When you can use the same card for both toys, you don't have to buy twice as many cards.

- ✔ Finally, consider buying an older MP3 player. Check out the auctions on eBay (www.ebay.com) or Yahoo! (www.yahoo.com). Just as people trade in their old cars when buying new ones, many people sell their old MP3 players when buying the latest big thing. Last look showed more than 1,000 players on eBay, with some going for just $75.

Choosing a Portable Player

When shopping for MP3 players, the following terms pop up either on the box or the advertisements. You might already know what some of them mean; others might be completely foreign. Either way, here's a look at what they mean.

Don't just buy a player without researching it a little bit. First, head to `http://groups.google.com/` and search for the name of the player you have your eye on. Chances are, that site will turn up discussions of many owners either praising or damning their purchase. The MP3 Hardware forums at MP3.com are another great place for finding information.

Skip protection

When you shake a CD player, the little laser thingy inside moves, making the sound skip. So, those clever engineers added *skip protection*. When your CD player starts reading the CD, it reads some of the song in advance, storing it in memory that isn't affected by movement.

Then, should the little laser doohickey get jostled, the player reads the music from the memory — the *buffer*. Skip protection technology keeps the song playing smoothly.

Sometimes skip protection is measured in seconds — the number of seconds of music that's read ahead. Other times, skip protection is measured by the amount of memory used to store the music. Either way, the larger the number, the smoother the song plays under rough conditions.

Radio tuner

Face it, most portable MP3 players can't store more than ten songs per disk. If you're taking off in the morning and returning later in the afternoon or evening, those ten songs might become monotonous.

That's why the best MP3 players toss in a few extra dollars of circuitry to include a radio tuner. That lets you hear your favorite stations when your MP3 tunes become tiring. It's definitely something to look for.

Microphone

Everybody stumbles on a key thought from time to time that could change their lives — if only they could remember it when they got home. So some MP3 players add a microphone for recording those thoughts that seem so important at the time.

Beware, however: MP3 players don't record sounds in MP3 format. They record them as a WAV file. (Chapter 1 describes WAV files and other sound formats.) An MP3 player also records sounds in a low-quality format that's fine for speech but lousy for everything else. Most limit the recordings to a few minutes, as well. Even if you do smuggle one into a concert, you'll get only a bad recording of the first part of one song.

Just tell me which MP3 player to buy!

I tried doing that in the first edition of the book. The first edition contains pictures and reviews of all the MP3 players on the market at that time. A week after the book came out, dozens more new players appeared, followed by more players every week after that. There's just no way a book can keep up.

Instead, I'll tell you how to cut through the promotional and marketing stuff and find out what users think about today's crop of MP3 players. Here's how to find the best MP3 player for your pocket, your car, or your home stereo:

✔ First, head to MP3.com (www.mp3.com) and click the MP3 Hardware button. The folks at MP3.com get all the new goodies before anybody else, so you'll find pictures, specs, and a review of each one. Here's the best part: After reading what the reviewer thinks of the product, click the Read User Reviews link. There, people log on to discuss the product and compare it to others on the market. People who've actually bought it say what they like and don't like about it. It's a great place for hands-on information, and the site separates reviews by portables, home stereos, and car players.

✔ Next, head for the Internet's Usenet, a spot where computer geeks from around the world meet to discuss just about everything. To search through the Usenet messages easily, head to the Google Usenet Archive (http://groups.google.com/). That service currently keeps track of all the Usenet messages posted since 1999. Type the name of the player you're considering and click the Search button. Wham! You see messages from anybody who's talked about that player in the past two years. Best yet, these messages are from *real* people — no company hype here.

✔ Finally, to find *everything* on the Internet about a particular MP3 player, head to the Google (www.google.com) search engine. You'll find chatter from owners and dealers and information from the player's Web site — just about anything related to the product. Another good search engine is Surfwax (www.surfwax.com). Surfwax searches bunches of search engines simultaneously and posts the results for your perusal. Some people like CNET.com (www.cnet.com) for reviews and information, too.

By using a combination of these techniques, you can find all the information you want about a particular player. Remember, however, that this is the Internet, so don't take any single message at its word. Posts that appear repeatedly from different people are more likely to be accurate than a post from one user.

Directory and sub-directory restrictions

Some people meticulously organize their MP3 collection. They create one folder called MP3 and then create folders inside that folder for each artist. Next, they create folders in each artist's folder, one for each album. This meticulous organization makes it easy to find songs on a huge hard drive.

However, some players don't recognize all this work. They want all the songs lumped together in a single folder. That makes it harder for you to pluck the right song from a big pile. It might just be a minor inconvenience, but beware of it, nonetheless.

ID tags

MP3 files contain more than music. The format includes space for people to add information about the music: The artist, song, album, type of music, recording year, and other interesting tidbits.

Even if a file is named incorrectly, an MP3 player can look at the tag (assuming that it's been filled out correctly) and find out what song is *really* inside the file.

The best players read ID tags and display the information on-screen, making it easy to see what's being played. The worst players ignore the ID tags and just display a number in place of the song's title.

Now the technical bit. As the MP3 format evolves, so does the ID tag format. In fact, it's gone through several incarnations, with the most popular being either ID3v1 or ID3v2. ID3v2 is growing in popularity because it holds more information about the song — even a picture of the CD cover, if desired. However, some players can handle only the earlier, ID3v1 tag. That frustrates people who have meticulously entered ID3v2 information into their 563 MP3 files.

Playback options

Does the player simply play all your songs in a row? Can you program them to play back in a certain order? Can it shuffle them randomly so that you don't get tired of the tunes as quickly? When it shuffles them randomly, does it always use the same random order? Don't laugh — it happens.

Power

Portable players come with batteries. But are the batteries replaceable or rechargeable? There is a tradeoff. Rechargeable batteries are cheaper in the long run, unless you're living in California during a power crisis. But if they run out during the afternoon, you can't run into a 7-Eleven and grab some new ones. You're stuck.

How long do the batteries last? And does an AC adapter come with the player, or do you have to buy it separately?

Accessories

Many MP3 players, eager to stand out among the competition, toss in some extra goodies: A power adapter that plugs into your car's cigarette lighter, for instance. How are the earphones? Does it have a carrying case? And, if you'll be jogging with it, does it come with a belt clip?

Playing MP3s through Your Home Stereo

Now that you have the CD that came with this book, you can play MP3 tunes on your computer. You might even have a portable player to listen to tunes when away from the computer. But serious music fans want a third player: One that hooks up to their home stereo to fill the house with music.

You can make the tunes come out of the home stereo in several ways:

- ✔ **Your computer's an MP3 player — connect it to your stereo.** The end of Chapter 6 shows you how to connect the right cables between the right holes in your computer and home stereo. If you have a spare computer and enough space for it to fit next to your home stereo, go for it.

- ✔ **Connect your portable MP3 player to your home stereo.** Just follow the instructions in the sidebar "Hooking up an MP3 player to a home stereo."

- ✔ **Head to a home stereo shop and buy one of the latest players.** These players handle CDs, DVDs, and CDs containing MP3 files. Unfortunately, the ones I've seen aren't very good quality. And if you already have a CD and DVD player, why buy another unit when two-thirds of its features are useless?

- ✔ **Hook up a transmitter to the back of your computer and a receiver to your home stereo's input jacks.** If they're not too far apart, you'll hear sound. Look for the Akoo.com Kima, the NetPlay Radio FMP3, and the Jensen Matrix. This stuff's still too esoteric to be found in mainstream stores, so search for them on www.google.com to find a mail-order store that currently stocks them.

Listening to MP3 Files in Your Car

You can play MP3 files from your home stereo, from your computer, and from a portable player using headphones. But MP3 hasn't quite broken through the final barrier — the automobile.

Hooking up an MP3 player to a home stereo

Hooking up an MP3 player to your home stereo is easy enough; just follow these steps:

1. **Turn down the volume on your stereo and MP3 player.**

2. **Buy a shielded Y-adapter cable — Radio Shack part number 42-2481.**

3. **Plug the cable's ⅛-inch stereo plug into your player's headphone jack.**

4. **Plug the cable's two RCA phono plugs into the stereo's Aux Input or Tape Input jacks.**

5. **Turn on the stereo and switch it to Tape Input or Aux Input.**

6. **Play an MP3 file and adjust the volume.**

For more complete instructions, refer to Chapter 6 and read the section on hooking up your computer's sound card to your home stereo. You use the same cable; the only difference is that you're using the MP3 player's headphone jack instead of the computer's Line Out jack.

Kenwood's 22-watt eXcelon Z919 takes the situation in stride, playing normal CDs as well as MP3 CDs that you create yourself on your home computer. It includes an equalizer, and way-cool swirlies on the dash. It also includes a price tag of $649 from Crutchfield (www.crutchfield.com).

Look for more in-dash CD players to appear this year, with increasingly lower price tags. Until they're on sale at local car stereo shops, here are some less expensive workarounds to consider:

- ✔ **Use a cassette player adapter:** If your car has a cassette player, check out Radio Shack's CD-to-Cassette Player Adapter (part number 12-1999). It looks like a cassette tape with a stereo cable hanging from one end. Plug the cable into your portable MP3 player's headphone jack, insert the cassette, and start listening to your MP3s through your car stereo. It sounds amazingly good. Well, at least compared to the road noise.

- ✔ **Use a wireless CD adapter:** Plug the cable from this small Radio Shack FM transmitter (part number 12-2051) into your portable MP3 player. Then tune your car's FM radio to the right frequency and listen to your MP3s.

- ✔ **Buy a car stereo with a CD Input jack:** Some car stereos lack a CD player. Instead, they have a CD Input jack. Plug a ⅛-inch stereo cable (Radio Shack part number 42-2420) between this jack and your portable MP3 player to hear MP3s through your car's stereo system.

- ✔ **Record MP3s onto cassettes:** After you hook up your computer's sound card to your home stereo, record the songs onto cassettes. If your car has a tape deck, you're ready to roll.

- ✔ **Burning MP3 songs onto a CD in audio format:** Does your car have a CD player? Then convert your MP3 songs back into standard *CD audio* format and copy them to a CD. (I cover how in Chapter 12.) You can't fit more than a dozen onto the CD, but at least you can hear them.

✔ **Connect a portable MP3 player to amplified speakers:** Take some amplified speakers — like the ones that come with your PC — and plug a portable MP3 player into them. Carry it all to your car and start listening. To change songs, just swap new cards in and out of the portable player.

✔ **Experiment with a prototype MP3 player:** Just because you can't pick up a prepackaged MP3 player for your car at the dealer doesn't mean that it doesn't exist. Many people currently build automobile MP3 players. For the latest list of links, check out www.mp3.com and click Hardware. The site keeps track of the latest car MP3 players, as well as their requirements, release dates, and, if available, prices.

Just like car stereos, dedicated MP3 players for cars can be ripped off. To avoid that, substitute your portable MP3 player. You can easily grab your portable MP3 player when you leave the car, keeping it safe.

Chapter 8

Listening To or Setting Up an MP3 Radio Station

. . . .

In This Chapter

▶ Discovering Internet radio stations

▶ Getting the scoop on SHOUTcast radio stations

▶ Figuring out what equipment you need to get started

▶ Tuning in to SHOUTcast

▶ Webcasting through SHOUTcast

. . . .

*I*f you've perused some of the earlier chapters, you're well aware of how MP3 technology turns PCs into jukeboxes packed with music. Portable MP3 players let you listen to "Stairway to Heaven" during the next Perseids meteor shower.

But wait, there's more: MP3 technology lets anybody tune in to the thousands of MP3 radio stations now heard through the Internet.

This chapter shows you how to tune in those stations and create your own personalized stations that play your favorite songs. Or, if you're hankering to be a DJ and willing to spend an hour or two configuring your computer's software, check out SHOUTcast, which gives you the chops to create your own radio station, capable of sharing your favorite music with listeners worldwide.

What's an Internet Radio Station?

Some people fill up their garages with stuff they just *know* they're going to use someday. They might not use it, but hey, it's there if they ever want it.

The same goes for MP3 files. Some people grab every MP3 they can find and stuff it onto their hard drive. They may not play the songs very often — if at all — but they've created one heck of a library. (If only they didn't take up quite so much hard drive space . . . .)

To combat the MP3 storage problem, many MP3 fans are eyeing an increasingly popular alternative, and that's Internet radio. Because MP3 files are so small, they can be broadcast — *Webcast* — across the Internet. And because the Internet allows for two-way communication, it's easier than ever to find or even create a radio station that plays your favorite music.

The more you think about it, the better those Webcasts sound, huh?

✔ Internet radio stations don't fill your hard drive with MP3 songs. Instead of saving the songs, you simply listen to them, just like any other radio. Depending on how you set up your software, you can also view the current song's name and creator.

✔ MusicMatch, Rolling Stone, MP3.com, Winamp, and hundreds of other Internet sites now broadcast music directly from their Web sites. If you don't like corporate stuff, head for SHOUTcast, which I describe in the next section. Many of those stations are run directly from the computers of music fans like yourself.

✔ Rolling Stone pollutes its Internet radio stations with commercials, unfortunately. Luckily, most Webcasting radio stations don't have commercials (thank goodness).

✔ The Internet carries an incredible variety of music, much more than what you'd hear within your local radio's reception area. Instead, you can listen to Korean pop, Indian sitars, African rhythms, or '60s rock, or stations that match your music mood for the day.

✔ The Internet lets you create "personalized" radio stations. MusicMatch, for instance, lets you choose your favorite artist, click a button, and hear a station playing music by that artist, as well as other musicians playing that type of music. If you allow it to do so, MusicMatch will even keep track of the MP3s you listen to and create a personalized radio station based on your own musical tastes. (I cover MusicMatch in chapter 11.)

✔ The better your modem connection, the better your music will sound. Cable and DSL users will have near-CD quality music. Stations won't sound nearly as good with a dial-up modem. But the music may still sound as good or better than your FM radio.

What's a SHOUTcast Radio Station?

Nullsoft, the corporate arm of the folks who created Winamp, created the popular SHOUTcast radio to let Winamp users share their musical tastes with the world.

If I Webcast, am I gonna get busted?

Like everything else associated with MP3s, the legalities of Webcasting are currently in a state of flux. Parts of the law are spelled out in vivid detail, especially the details of how to pay $20 for a "statutory license" that handles the royalty payments. To qualify for the statutory license, however, Webcasters must meet a healthy list of requirements. Here are just a few:

✔ In any three-hour period, you can't play more than three songs from a particular album, nor more than two consecutively, and you can't play four songs by a particular artist or boxed set, including no more than three songs consecutively.

✔ You can't say in advance what particular song you'll play, nor when you'll play it.

✔ If you're continuously playing a recorded program, the show must be longer than three hours long.

✔ You must identify the song, the album, and the artist when Webcasting. (SHOUTcast handles this, so you're safe.)

✔ You can't encourage listeners to copy your transmissions, nor allow them to make copies, if possible.

✔ You must pay royalties.

As of this writing, nobody's decided on a scheme for calculating royalty payments. The easiest way, however, is to operate under a "statutory license" by filing an "Initial Notice" with the Copyright Office before Webcasting.

This "Initial Notice" should be sent with a $20 filing fee to: the Library of Congress, Copyright Office, Licensing Division, 101 Independence Avenue, S.E., Washington, DC 20557-6400.

For the most current information on Webcasting legalities, contact the RIAA at www.riaa.com or www.radiospy.com. Finally, to read the law yourself, head to http://lcweb.loc.gov/copyright/legislation/dmca.pdf and read the text with Adobe Acrobat.

Tuning in to a SHOUTcast radio station is pretty easy. First, make sure that you've installed a copy of Winamp. (Use the copy included on this book's CD, or grab a copy at www.winamp.com.) Next, log on to SHOUTcast at www.shoutcast.com, and you're ready to start listening.

As shown in Figure 8-1, SHOUTcast currently has 6,424 listeners tuned in to 1,477 different Internet radio stations. Click a station from the list, and Winamp begins playing the station's music. The next section describes the process in more detail.

✔ Radio stations aren't *broadcast* through the Internet. The term "broadcast" refers to airwave transmissions. No, Internet radio stations are being *Webcast*. (Some Internet radio DJs are picky about that.)

✔ A SHOUTcast radio station is essentially an Internet "feed" from a copy of Winamp running on somebody's computer. Basically, you're listening to what's playing on the Webcaster's copy of Winamp. When you tune in, you start listening in the middle of the stream — a song won't start at the beginning.

✔ By adding additional software and tweaking your settings, you can configure your own copy of Winamp to Webcast over SHOUTcast. Depending on the speed of your Internet connection, you're limited to anywhere from one listener to several hundred.

✔ It's *much* more complicated to Webcast your own station than it is to listen to an existing station. You can still do it, though, as you find out in an upcoming section.

✔ The faster your modem, the better the stations will sound when listening. The same goes for Webcasting: Faster modems let more people listen.

✔ Yes, it's completely legal to listen to Internet radio, and it's free. If you're Webcasting your own station, however, head for the Recording Industry Association of America Web site (www.riaa.com) to see its recommended procedures.

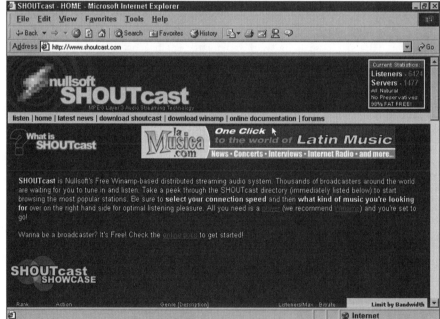

Figure 8-1:
More than 6,000 people currently listen to nearly 1,500 different Internet radio stations through SHOUTcast.

What Equipment Do I Need for SHOUTcast?

Forget about the transmission towers, stacks of paperwork, huge legal fees, or even an expensive radio. To listen or broadcast on SHOUTcast, you need the following equipment:

✔ **A computer that's powerful enough to play MP3s through Winamp.** I talk about Winamp extensively in Chapter 6.

✔ **A copy of Winamp.** Any version above 2.5 will do. You can use the copy on this book's CD or download the latest version from www.winamp.com.

✔ **A modem.** You can listen and broadcast with a 56K modem, although the sound improves considerably as your modem speed increases.

✔ **SHOUTcast software.** To set up your own station, download the required software on the SHOUTcast Web site at www.shoutcast.com.

If you're trying to Webcast through SHOUTcast with a dial-up connection, you can reach only one listener. Your modem simply isn't fast enough. Bummer. To reach more listeners, you need ISDN, DSL, a cable modem, or something even faster.

Listening to SHOUTcast

First, make *sure* that you've installed a copy of Winamp. Nullsoft created Winamp and SHOUTcast to work together. Nullsoft recommends that Mac users install Audion (www.panic.com), also found on this book's CD.

After you install your copy of Winamp, follow these instructions to tune in to a station:

1. **Make sure that Winamp has registered the PLS file extension.**

   After installation, Winamp is automatically configured to play MP3s and most other sound file types. But make sure that Windows knows to send the SHOUTcast Webcast to Winamp. Open Winamp and press Ctrl+P. Then, as shown in Figure 8-2, make sure that PLS is highlighted in the File types list along with MP3 and other optional file types.

Figure 8-2: Make sure that pls is highlighted in the Winamp Associated Extensions menu, as shown here.

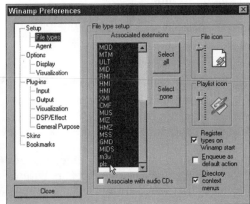

2. **Head to SHOUTcast at** www.shoutcast.com **with your Internet browser.**

   You needn't move past the first page to begin listening.

3. **Choose a station matched for your modem speed.**

   First, examine the station's descriptions until you find one that you like. When you first log on, SHOUTcast displays stations sorted by popularity.

   Don't like the popular stations? Click the List by Genre arrow, choose your type of music from the list that pops down, and click the List button. Or you can type a word describing your musical tastes in the Search for box and click Search. Either way, SHOUTcast dishes up currently broadcasting stations that meet your needs.

   Next, look in the column on the far right to find the *bit rate* for the stations you're interested in. Be careful to choose a station that your modem can handle. A modem with a 56K dial-up connection should choose stations transmitting at less than 56, for example, as shown in Figure 8-3. If you start receiving skips or gaps in the sound, choose a station that's Webcasting at a lower bit rate.

Figure 8-3:
Choose a station that Webcasts at a bit rate that's lower than your modem speed, or the sound will skip.

72	Tune In! Chat!	[World Asian] JPOPSTOP - Pleasing Japanese Pop Music for You! Now Playing: YoshimuraYumi - SoloSolo - VACATION	8/500	128
73	Tune In! Chat!	[Techno Trance Epic] CLUSTER Tag's Trance Trip - The All Groove Station Now Playing: DJ Halon - Passions	8/500	24
74	Tune In! Chat!	[Various] DeinChatRadio.de Now Playing: Saturday Night Party "live" mit Beasty	8/32	18
75	Tune In! Chat!	[t] Inlive: yyyyCJyyyy [AIM] Now Playing: -	8/500	128
76	Tune In! Chat!	[inlive.co.kr] Inlive: Easy Cast [AIM] Now Playing: 04- (Prayer)	7/500	96
77	Tune In! Chat!	[various] XhWeB - DyNet - Monterrey Mexico [ICQ] Now Playing: Alejandro Sanz - Cuando nadie me ve	7/5000	24
78	Tune In! Chat!	[Ambient Techno Downt] Groove Salad 24kb - A nicely chilled plate of ambient beats and grooves. 56 and 128k Also Available! [ICQ] Now Playing: Fila Brazillia - Heat Death Of The Universe	7/200	24

4. **Click the station's Tune In! button.**

   Click the Tune In! button (see Figure 8-4), and Winamp begins playing the station.

5. **Configure your browser, if necessary.**

   Depending on how your browser is configured, this step might take place when you tune in to a station.

   Internet Explorer: When you tune in to a SHOUTcast station, Internet Explorer sometimes sends a message (see Figure 8-5), asking whether it should Open this file from its current location or Save this file to disk. Select the first option — opening the file. If possible, uncheck the box marked Always Ask Before Opening This Type of File. Without this option checked, Internet Explorer will always begin playing playlists when you click them.

My modem keeps disconnecting me after a half hour!

As you kick back and listen to Internet radio stations, some Internet Service Providers think you're no longer using the Internet. After all, you haven't pressed a key in awhile, eh? So, the ISP automatically disconnects you. That leaves its phone line open for a more active subscriber to use.

Also, Windows sometimes tries to protect you by disconnecting your connection.

How can you stop this radio rudeness? Unfortunately, different ISPs handle the situation in different ways. Some cable modems offer 24-hour service — you can listen all the time without problems. Other services just dump you when you haven't used the keyboard for awhile.

Dial-up connections cause the most problems. Here are a few solutions to avoid the dastardly dial-up disconnect.

The simplest solution is to watch for the ISP's automatic disconnection warning, and click "Do not disconnect." Distracting, but livable. If you _do_ get disconnected, click the play button on Winamp, and it will automatically try to connect and play the same station.

Although you can't always stop your ISP from disconnecting you, you can make sure that Windows doesn't do the disconnecting. Try these settings for Windows 95, Windows 98, and Windows Me.

For Windows 95:

1. **Click the Start button and choose Control Panel from the Settings option.**

2. **Double-click the Internet icon.**

3. **Select the Connection tab.**

4. **Remove any check mark in the box next to Disconnect if Idle for ___ Minutes.**

5. **Click Apply.**

6. **Click OK to close the open windows.**

For Windows 98, Second Edition:

1. **Click the Start button and choose Control Panel from the Settings option.**

2. **Double-click the Internet Options icon.**

3. **Select the Connections tab.**

4. **Select the Settings button.**

5. **Click the Advanced button.**

6. **Remove any check marks next to options saying Disconnect.**

7. **Click OK to remove the open windows.**

For Windows 98, First Edition:

The sequence is the same as for Windows 98, Second Edition, except for a few areas. The Control Panel icon is labeled simply Internet in Step 2. And Step 6 provides only one option labeled Disconnect; so make sure that it's not checked.

For Windows Me:

1. **Click the Start button and choose Control Panel from the Settings option.**

2. **Double-click the Internet Options icon.**

3. **Select the Connections tab.**

4. **Click the Properties button.**

5. **Click the Dialing tab.**

6. **Remove the check mark in the Enable Idle Disconnect box.**

7. **Click the OK buttons to close the windows.**

To tell which version of Windows you have, right-click the My Computer icon on your desktop and choose Properties. A window appears, listing your particular version.

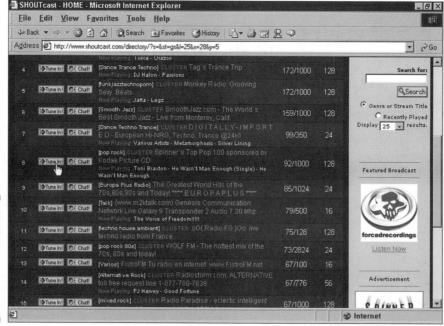

Figure 8-4:
Click the
Tune in!
button to
begin
listening to
the station.

Figure 8-5:
Choose
Internet
Explorer's
Open This
File from Its
Current
Location
option when
tuning in
to a
SHOUTcast
station.

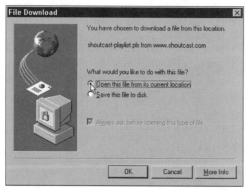

Netscape Navigator: When you first click a SHOUTcast station, Netscape
brings up the box in Figure 8-6 with four buttons: More Info, Pick App,
Save File, and Cancel. Click Pick App, and when the next box appears,
type the location and name of Winamp. (If you chose the default Winamp
location during installation, you should type `C:\program`
`files\winamp\winamp.exe`.) Click OK, and you're through.

Figure 8-6:
When
Netscape
first
receives a
SHOUTcast
Webcast
and displays
this box,
click the
Pick App
button.

Your computer loads Winamp and begins playing the station.

6. **If that station turns out to be a drag, click a different one.**

After a few moments, Winamp will begin playing the new station's sounds. That's it — unless you want some more information, which appears in the following list.

✔ The next time you load Winamp, the program remembers which station it previously played. Click the Winamp Play button — the same button that starts playing MP3 files — and, if the station is still Webcasting, Winamp will begin playing the station.

✔ Can't find a cool station you heard a few days back? Load Winamp and press Ctrl+L to see the Open Location window. Click the downward pointing arrow, and Winamp lists all the locations of the last few dozen stations you've listened to. Click each one until you find your favorite.

✔ Clinging to a Macintosh? You're not left out, thanks to Audion (www. audion.com). This program's so hot, thieving hackers are begging for registration serial numbers all over the Net. Check out the 15-day demo included on this book's CD, and you'll know why they're drooling. (And the full version, which allows encoding, is only around $30, fer cryin' out loud!)

✔ When listening with a low-speed, dial-up modem connection, any sort of Web surfing or page flipping often causes skips in the sound. The solution? Don't Web surf while listening, or get a cable, DSL, or faster modem.

✔ Using a proxy server on a network? You can still listen, if you tell Winamp about it. Load Winamp, press Ctrl+P, and click Setup. Under Internet Settings, click the button marked Using LAN Internet connection. Then type your Proxy into the box labeled HTTP proxy: 'Server:Port'. I use Wingate to let my networked computers share a single cable modem, so I type **wingate:80**.

✔ Modems rarely receive information at their labeled speed. A 56K modem usually can't keep up with a 56 Kbps SHOUTcast Webcast. That's because 56K modems usually receive at around 32K to 40K per second, depending on their brand and the quality of the Internet connection. Similarly, 28K modems can handle 24 Kbps and lower SHOUTcasts. Luckily, SHOUTcast carries stations that Webcast at a variety of rates to support many modems.

✔ To find out more information about a particular station, slide your mouse over the words in the site's Genre (Description) column and look for underlined words. The underlined words usually link to the station's Web site, which often displays the information you're looking for about the station.

✔ When you connect your computer to a home stereo and use a cable modem, some Webcasts sound just as good or better than an FM radio station. (Chapter 6 shows how to hook up your computer to your home stereo.)

Setting Up Your Own SHOUTcast Radio Station

When you've grown familiar with listening to Webcasts, and you're ready to set up your own station, these instructions will put your tunes on the Net. The good part is that it's free. The horrible part is that it's dreadfully complicated, and generally accompanied by much gnashing of teeth.

First, don't try Webcasting unless you're running a reasonably fast (300 MHz) or faster PC running Windows 95, 98, Me, XP, NT, or 2000. You'll need Winamp 2.65 or better, plus a whole lotta MP3s.

You need to have an Internet Service Provider, which you probably already have or you couldn't have downloaded these goodies. Make sure that you're using a decent ISP that keeps everything flowing smoothly.

Finally, many ISPs will shut you down if you're caught running a server from your computer. (My ISP, Cox Cable, doesn't permit home users to run servers from their computers, but I've snuck one up for a few hours here and there.)

1. **Log on to the SHOUTcast Home page (**`www.shoutcast.com`**) with your Internet browser and click the Download SHOUTcast button.**

As you can see in the margin, the Download SHOUTcast button is part of a string of options listed across the top of the page.

When you click the Download SHOUTcast button, the SHOUTcast download page appears.

Three buttons appear on the page:

- Be a Listener
- Be a D.J.
- Be a Server

2. Click the Be a D.J. button.

A new page appears, as shown in Figure 8-7, containing all the necessary enhancements for Webcasting needed for Winamp. The rest of these steps walk you through each of the enhancements.

3. Make sure that you're using Winamp 2.65 or newer.

Feel free to use the copy included on this book's bundled CD. Or grab a new copy by heading to the Winamp Web site (`www.winamp.com`). Take a shortcut there by clicking the word Home on the SHOUTcast download page you reached in Step 1.

Already have a copy of Winamp? Make sure that it's Version 2.50 or higher by watching the program as it first loads. The version number should appear where the song's title normally appears. Or press the F1 key; when the About Winamp box appears, click the word Winamp. The version number appears at the bottom of the screen. (The letter *v* is in front of the version number.)

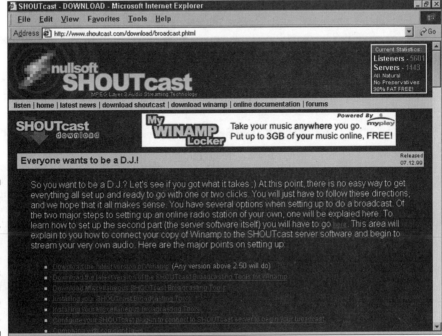

Figure 8-7: The Everybody Wants to Be a D.J. page contains information on how to Webcast.

4. **Download and install the SHOUTcast Broadcasting Tools for Winamp.**

   The SHOUTcast Broadcasting Tools consist of two things. You need to download a special plug-in for Winamp, covered in this step, and you need a special MP3 decoder for Windows (covered in Step 5).

   When you click this line, the page jumps to the section about downloading the SHOUTcast DSP Broadcasting Tools (refer to Figure 8-7). Find the line mentioning the SHOUTcast DSP Plug-in and choose the <u>click here</u> link to begin the download. Your browser downloads the file to whatever directory you choose.

   Make sure Winamp isn't running; then install the downloaded DSP Plug-in program, following its instructions. (In addition to installing the techie stuff, it places a cute little How-To movie on your hard drive. It's hidden in the Winamp area of your Start button menu.)

   This particular plug-in sends the music currently played by Winamp to the SHOUTcast server, where it can be Webcast. It's considered the *source*.

5. **Download and install the Microsoft Netshow Server Tools.**

   Now you need a special MP3 decoder for Webcasting, and it's included with the Microsoft Netshow Server Tools. (The tools are used mainly for corporate PowerPoint users, but we're grabbing them for the freebie MP3 decoder that's tossed inside.)

   Because of licensing agreements, Nullsoft can't offer this free decoder on its site, so download the 4MB Netshow Tools from the Microsoft Web site.

   After downloading the decoder, run the program `NSTOOLS.EXE` to install it. The decoder allows you to Webcast as high as 56 Kbps — a reasonably decent rate. Restart your computer if the Installation program asks you to.

6. **Open Winamp and press Ctrl+P to begin configuring the software.**

   This is the beginning of the hard part, although the folks at Winamp have made it easier over the years.

7. **Click the DSP/Effect area and choose SHOUTcast Source for Winamp.**

   Figure 8-8 shows where to click.

   The SHOUTcast window appears, as does its tiny icon, which appears in your toolbar near the clock. (It's shown in the margin.) Clicking the icon at any time brings up the SHOUTcast source. Right now, however, ignore both the SHOUTcast source window and its icon, and look at the Preferences window.

8. **Click the Configure button at the bottom of the Preferences window.**

   A new window pops up, shown in Figure 8-9. (I told you this was complicated.)

Make sure that the Enable Low-Pass Filtering box is checked and that there's no check mark in the Enable Advanced Recording Mode box. Click OK to close the window.

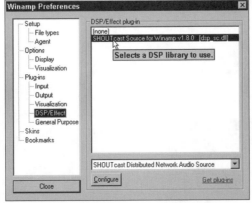

Figure 8-8: Open Winamp, press Ctrl+P, and click the DSP/Effect area.

9. **Click the Server's Edit button from within the SHOUTcast source window.**

You may have to click the SHOUTcast source icon from its location by the clock. When the source window appears, click the window's Edit button in the top-right corner, as shown in Figure 8-10, and a new window appears (see Figure 8-11).

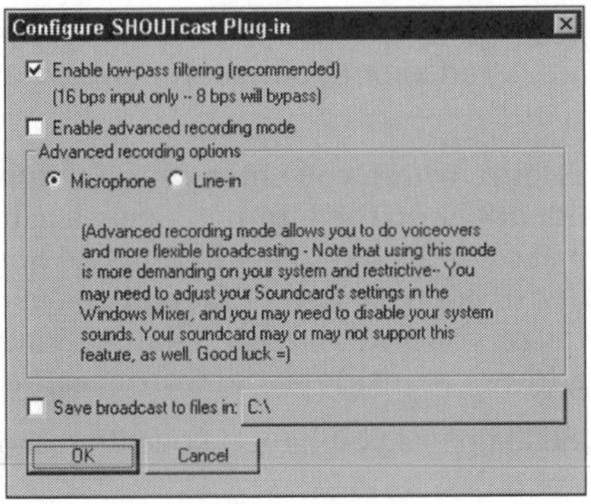

Figure 8-9: The Enable Low-Pass Filtering box is checked, and the Enable Advanced Recording Mode box is not.

Figure 8-10:
Click the
Edit button
to configure
your server.

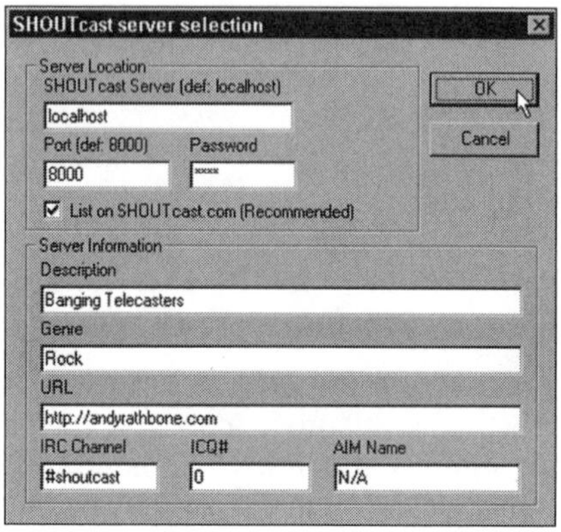

Figure 8-11:
Fill out the
window's
boxes with
information
about your
station and
its server.

10. Fill out the SHOUTcast server selection window.

When the box pops up (see Figure 8-11), it's time to fill out the boxes with information you've gathered about your server and your new radio station. Here's what to fill out:

- **SHOUTcast Server:** Here's where you enter your IP Address — your computer's unique identifier on the Internet. Using a cable modem, or something else that's connected to the Internet 24 hours a day? Then you have a *static* IP address. Enter that address here. If you're using a dial-up server, or you don't have a 24-hour connection, you have a dynamic IP address — just type the word **localhost**.

- **Port:** Leave this at 8000 unless you have a specific reason to change it.

- **Password:** Make up a password, write it down, and enter it here. (You'll need to remember it later.)

- **List on SHOUTcast.com:** Click to place a check mark in this box. This box ensures that your station is listed on SHOUTcast's Web site so that people can find it and listen.

- **Description:** Describe your station's contents here.

- **Genre:** Enter the type of music you play.

- **URL:** Enter your Web page where people can find out more information about your station.

- **IRC Channel:** Short for Internet Relay Chat; enter this number if you have one. (It's a way for listeners to chat with you.)

- **ICQ#:** Enter this, if you have one. (It's yet another chat system.)

- **AIM Name:** Short for America Online Instant Messenger; it's yet another chat system.

11. **Click the OK button in the SHOUTcast Server Selection box.**

    That saves your changes and returns you to the SHOUTcast Source box.

12. **Click the Edit button to the right of the Format line to open the Format Selection dialog box.**

13. **Click the Edit button beneath the Edit button you clicked in Step 9.**

    Make sure that MPEG Layer-3 is chosen under Format. (It's probably already selected.)

    That leaves only one more thing to change: Attributes. Unfortunately, bunches of choices are available, as shown in Figure 8-12.

Figure 8-12:
Choose the right attributes for your combination of modem speed and number of listeners.

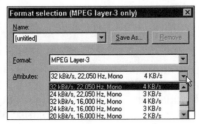

14. **Review the following points and then choose an Attribute from the drop-down list:**

    - Decide the speed you want to broadcast at, measured in Kbps. Then decide whether you want to broadcast in stereo. (That's a no-no if you're using a dial-up line.) The ReadMe file that came with your SHOUTcast Winamp Plug-in (open it in Notepad) explains the speeds to choose depending on your modem's speed.

- Use a speed of 24 Kbps until you're sure everything works; then gradually increase the rate.

- To enter your Attributes information, click the downward pointing arrow in the Attributes box and search for your combination of speed, stereo/mono, and the largest number in the Hz column that your speed can support.

- Make sure that your Hz choice is a multiple of 11 — a selection of 44, 22, or 11 kHz makes your Webcast available to the largest number of listeners. Found that magic attribute number? Click OK to close the window.

At this point, you've set up Winamp, and your source is ready. Now it's time to download and set up the SHOUTcast server software on your computer.

15. Log on to SHOUTcast's Home page with your Internet browser and click the Download SHOUTcast button.

This button is part of a string of options listed across the top of the page. Feeling a sense of déjà vu? Yep — you were here before in Step 1.

16. Click the Be a Server button.

Last time you were here, you clicked the Be a D.J. button. That led you to configure Winamp as the source for your tunes. Now, it's time to set up the SHOUTcast server software to send those tunes out onto the Internet.

(Or, if you're still confused about Steps 1-13, click the Be a D.J. button again and retrace your steps.)

Setting up the server requires three steps. Here goes.

17. Download the latest version of SHOUTcast Server.

Click the Download Now button and read the license agreement. If you agree to the legalese, click the Proceed to Downloading link and download the version for your particular operating system. You'll probably choose Windows — unless you're running FreeBSD, Linux, or Solaris Sparc. Macintosh users can broadcast MP3 radio stations with MacAmp 2.0 (www.subband.com/macamp/). The popular player now has broadcast capabilities.

Save the file to a spot on your computer where you can remember to find it in the next step.

18. Run the downloaded SHOUTcast Server file.

After the program installs itself into a SHOUTcast folder in your C drive's Programs folder, its ReadMe file pops up.

19. Read the ReadMe file.

Yes, it's complicated, but you must read it in order to figure out what's going on. The biggest problem is your Internet connection. If you want to broadcast to 100 listeners at a mere 24 Kbps, you need 2,400 Kbps, or 2.4 Mbps of bandwidth. An average cable modem has only around 750 Kbps — barely enough to dish up a half-dozen listeners.

Also, you want a *clear* connection: no proxies, firewalls, networks sharing modems, and other conveniences.

When you installed the program, it installed the SHOUTcast Distributed Network Audio Server (DNAS). The DNAS accepts the broadcast feed from your newly configured Winamp; it then broadcasts that sound over the Internet to your listeners. It also lists your broadcast on the SHOUTcast Web site.

20. Edit the SHOUTcast DNAS configuration file.

Click the Windows Start button, choose Programs, and click SHOUTcast DNAS. From there, choose Edit SHOUTcast DNAS configuration, and an odd-looking file, shown in Figure 8-13, appears on-screen.

Most of this file consists of comments and instructions. (Any line beginning with a semicolon or the [symbol is a comment or label and shouldn't be changed.) Only the following lines need an ogle; be sure that the values match what you entered in Step 10:

- **MaxUser:** Choose a conservative number of maximum users for your server. Multiply your modem's speed by 0.9, and divide that by your bit rate — 24. For example, a 56K modem's dial-up connection would support two users.

  Best yet, start with a MaxUser of 1, just to get the thing up and running. Then you can increase your users as you fine tune everything.

- **Password=:** This must be the same password that you entered in Step 10.

- **PortBase=8000:** Make sure that this number is the same as the number you typed in the Port box in Figure 8-11. (Because you probably didn't change it in Step 10, you won't need to change it here.)

Make sure that all the things you enter here correspond to what you entered in Step 10.

21. Load the SHOUTcast Server.

Click the Windows Start button, choose Programs, and click SHOUTcast DNAS. From there, choose Edit. The server leaps to the screen, waiting for you to run Winamp. It places its tiny icon next to the clock on the Windows taskbar.

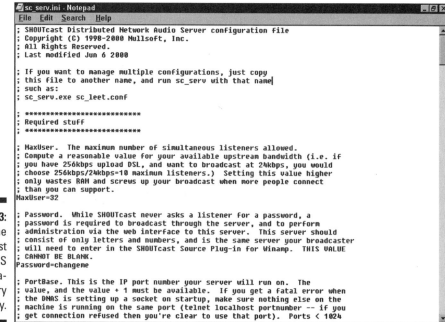

Figure 8-13:
Edit the
SHOUTcast
DNAS
configura-
tion file very
carefully.

22. **Load Winamp and click the Connect button to start Webcasting.**

Watch the words next to the Connect window. They should say, `Connecting to Host` and, finally, list the number of bytes of music you've Webcast. If everything's worked out the way it should, you're sharing your tunes with the world. If not, you'll probably see some sort of an error message.

And if you do see an error message? Your first step is to read the ReadMe files that came with the Winamp plug-in and the SHOUTcast server program. There's some complicated stuff in there, and a single mistake can ruin everything.

✓ Still having problems? Head to the SHOUTcast Online Documentation at `www.shoutcast.com/support/docs/`. You'll find fairly readable descriptions of how to fix problems.

✓ Read the SHOUTcast Web site forums. If something's confusing to you, it will have already confused somebody else. Chances are, you'll find an answer there.

✓ Before posting on the SHOUTcast Web site forum, however, be sure to pour over the ReadMe files and the Online Documentation. Although forum members are willing to help people with problems, they're often hostile at helping people who haven't taken the time to grasp the basics of Internet Webcasting.

- For live Webcasts, download the Live Input plug-in. It lets you Webcast live audio — talk shows, band jams, whatever. After downloading the plug-in into your Winamp Plug-in folder (as I describe in Chapter 6), open Winamp, press Ctrl+L, and type **linerec://** to Webcast live audio.

- SHOUTcast offers some promos that do play along with your playlists — things like, "Milking our bandwidth for all it's worth with SHOUTcast streaming audio!"

- Several other Web sites, such as MP3Spy (www.mp3spy.com) and Live365 (www.live365.com), help you create Internet radio stations. Live365 broadcasts from its own server, for instance, so you don't have to broadcast through your own computer and ISP. However, you need to upload all your songs to that site so that they can be broadcast.

Part III
Creating Your Own MP3 Files

The 5th Wave   By Rich Tennant

"Get ready, Mona. I just downloaded 'Mickey' by Starfox."

In this part . . .

When I was a nerdy little kid, I collected TV theme songs. Whenever a show started, I ran up with my Radio Shack tape recorder, put the microphone up by the TV's speaker, and recorded shows like *The Beverly Hillbillies, The Jetsons,* and *The Rockford Files* — if I could stay up that late.

Now, as a nerdy adult, my equipment and tastes have changed. Instead of a cheap tape recorder and microphone, I carry around an Archos Jukebox 6000 portable MP3 player that holds more than 100 CDs worth of music.

This part of the book shows how to turn CDs into MP3s, but it also covers creating MP3s from albums and tapes. It even shows how to take your vacation movies of a Hawaiian beach, convert the sound into MP3, and loop it — layering your room with a relaxing environmental ambience.

And if you do have a hankering for the *Speed Racer* theme song, this part of the book shows how to capture it.

Chapter 9

Ripping Songs from a CD, Album, TV, Radio, Tape, or Microphone

. . . .

In This Chapter

▶ Understanding and using Ripper software

▶ Ripping sounds from a CD

▶ Recording sound from albums

▶ Recording sound from the TV

▶ Recording sound from a tape

▶ Recording sound from a microphone

▶ Editing recorded music or sound

. . . .

The term *ripping* basically means copying sounds from a CD onto your hard drive. MP3 aficionados use the word *ripping* because they're tearing the digital sound from CD and copying those numbers onto their hard drive. Besides, ripping sounds more cool than copying.

This chapter shows how to rip songs from your own CDs into your computer, where you convert them into MP3 files. It also shows you how to record albums, camcorder soundtracks, TV shows, videotapes, or any other noise-makers onto your hard drive. Once there, you can clean up the sounds so they're ready to be converted into MP3s.

If you're looking for the simplest method of converting CDs into MP3s, head for Chapter 11, which covers software designed especially for turning CDs into MP3 files in one easy step. But if you're creating MP3s from something besides CDs or if you're looking for tips to make the cleanest rips possible, stick around.

Why Use a Ripper?

Creating an MP3 requires two steps. First, rip the CD's contents onto the hard drive; then, encode the contents into MP3 files.

When you rip the sounds into your computer, the Ripper software stores the CD's music files in a WAV format. (Chapter 1 describes the differences in file formats.)

Your computer can play these newly created WAV files without problem; both Winamp and Windows Media Player do the job. So, why not stick with WAV files? Because WAV files are huge, uncompressed files of 40MB to 50MB or, in the case of a rocking Grateful Dead live jam, 200MB.

Converting the WAV files into MP3 files is called *encoding*. (Encoding gets its coverage in Chapter 10.)

✔ In the early days, people needed two pieces of software to create MP3s. The first software ripped the sounds from the CD; the second piece encoded the sounds into MP3 files. Today, all-in-one programs, such as MusicMatch, AudioCatalyst, and RealJukebox, perform both chores at the same time: You insert the CD and click a button, and the software automatically transforms the songs directly into MP3 files.

✔ Some MP3 purists dislike all-in-one software because they lose control over the sound quality. When the software automatically turns the CD's songs into MP3s, it bypasses the WAV file step, which leaves no way to edit the WAV file to correct any flaws in the rips.

✔ Plus, not everybody rips CDs exclusively. Some people convert their aging album collection into MP3s for easier storage and to get rid of that stinky mildew smell. They need that extra step of cleaning up the sounds before encoding them into MP3s.

✔ Ripping has nothing to do with *Raster Image Processing,* also called *RIPping,* which refers to the conversion of a PostScript file to a high-resolution bitmap used in fancy printing work.

✔ Ripping doesn't hurt CDs.

✔ Open My Computer and stick a CD into your disc drive. Right-click the disc drive, choose Explorer, and view the CD with the Windows Explorer. Instead of seeing song names, you see a bunch of 1K files named `Track01.CDA`, `Track02.CDA`, and so on. Strangely enough, these aren't the songs. Those are *pointers* to the song's location on the CD. Ripping software examines the CDA files to find the songs and then copies those songs to your hard drive.

✔ Popular sound-editing programs like Cool Edit 2000 ($69 at `www.syntrillium.com`) and SoundForge XP ($59 at `www.soundforge.com`) enhance, filter, mix, and clean up dirty WAV files. They remove pops from an album, for example, or fix CD rips that don't sound right. A copy of Cool Edit 2000 awaits you on this book's CD.

How Do I Rip Songs from a CD?

Start the Ripper software, insert the CD, choose the songs, and click the software's Copy option. The software grabs the Compact Disc Audio (CDA) straight from the CD and saves the sound as a WAV file on your hard drive.

You don't even need a sound card; the CD's music (which is already stored on the CD using numbers to represent the sounds) becomes numbers on your hard drive.

Ripping CDs, known technically as *Digital Audio Extraction* (DAE), doesn't work on all CD players, unfortunately, mostly the older ones. If your drive can't, it's time to buy a new one. (Chapter 2 shows how to install it.) The latest list of Ripper software lurks at `http://dailymp3.com/cdrippers.html`. Figure 9-1 shows one popular ripper, WinDAC32, ripping a CD. (When ripped, the song turned into a 43.5MB WAV file.) A Ripper is rarely free, a few are shareware, and most are commercial.

Figure 9-1: WinDAC, a popular standalone ripper, prepares to copy a 43.93MB song onto the hard drive, where it can be encoded into an MP3 file.

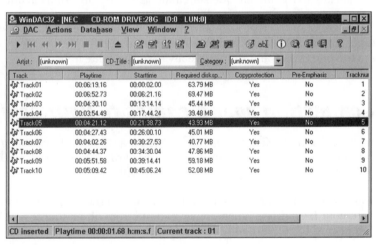

The songs on the CD shown in Figure 9-1 range from 39.48MB to 69.47MB. Ripping the entire CD would require more than 507MB of hard drive space.

✔ WAV files consume *lots* of room. If your hard drive lacks at least 600MB of free space, rip the songs one at a time. Encode the ripped song to MP3 format, delete its WAV file, and move on to the next file.

✔ Hard drive not big enough? Chapter 2 contains tips on installing a second drive or using an Iomega Jaz drive, a standard for audio storage.

✔ Bought a blazingly fast 24x speed drive? It'll never rip audio that quickly. That rating shows how fast the drive *reads* a CD's information. Rippers need a CD to *send* data. In fact, for the best quality rips, choose single speed. If you try to rip at too fast a speed, the sound file might contain skips and pops. Experiment until you find the right rate.

✔ Immediately after ripping a CD, listen to the WAV file in Windows Media Player or Winamp. If the sound has skips, pops, unwanted noise, or other distortion, tell the software to rip at a lower speed.

✔ Feel free to clean up a CD's WAV file using any of the sound-editing programs that I discuss later in this chapter.

Recording from Sources besides CDs

Although rippers create WAV files from CDs for later encoding into MP3s, that's not usually their best function anymore. For creating MP3s specifically from your CDs, check out MusicMatch in Chapter 11. That software's designed specifically to rip and encode simultaneously, creating MP3s in one step.

But if you want to create MP3s from something besides CDs — records, tapes, radios, TVs, camcorders, or similar sounds — the next few sections are the ones you want. Rippers really earn their due here.

Connecting sound cables to your computer

Whereas ripping refers to copying sound off a CD — and bypassing the sound card in the process — you need the sound card when creating MP3s from a turntable, TV set, VCR, camcorder, or microphone.

Sounds are stored as numbers on the CD, which the ripper merely copies onto your hard drive. When copying sound from other sources, you need the sound card to convert audible sound into numbers.

To grab audio from those sources, record the sound through your sound card. You can set up your computer to capture audio by connecting the output cables from your sound source into the Line In jack on your sound card.

This section shows how to connect the appropriate cables for recording the sound onto your hard drive.

Tools you need: The appropriate cable (see Table 9-1) to connect from the sound source to the computer's sound card.

Cost: About $5 to $10, if the sound card doesn't already include the correct cable.

Stuff to watch out for: Sound cards rarely label their jacks well. Instead of using big letters, they use bizarre pictures or weird circles. And if the jacks on the back of your sound card aren't marked, you'll have to dig around for the manual.

Follow these steps to connect a cable from your album, tape, VCR, camcorder, or TV set to your sound card's input jack for recording:

1. **Turn down the volume on your sound card and sound source.**

   You don't want to hear any speaker-shattering pops when pushing cables into jacks.

2. **Find the correct cables for your sound device and your sound card.**

   Different components use different cables; Table 9-1 shows what cable to use. Although most stereo stores carry these cables, Radio Shack is always a good last resort.

   An ⅛-inch jack is often called a "mini-jack" at electronics stores.

Table 9-1	Cables for Connecting a Device to a Sound Card	
This Device	*Needs This Cable*	*Radio Shack Part Number*
Turntable, VCR, tape deck, or stereo TV	Y-cable with one pair of RCA jacks on one end and a ⅛-inch stereo plug on the other	42-2481 for six feet; 42-2475 for three feet
Mono TV	Y-cable with a single RCA jack for the TV and a ⅛-inch stereo plug on the other	42-2444
Camcorder	Y-cable with two RCA jacks for the camcorder and one ½-inch stereo plug for the sound card. Camcorders with ⅛-inch audio jacks (or headphone jacks) need an ⅛-inch stereo jack on each end of a cable.	42-2481 for six feet; 42-2475 for three feet. Camcorders with ⅛-inch audio jacks need 42-2607.
Microphone with ¼-inch plug	Plug the microphone's cord into a ¼-inch to ⅛-inch adapter, then plug it into the sound card's MIC jack.	274-047 for adapter
Microphone with ⅛-inch plug	Plug the microphone directly into the sound card's MIC jack.	No adapter needed

3. Connect one end of the cable to your sound device.

Check the back of your VCR, camcorder, turntable, stereo, or TV for output jacks. You should see a pair of stubby little metal heads (RCA jacks) along one side. If it's not stereo, there's only one little stub. If you're lucky, they're labeled.

Take the Y-cable adapter, like the one in Figure 9-2, and plug the cable's two RCA jacks into those output jacks, making sure that the red jack goes into the red plug. (That's for the right speaker.)

If your camcorder has an ⅛-inch stereo jack (or headphone jack), plug your cable into it.

Figure 9-2:
The ⅛-inch plug goes into your sound card's Line In jack; the two RCA jacks connect to the VCR camcorder, turntable, or other device.

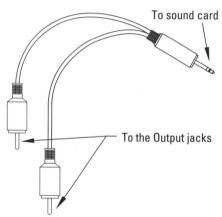

To sound card

To the Output jacks

4. Connect the cable's ⅛-inch plug into your sound card's Line In jack.

Make extra sure the cable doesn't mistakenly push into the other nearby jacks.

5. Adjust the mixer levels.

Now, start playing your turntable, camcorder, or whatever else you're trying to record. This is where recording becomes an art: You carefully adjust the volume level through the Windows mixing board while watching the recording software's volume level to make sure the incoming sound is not too loud or soft.

To see the Windows built-in mixing board, double-click the speaker icon in the screen's bottom-right corner. When the mixing board appears, choose Properties from the Options menu, as shown in Figure 9-3.

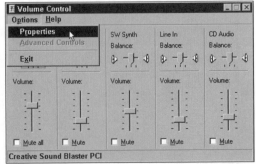

Figure 9-3:
Choose
Properties
from the
Options
menu.

Because you want to record the incoming sounds, choose Recording from the Properties window. Click in any empty box to put a check mark inside it; doing so shows all the options of what you're able to record.

Click OK, and the Recording Control window appears. Because you're recording from the sound card's Line In jack, select the Line In box, as shown in Figure 9-4.

Figure 9-4:
Choose the
Line In
Balance box
and slide
the meter up
or down
until the
recording
level looks
right in your
recording
software's
meter.

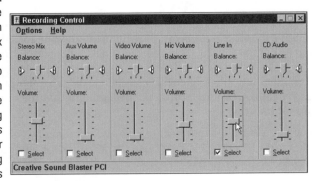

Now turn on the volume meter — sometimes called a VU meter — on your recording software — Cool Edit 2000, in this case. Slide the mixing window's Line In bar up or down until the sound level in its adjacent meter looks just right: The Windows meter should stay below the red levels, and the recording software's meter should come close to — but not reach or surpass — 0 on the control bar.

See how the mouse pointer slides the bar up or down in Figure 9-5? When you slide the bar to adjust the volume coming in through the Line In jack, the volume meter along the bottom of Cool Edit 2000 moves back and forth accordingly.

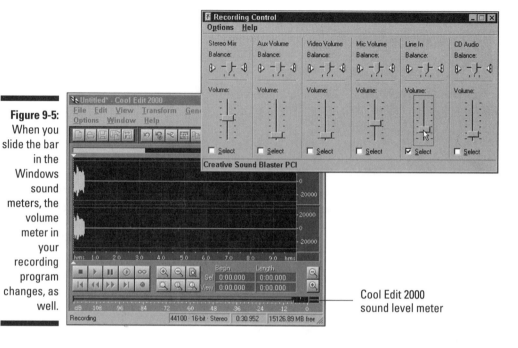

Figure 9-5:
When you slide the bar in the Windows sound meters, the volume meter in your recording program changes, as well.

Cool Edit 2000 sound level meter

6. Listen in through your sound card's speakers.

The incoming sound should begin playing through your sound card's speakers.

✔ If you don't hear anything, check the sound card's mixer software. Make sure that the Line In or Line button is checked and that the controller is slid up about halfway.

✔ Keep checking your cable connections as well. You're always aiming for the sound card's Line In jack. Don't use the Mic jack for anything but microphones, or the sound will be awful.

✔ Be sure to experiment a few times by recording at different levels. Sooner or later, you'll find one that sounds right. You might have to change the level for everything you record.

✔ To listen to your computer through your home stereo's speakers, flip back to Chapter 6. That chapter shows you how to connect cables in the proper direction.

Recording songs from albums

Albums may be a joy for listening, but they're a pain to store. Plus, you always worry about when it's time to change the needle. Playing any rare singles? Don't they deteriorate each time they're played?

Converting albums to MP3 combats these problems and adds an advantage: Because the sounds originated from an album, the MP3 still holds some of that warm vinyl feel — none of that sterile CD feeling. The majority of portable MP3 players easily hold a full album.

Some all-in-one software records albums and converts them to MP3s on the fly, but that skips the WAV stage. Without this intermediate stage, you have no way to remove any recording flaws before the final encoding.

These steps show how to record songs from an album and save them as WAV files — where you can touch them up before turning them into MP3s.

1. **Clean the album.**

   The cleaner the album, the cleaner the sound. Try these cleaning tips:

   - Wash both sides of the album with a lint-free cloth. Most music stores sell record-cleaning brushes designed expressly for removing dust.

   - To remove extra-stubborn goo from the grooves, try a mixture of 50/50 rubbing alcohol and distilled water. Lacking that, small amounts of baby shampoo can do the trick. Be sure to rinse well.

   - Always wash the record with a circular motion; don't scrub "across grain" as it might scratch the grooves. When you finish cleaning, dry the album and only touch it by the edges.

   - If it's an important album — a rare import, or an old 78 — check the phone directory for professional record-cleaning services found in many big cities. They can often remove any extra-persistent grunge from the vinyl.

2. **Clean the turntable's needle.**

   Wipe it off with the little brush that comes with the turntable. Lost yours? Pick one up at the music or stereo store. They're cheap.

3. **Connect the turntable's output cables to your sound card.**

   See the "Connecting sound cables to your computer" section, earlier in this chapter.

4. **Adjust your recording level.**

   See the long black bar along the bottom of Cool Edit 2000 in Figure 9-5? That's the recording monitor. It flashes according to the incoming volume levels.

   Start playing your album and watch the monitor. If it flashes too close to the right end, turn down the volume going into the sound card, or use the sound card's mixer program to turn down the incoming sound. (I cover how in this chapter's "Connecting sound cables to your computer" section.)

If the level's too high, it will distort; if it's too low, you'll hear background noise. Take your time to find the right level before recording. Be patient.

5. **Start the recording software.**

   Begin recording using Cool Edit 2000, or another recording-and-editing package. (MusicMatch can also record albums — as I describe in Chapter 11 — but it can't edit the resulting WAV files.)

6. **Play the album.**

   Be sure to press the Record button on your recording software *before* playing the album. Don't worry about the initial plop when the needle falls onto the record or the empty space before the first song. You easily edit out those sounds later, as I describe in the "Editing Recorded Music or Sounds" section.

✔ Hear a persistent humming sound in the background? Plug your turntable into the "unswitched AC adapter" on your receiver or amplifier. If you can't find the unswitched adapter, try plugging your computer and turntable into the same wall outlet. (Use an adapter, if needed.) The two devices then share a common ground.

✔ Remember to record at a level that's very close to the 0 on the recording level — but never too close. Otherwise, the recording won't sound loud compared to others, like MP3s created from CDs.

✔ Recording an old mono album? You might only hear the sound on one speaker. You can correct this with sound-editing software, however, as I explain later in the "Editing Recorded Music or Sounds" section.

✔ Record the entire album's first side and save that as a single WAV file. Then do the same with the flip side. It's very easy to separate the tracks into separate files using Cool Edit 2000, Sound Forge, or other sound-editing software.

✔ In the eyes of the law, converting albums to MP3 files isn't any different from copying CDs. You can keep the file for your own personal use, but don't give it away or sell it or you might be violating copyrights.

Recording from tapes, camcorders, a microphone, or TVs

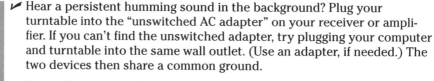

Recording from TVs, audio tapes, or videotapes works the same as recording from an album. Why would you want to? Well, perhaps you want an MP3 file of that hot new band playing on David Letterman in the wee hours.

Or maybe you videotaped a Hawaiian luau last summer, complete with fire-walkers and mystic drumbeats. (You would be surprised at the sound quality from today's camcorders.)

Here's how to copy those sounds to your hard drive, where they can be cleaned up and converted to an MP3 file.

1. **Connect the sound source's output cables to your sound card.**

   I describe how in the "Connecting sound cables to your computer" section, earlier in this chapter. Basically, you connect the Output cables of your sound source to your sound card's ⅛-inch Line In jack. Table 9-1 shows the required cables.

   Remember that *everything* plugs into the sound card's Line In jack except a microphone. Microphones must plug into the sound card's Mic jack.

2. **Adjust your recording levels and start recording.**

   Check out Steps 4 and 5 in the "Recording songs from albums" section; everything's the same. Make sure that you begin recording *before* your sound begins playing. You can always edit out any unwanted garbage later, but if the ukulele starts playing *before* you push the recording software's Record button, you'll need to start over.

3. **Click the Stop button when through.**

   Grabbed the sound? Hit the Stop button on the recording software; then stop the sound source. It's now time to clean up the sound, as I describe in this chapter's "Editing Recorded Music or Sounds" section.

Just because you can grab a TV performance off the air doesn't mean you own it. The same goes for a band playing at a local street fair. You can keep the soundtrack for your own personal use, but don't give it away or sell it, or you might be violating copyrights.

Editing Recorded Music or Sounds

After you record the music or sounds and save them as immense WAV files on the hard drive, you can convert them straight to MP3s using the encoder programs described in Chapter 10.

But while the file's still in WAV format, there's no excuse not to touch it up a little bit. Remove those clicks and pops from the album. Edit the TV recording so it starts the moment David Letterman says, "And now, here's . . . ."

The following sections describe some tips for editing WAV files down to the best possible recording.

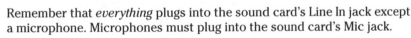

Making mono recordings play on both speakers

When recording from a mono source — a single microphone or a TV with only one speaker — the computer fills only one side of its stereo signal with the sound. You can't get true stereo from a mono recording, but you can fake it.

Tell your sound-editing software to copy the recorded track onto the other, empty track. For instance, if the sound's only recorded on the right side, duplicate it to the left side, too.

The sound-editing software can match up the two tracks so that they're identically positioned. Save the resulting file, and your mono sound will now play over both speakers. It's still not stereo, but it's much better than only one speaker.

Cutting out the bad parts

When you record something through a sound editor like Cool Edit 2000, the software shows a pictures of the sound waves, like in Figure 9-6.

Sound-editing software works much like word processing software. You position the cursor in different places to choose sections for cutting and copying, or to move highlighted segments to different locations.

Figure 9-6:
Cool Edit
2000 and
other
sound-
editing
packages
show
recorded
sounds as
a picture.

Ripping audio from the Internet

Saving audio or music sent in a "live stream" from the Internet is a copyright violation. That's why most sound programs won't let you save incoming RealAudio programs and other streams. (You can always bypass copy-protection schemes by sticking a microphone next to your PC's speakers, but that rarely sounds very good.)

Versions of Winamp before Version 2.10 could save streamed MP3 files, but that function is disabled in the current versions. (Head for www.winampheaven.com to check out every version of Winamp ever released.) Older versions of Windows Media Player save streamed MP3 files in your Windows Temporary folder, if you take a peek.

The first editing step is to find the beginning and end of your recorded sounds so you can trim off the unnecessary sounds. Use the software's Zoom or Magnify commands (those little magnifying glass icons along the bottom) to magnify your view of the sound. That gives you a better picture of when sounds start and stop.

A tall wave means a loud sound; very small waves (or no waves) mean no sound.

Figure 9-7 shows a live recording saved in Cool Edit 2000. Notice how the sound wave comes to an abrupt stop near where the cursor points in Figure 9-7? That's the end of the song, and you can delete anything past that point. Double-check by clicking at the ending point and pressing the Play button. The software plays any sounds past that point, letting you make sure they're not needed.

Highlight all the sound waves past your chosen ending point, press the Delete key, and Cool Edit 2000 chops it out.

Here are some more editing tips:

- ✔ Listen to your file from the beginning to see when it actually starts. Click at the actual starting point, highlight the material in front of it, and delete it, too. Your resulting file is now trimmed to its exact size.

- ✔ Having trouble finding the exact spot to trim? Use the magnify command to zoom in until you can spot individual sound waves. That makes it very easy to choose the exact spot.

- ✔ Prefer a nice fade out on a recording? Choose where you would like the fade out to begin, highlight the sound from that spot onward, and choose the software's fade option. The software will make the sound fade away, like the ending of many songs.

✔ When dealing with a noisy recording, check your sound-editing software's filter and noise reduction menus. Many of them can reduce the pops of a crackling album and cut out some hiss from tapes.

✔ The more money you spend on your sound-editing software, the more tricks it has for manipulating sound. Sound Forge and the professional version of Cool Edit may be expensive, but they're full of features not found on less-expensive software. They have plenty of Undo features, so you can go back to normal if an auditory experiment goes awry.

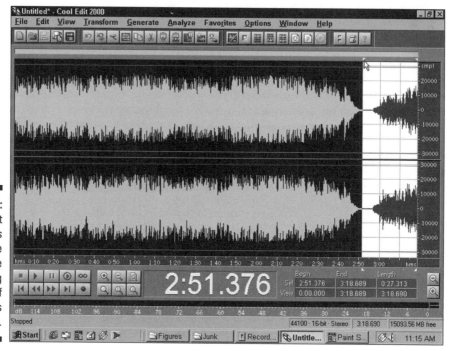

Figure 9-7: Cool Edit 2000 shows where the sound file ends, letting you trim off any excess sounds.

Chapter 10

Completing the MP3 File with an Encoder

Chances are, you won't need to read this chapter. If you're just converting your CDs into MP3s, move ahead to Chapter 11. It covers software designed expressly for that purpose.

But if you're converting something besides a CD — or you want to convert a WAV file into an MP3, this is the spot. Besides, this chapter explains all that codec stuff you're bound to hear MP3 fans talk about.

What's a Codec?

Short for compression/decompression, a *codec* is the computer coding technology used to compress a file and then expand it when needed. MP3 stands for MPEG-1, Layer 3 because that's the name of the MP3 *standard* — the official name for the original codec used for creating MP3 files.

MP3 began in 1987 when Germany's Fraunhofer Institute and France's Thomson Consumer Electronics began researching new ways to compress audio. The Moving Picture Experts Group (MPEG), a designator of Official Standards, liked one of the concepts so much it declared that codec to be an official standard — MPEG-1 Layer 3, known as simply *MP3*. The timing of MP3 caught the recording industry by surprise. Until fairly recently, computers weren't powerful enough to compress CD-quality audio into such easily saved files. The creation of MP3 technology matched the timing of Pentium computers and fast modems, leading to a worldwide sonic boom of MP3 popularity on the Internet.

- MP3 certainly isn't the only type of codec. Sound and video can be compressed in many ways. However, MP3 is one of the best ways to compress sound while still retaining almost CD-quality sound.

- Interesting factoid: France's Thomson Consumer Electronics, one of the creators of MP3, is putting out the Lyra portable MP3 player under the RCA brand name. As the Lyra loads MP3 files, it converts them into MPX files as a security measure, so the files can't be moved to other players or computers. This inconvenience destroyed sales.

- Files aren't the only things using codecs. Streaming audio or video — music or movies that flow into your computer over the Internet — also use codecs. Compressing things before sending them saves download time, because the receiving computer can decompress them upon arrival. Video, too, is compressed using codecs.

- MPEG stands for Moving Pictures Experts Group, a bunch of programmer types who think up new ways to compress digitized sound and video and then think of imaginative new names to call the compression schemes: MPEG-1 Layer 3, for example, as well as MPEG-2, MPEG-4, and MPEG-7.

- MPEG-1 comes in several layers, but almost all MP3 files use the Layer 3 standard. It sounds better than other standards (Layers 1 and 2) because it's more complex, requiring more processing power to handle the compression and decompression chores.

- You'll find more technical information than you can stomach at the MPEG Organization's Official Web site, `www.cselt.it/mpeg/`, seen in Figure 10-1, as well as the layman-oriented `www.askmp3.com`. (Try `www.mpeg.org` if you can't get through there.)

Which Codec Is Best?

Just as gourmets never agree on the best wine (or even the best way to create wine), programmers can never agree on the best codec — the backbone of MP3.

All files encoded using MP3 technology must be able to play on all MP3 players. However, just as different types and brands of cassette tape work in everybody's player, different types of codecs can create MP3 files that play on all MP3 players.

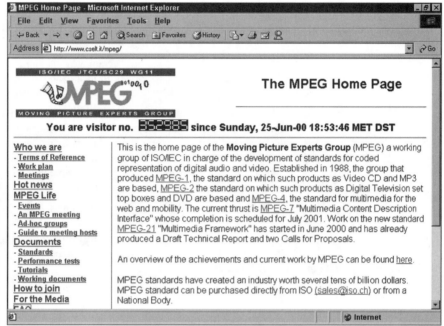

MPEG Home Page - Microsoft Internet Explorer

File   Edit   View   Favorites   Tools   Help

Back ▾ → ▾ ⊘ ⟳ ⌂   Search Favorites History   ▾ ⬒ ⬓ ⬔

Address http://www.cselt.it/mpeg/   Go

ISO/IEC JTC1/SC29 WG11

The MPEG Home Page

MOVING PICTURE EXPERTS GROUP

You are visitor no. [352295] **since Sunday, 25-Jun-00 18:53:46 MET DST**

Who we are
- Terms of Reference
- Work plan
- Meetings
Hot news
MPEG Life
- Events
- An MPEG meeting
- Ad-hoc groups
- Guide to meeting hosts
Documents
- Standards
- Performance tests
- Tutorials
- Working documents
How to join
For the Media

This is the home page of the **Moving Picture Experts Group** (MPEG) a working group of ISO/IEC in charge of the development of standards for coded representation of digital audio and video. Established in 1988, the group that produced MPEG-1, the standard on which such products as Video CD and MP3 are based, MPEG-2 the standard on which such products as Digital Television set top boxes and DVD are based and MPEG-4, the standard for multimedia for the web and mobility. The current thrust is MPEG-7 "Multimedia Content Description Interface" whose completion is scheduled for July 2001. Work on the new standard MPEG-21 "Multimedia Framework" has started in June 2000 and has already produced a Draft Technical Report and two Calls for Proposals.

An overview of the achievements and current work by MPEG can be found here.

MPEG standards have created an industry worth several tens of billion dollars. MPEG standard can be purchased directly from ISO (sales@iso.ch) or from a National Body.

Internet

Figure 10-1:
The MPEG
Web site
contains a
vast amount
of technical
information
on MP3.

And just as the same basic components form the basis for each brand of tape, the original Fraunhofer programming work forms the backbone for nearly every MP3 codec. In fact, Fraunhofer has shut down several encoding programs for alleged copyright violations. Most commercial programs pay a license to Fraunhofer to use its technology.

Some codecs start with the Fraunhofer codec and then alter it slightly, changing the way it compresses the sound into the MP3 standard. Some codecs require more time and processing power, but create better-sounding MP3 files. Others are quick, but not as effective.

REMEMBER

✔ All encoder software uses a type of MP3 codec to convert standard audio files — WAV files, see Chapter 9 — into MP3 files, shrinking the file to the defined MP3 standards.

✔ Because Fraunhofer came up with the original MP3 codec, it's generally regarded as one of the best quality, and it's usually the basis for other MP3 codecs.

✔ Different types of MP3 codecs are out there — Xing, BladeEnc, and others. To choose the best, simply listen to them all and choose the one that sounds best to you. Try listening through headphones, or ask around on the newsgroups that I describe in Chapter 4.

Okay, how do they compress an MP3 file's sound?

Human hearing isn't anywhere near perfect. Dogs can hear more accurately; you've probably heard them start howling several minutes before the fire engine passes by.

MP3 takes advantage of the human ear's imperfections by editing out the sounds and tones that humans can't hear. It does that by taking the audio file and dividing it into a bunch of separate frequency bands. The software then examines the bands and decides which portions of the bands are inaudible to the average human.

Imagine a piano player trying to play on a broken piano. You'd hear the player's fingers hitting the keys, as well as occasional grunts of

excitement. When you fix the piano and it begins to play, the piano sound now masks out the once audible grunts and finger noises.

Similarly, a particular loud sound in a song masks out lower-volume sounds. So, when the compression software examines the layers of sound frequencies, it saves the loud layer, but discards adjacent layers containing quieter, drowned-out sounds.

By eliminating sounds on the inaudible frequencies, MP3 reduces the file's size. Humans won't notice much, if any, difference, but your dog might. Don't use MP3 on music your dog enjoys.

Using an Encoder

All encoders work the same way. First, select your recorded sound file (anything ripped using the steps in Chapter 9) and select the desired quality level. Then press the Encode button and twiddle your thumbs for a while.

Choosing the quality level is pretty much a no-brainer. The MP3 standard calls for files to be encoded at 128 Kbps, 44k Hz, stereo. If you want your songs to be encoded with the best compromise between quality and file size, use those settings.

- ✔ Not all encoders let you create MP3 files at those settings, however. In fact, many shareware versions of programs use that fact to encourage people to register and pay for a program. After you send in the money, the program permits you to encode at the standard 128 Kbps. RealAudio RealJukebox, for instance, encodes at 96 rather than 128 Kbps until you pay for the upgrade.

- ✔ The freely available Fraunhofer codec used by the Windows latest version of Media Player can only encode up to 56 bits per second, and 22 kHz stereo. If you buy the advanced codec from Opticom (www.opticom.de) for $49.95, you can reach the normal MP3 quality levels.

- ✔ MusicMatch can encode WAV files into MP3 files at 128 bits. If you're looking for an encoder to convert your WAV files, check out the copy on this book's CD.

✔ Actually, MusicMatch can encode MP3 files up to 320 Kbps. Some audio-philes say this creates better sounding files. Most people can't hear the difference, however, and the resulting files are huge in comparison, defeating the purpose of MP3.

Filling Out ID Tags

After you've encoded your file, there's one last step: Filling out the song's ID tag. MP3 files contain more than just music. There's room inside the file to store information about the song itself: its name, composer, artist, album, length, and other pertinent information.

To fill out an ID tag of a newly created MP3 file — or any MP3 file — load it into Winamp and double-click on its name. A box appears, as seen in Figure 10-2.

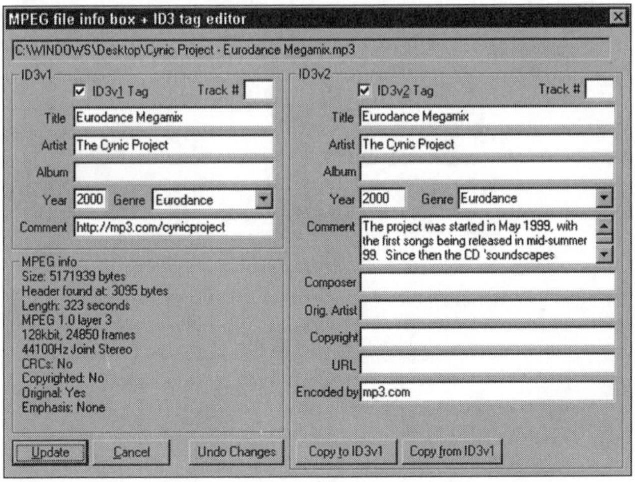

Figure 10-2:
Double-click
a file's name
in Winamp
to call up its
ID tag for
editing.

In Figure 10-2, Winamp displays the ID tag information about an MP3 file, Cynic Project's Eurodance Megamix.

Now for the complicated part. First, ID tags sometimes aren't called ID tags. They're often called *ID3* tags. And, like most other bits of computer unpleas-antness, ID3 tags have moved through several versions, each confusing things a little big more. So some programs, like Winamp, display the information stored in both tag formats.

The left side of Figure 10-2 shows the first version of the ID3 tag. Known as ID3v1, the tag includes space for the song's track number (its order on the CD), title, artist, album, recording year, genre, and a tiny comment.

Can't I install one codec for *all* my programs to use?

Some codecs don't come built in to separate programs. Instead, they're Windows "plug-ins" known as Audio Codec Managers (ACM). Once installed, as shown in the figure below, any Windows audio recording program can use the ACM — Cool Edit, Sound Forge, or even Windows Sound Recorder — to create MP3s.

You'll find a free Fraunhofer ACM codec for creating MP3s in Windows Media Player 6.0 and above (Media Player is available at the download section of www.microsoft.com) or by downloading Microsoft's Net Show development.

The freebie ACM Fraunhofer codec can decode 128-bit or better MP3 files — it sounds great. However, it only allows encoding up to 56K at 22,050 kHz stereo, which is far from the average quality MP3 file. To up the quality to normal levels, you must buy the advanced codec from Opticom (www.opticom.de) for $49.

Or, do what many people are doing. MusicMatch comes with the codec for converting WAV files into MP3s at top quality, so feel free to use that. (It's on this book's CD.)

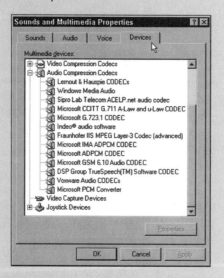

MP3 users quickly tired of the restrictive format, so the tag engineers released the ID3v2 tag, which appears on the right side of Figure 10-2. That tag includes more space for each description, a lengthy comment area, and additional spaces for more detailed information.

Why should anybody care about ID tags when the file's name usually already contains the artist's name and song title? Because the larger your collection grows, the more difficult it becomes to keep track of your songs. With properly filled-out ID tags, players can find songs more easily and play them on demand.

✔ Some programs, such as MusicMatch and BladeENC, automatically fill out every song's tag as they create the MP3. The programs read a special code number on the CD and dial the Internet's Gracenote CDDB database. There, the programs grab the CD's proper song and artist information and automatically insert the information into the proper tag areas. (Figure 10-3 shows how the system works.)

✔ Many MP3 songs downloaded from the Internet lack any tag information. Luckily, some programs can read a file's name to find the artist and song information and then fill out the tag automatically.

You'll find many tagging programs — as well as tag information — at `www.id3.org`.

✔ Napster, which I describe in Chapter 5, searches through an MP3 file's ID tag information as well as its file name when looking for songs.

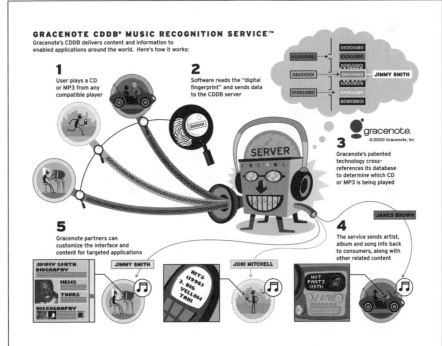

Figure 10-3: The best programs automatically fill in an MP3 song's tags by contacting the Internet's CDDB database.

Chapter 11

MusicMatch's All-in-One Software: From CD to MP3

*S*ome software performs a single task, stops, and lets another program take over. CD rippers, for example, copy music from your CD onto your hard drive. The encoders then go to work, converting the ripped — a fancy word for extracted — WAV files into MP3s.

MusicMatch Jukebox, by contrast, plans the menu, cooks the meal, and delivers it to the table. When you insert the CD and click a button, a window appears, listing the song titles. Click the songs you want encoded, and the software automatically converts them into MP3s.

The program can even record files from albums, stopping to separate record tracks into separate songs. It converts MP3s into WAV files and then burns them onto a CD for you to play in your car or home stereo. It can even download MP3s into your portable MP3 player.

Looking for Internet radio stations? MusicMatch not only tunes them in, it creates them based on your own personal tastes. To sample the best MP3 has to offer, you really needn't go further than MusicMatch.

Best of all, MusicMatch Jukebox comes free on the CD in the back of this book. This chapter shows you how to install it and put it to work.

Installing MusicMatch Jukebox

MusicMatch Jukebox works only on Windows 95, Windows 98, and Windows NT 4 or newer operating systems. Plus, your computer must be a Pentium 166 MHz or faster. If your system doesn't meet these specifications, the software will probably give up during the installation process. Finally, some older CD-ROM drives can't handle ripping. If your drive has trouble, it may need an upgrade.

The MusicMatch Jukebox installation process doesn't differ much from most software packages. Feel free to follow the on-screen directions, referring to these steps if you encounter a head-scratcher.

Follow these steps to install MusicMatch from the CD that accompanies this book:

1. **Close any programs before you begin the setup process.**

   Do this before installing *any* program. Sometimes programs share resources, and when a new program tries to butt in, everybody's unhappy.

 2. **Insert the CD bound into the back of this book into your CD-ROM drive, and choose the MusicMatch installation.**

   If you're installing a version you've downloaded, click the setup program's icon. Either way, the MusicMatch icon looks like the one in the margin.

3. **Click the Next button at the Welcome screen.**

4. **Read the License Agreement and click Yes.**

   Finished all 25 pages and accept every one of the terms? Then click the Yes button. Don't like the terms? Then click No, which means no software for you.

5. **Fill out the User Registration information and click Next.**

   When registering any software, look carefully for buttons that authorize the company to send you special offers. What's *special* to them could be junk mail to you.

6. **Decide how private you are with your listening habits and click Next.**

   Here, you decide whether to let MusicMatch keep track of the music you listen to on its program. If you choose Yes, the program keeps track of the songs you play and sends an updated song list to the corporate servers every few days.

- **Pros:** After MusicMatch knows your favorite artists, it creates your own personalized Internet radio station with music you'll probably like. Best yet, the station plays the same mainstream artists you hear on the radio today.

- **Cons:** Who likes a nosy corporation?

To let MusicMatch know what you listen to, click Yes. To keep your listening habits private, click No. (You can always go back and change this later.)

7. **Choose Express or Custom installation and click Next.**

   Choose Express and MusicMatch installs itself automatically. (Go for this one.)

   Choose Custom if you're picky about your PC and want to choose what parts of MusicMatch to install and its location on your hard drive.

8. **Click Finish.**

   You're through, and MusicMatch is ready to handle all aspects of your MP3 collection: Creating MP3s, playing Internet radio stations, organizing your collection, editing tags, and other MP3 chores. An icon for MusicMatch Jukebox now rests on your desktop, ready to be clicked into action.

   As shown in Figure 11-1, MusicMatch opens with a friendly screen offering quick tips on how to use the program's main features.

Figure 11-1: Click any Getting Started icon for quick tips on MusicMatch features.

Putting MusicMatch to Work

MusicMatch Jukebox handles just about every aspect of the MP3 world. In fact, it can do so much that completing a simple task may sometimes seem confusing. The next few sections show how to make MusicMatch automate those tasks that once took hours of work.

Making MP3 files from a CD

MusicMatch can convert an entire CD all at once, or just convert the songs you choose. Either way, follow these steps to rev up the MusicMatch MP3 creator and start creating MP3s:

1. **Start MusicMatch by double-clicking its icon on your desktop.**

   Or start MusicMatch from your Start button, depending on where you told the program to lodge itself during the installation process. The program leaps into action, accompanied by its oft-bothersome Welcome Tips window.

   Feel free to close the Welcome Tips window by clicking the little box in its top-right corner. To keep it from reappearing, click in the box marked Show Welcome Tips at Startup; that removes the check mark, and the box no longer appears.

   Just like Winamp, which I discuss in Chapter 6, MusicMatch consists of several detachable windows. The Recorder window, only necessary while creating MP3s, lists a CD's songs. The My Library window, in the middle, is where the MP3s stay organized by CD for easy access.

   Don't see MusicMatch's Recorder window? Choose View from the MusicMatch window's Options command, and select Show Recorder.

   Finally, the MusicMatch Jukebox's control window sits on top, ready to play any selected CDs or MP3s.

   Windows always needs to know which player should play your MP3 files when you double-click them. If you have more than one MP3 player, the players often fight for that privilege. That's why MusicMatch sometimes says `Another application has associated file types playable by the MusicMatch Jukebox`. It then asks if MusicMatch should be your default player. I choose No, leaving Winamp as my default player — it loads more quickly. Besides, even when not the default player, MusicMatch still plays any MP3s that you load into the program.

2. **Insert a music CD into your CD-ROM drive and click the red REC button.**

   When a CD is inserted into the drive, MusicMatch uses your Internet account to dial up CDDB (`www.cddb.com`), a vast database of CD titles and the accompanying songs. Figure 11-2 shows how MusicMatch correctly identified my Jimmy Cliff CD and automatically entered all the CD's song titles in the Recorder window.

Figure 11-2:
When you insert a new CD, Music-Match consults an Internet database and automatically enters the album and track titles.

No Internet connection? Start reading the CD's label and type in the titles yourself.

Although Gracenote's CDDB database holds an enormous amount of CDs, it occasionally misses a few releases from smaller labels. Instead, it lists the songs as Track 01, Track 02, and so on. To add them yourself, click each track name as seen on the left side of the window (see Figure 11-3) and type the correct name. Then click the window's right side to enter the Artist and Title names.

Figure 11-3:
To enter titles manually, click Track 01, Track 02, and so on, and start typing.

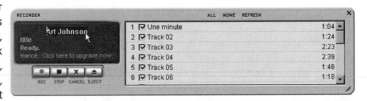

3. Choose the songs to be converted, or click All to select them all.

Normally, the Recorder window pops up with all the titles checked. If you don't want to convert all the songs to MP3, click to remove check marks from the titles that you don't want.

Be sure to stop the CD from playing. Although MusicMatch can convert a CD while it's playing, it's much slower and more prone to error.

4. **Click the Recorder window's Record button to begin converting songs to MP3 files.**

   The first time MusicMatch creates MP3 files, it must examine your CD's configuration, as shown in Figure 11-4. This takes the program 10 to 30 seconds to finish. (You have to do this only once.) The program then converts the songs, storing the MP3 files on your hard drive. (Chances are, they're stored in the My Music folder inside your My Documents folder.)

Figure 11-4:
MusicMatch examines your CD drive to make sure everything is okay.

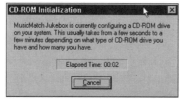

✔ As the program encodes your CD's songs, it lists the newly created MP3s in the My Library window (which I discuss in the next section) for easy access later. They're sorted by artist, album, and genre.

✔ If your new MP3 file sounds weird, you may be pushing your processor too hard. MusicMatch Jukebox rips and encodes in a single step, so it requires more processing power than plain encoders.

✔ Don't use your laptop with MusicMatch. The CD-ROM drives built into laptops are built for energy conservation, not smooth reading. Laptops play MP3s okay, but usually do a terrible job of creating them.

✔ MusicMatch works great, but it works better when you buy the upgrade. A $19.99 registration fee buys a secret code. When entered into the program, the code instantly unlocks the goodies. (A $39.99 fee grants lifetime free upgrades.) The upgraded program converts CDs into MP3s much faster, burns CDs up to 12 times faster, lets you print CD covers with original album art and track info, and other features.

✔ Some people intentionally encode files at 96 Kbps or lower or use the Windows Media Audio (WMA) format instead of MP3. The files will be smaller, letting you squeeze more of them into your portable MP3 player. Actually, you probably can't tell that much sound difference between the two when you're on a skateboard doing a one-footed, nose-boned tail-grab. (Make sure that your portable player can handle the WMA format before using it, though.)

Playing MP3 files

MusicMatch displays your MP3s in a list in the My Library window, just like books stacked on a shelf. But the files are a lot easier to organize than CDs or albums. Here's how to find a song or group of songs and play them:

1. **Find the songs you want to play.**

   Click the My Library tab, and the My Library window drops down, as shown in Figure 11-5.

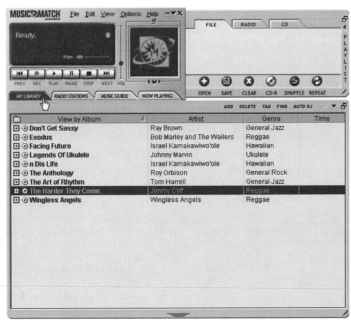

Figure 11-5:
Click the My Library tab to see your MP3 collection.

First, notice the words View by Album, Artist, Genre, and Time along the top of the My Library window. Click any of those words to sort the MP3s in the list by that category. Clicking Artist, for instance, sorts the songs by the musicians who created them. Click View by Album, and the songs are sorted alphabetically by their CD's name (refer to Figure 11-5).

There's more, though. Click the tiny folder icon in the upper-left corner, as shown in Figure 11-6, and MusicMatch offers to display your music in other ways, sorting them by Moods, Preferences, Tempos, and Year. Or, choose All Tracks to see every song in the collection (see Figure 11-7).

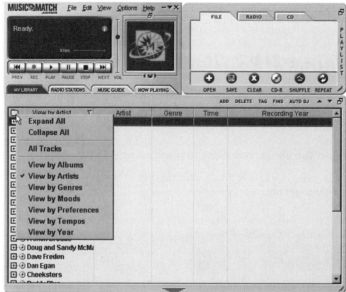

Figure 11-6: Click the tiny folder icon beneath the My Library tab to view your collection in different ways.

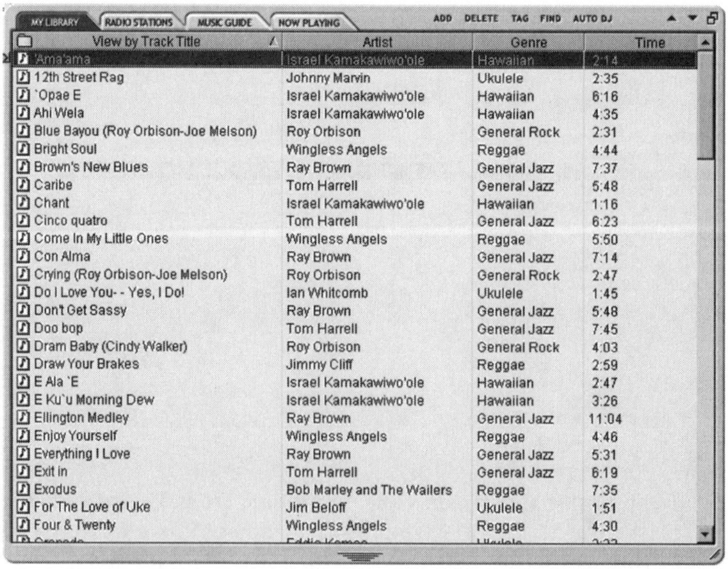

Figure 11-7: Choosing the All Tracks option displays every song in your collection.

2. Select the songs to play.

Select songs the same way you select files in Windows. Hold down Ctrl and click files to select them one by one. Alternatively, you can click one file, hold down Shift, and click another file to highlight all the files between the two you clicked. Or, you can lasso a bunch of files by holding down the mouse button and circling the files with the mouse pointer.

3. Place the songs into the Playlist window.

After you select your files and they're highlighted, right-click and choose Add Track(s) to Playlist. (Or, just drag and drop the songs into the Playlist window.) The songs appear in the Playlist window, as shown in Figure 11-8, and automatically begin playing.

Figure 11-8: Songs added to the playlist begin playing automatically.

Here's how to get the most out of your playlists:

✔ **Found a killer collection of songs that you want to hear over and over again?** Move the songs to the Playlist window and save the playlist for playing again. Click the Save button in the Playlist window and type a name for your killer list. To bring that group of songs back into the Playlist window, click Open, click the Playlists icon, and choose your saved list.

✔ **In a mood for jazz?** View your My Library list by Genre. Then drag the word Jazz to the playlist. All your songs categorized under Jazz appear in your playlist.

✔ **Using a network?** Feel free to drag and drop songs from networked computers into your Playlist window. They're often a little slow to load, but they'll play just fine. Make sure that you're not dragging from networked drives that have passwords, however, or MusicMatch might freeze up.

✔ **Tired of a playlist?** Click the Clear button. That removes all the songs from the Playlist window, letting you start over.

✔ **Not sure what a button does in MusicMatch?** Rest your mouse pointer over the confusing item and a helpful message usually explains its function.

✔ **Want to play random selections from your entire music library?** Drag your entire library to the Playlist window, right-click anywhere in the list, choose Select All, and then choose Add Track(s) to Playlist. The entire list appears in the Playlist window. Then choose Shuffle. MusicMatch plays your entire collection, shifting randomly from song to song like a radio station.

✔ **Want to easily add tracks to your playlist?** You don't need to use the My Library window to add tracks. Just click the Playlist window's Open button. From there, you can add all your tracks, certain albums, certain genres or artists, tunes from your CD player, or even tunes that aren't in your My Library area.

Adding tag information and CD art

Here's a little trick. Every MP3 file contains a special built-in storage space for the song's title, CD, recording date, genre, and other information. MusicMatch automatically fills out most of that information, known as an *ID tag*, as soon as you encode the CD.

But here's how to grab the CD's cover art, as well. You don't need a scanner, and you don't even have to use your CD's original art. Just follow these steps and MusicMatch automatically displays your CD's cover art whenever it plays a song from that CD.

1. **Drag any MP3 song to the MusicMatch Playlist window.**

   The song begins to play.

2. **Choose the Now Playing tab to see your currently playing CD's cover.**

   MusicMatch dials the Internet and shows you information about the artist currently playing. If you're lucky, the cover of your currently playing CD appears, as shown in Figure 11-9. Hurrah! Move to Step 3.

   If you're not lucky, try going to Amazon.com (www.amazon.com). In fact, that site is often easier to work with, anyway. When Amazon comes up, look for its Search area in the upper-left corner. In the drop-down menu, choose Popular Music. Then, in the second box, type the name of your CD and artist (see Figure 11-10). Amazon should display the cover of your CD.

Figure 11-9:
Songs
added to
the playlist
begin
playing
automati-
cally.

 **Figure 11-10:**
Find your CD
on Amazon
by
searching
for its name
and artist in
the Popular
Music
search box.

3. **Right-click the CD cover from within your Internet browser, choose Copy from the menu, and close your browser.**

   As shown in Figure 11-11, choose Copy to copy the CD's cover to the Windows Clipboard. Close your browser; you don't need it anymore.

4. **Choose Edit from the MusicMatch Options menu, and choose Paste/Tag Art from Clipboard.**

   Wham! Your CD cover appears in MusicMatch, as shown in Figure 11-12.

Figure 11-11:
Right-click
your CD's
cover from
the Web
page, and
choose
Copy to
copy the art
to the
Windows
Clipboard.

Figure 11-12:
The CD
cover now
appears in
MusicMatch
whenever
you play
that song.

Creating MP3s from Albums or Other Sources

If you don't need to do any sound editing of your albums, camcorders, or other sound sources, MusicMatch creates MP3s from them just as easily as it does from CDs.

Connect a Y cable from your audio source, and plug it into your sound card's Line In jack, as I describe in Chapter 9. Then perform the following steps:

1. Choose Recorder from the MusicMatch Jukebox Options menu.

How do I change an entire CD's tags simultaneously?

Keeping a song's tag correct is important, but changing the tag can be awfully tedious. For instance, when you copy a CD's cover art from the Web, you want every song on the CD to have that cover art. And, if you decide to add the CD's recording year to the tag, do you really want to edit the tags for *all* the songs individually?

Luckily, MusicMatch does the work for you, changing the tags of many songs simultaneously.

1. **Right-click the album you want to change in the My Library window — or highlight all the songs you want to change simultaneously — and choose Edit Track Tag(s) from the pop-up window.**

   The Edit Track Tag(s) window appears, listing all the songs you selected.

2. **Click the Select All button to highlight all the songs.**

   Notice how all the fields are grayed out.

3. **Click the little white box next to the item you want to change for all the highlighted songs.**

   For example, click the little white box next to where the CD's cover art should appear.

4. **Update the field that you selected in Step 3 (by pasting in the cover art, for example) and click the OK button.**

   MusicMatch updates the tags of all the highlighted songs simultaneously. If you updated the art, for example, all the songs will now have the CD cover in their tag.

2. **Choose Source from the menu that emerges, and select Line In.**

   Start playing your sound to adjust the mixer settings.

3. **Open your Windows Mixer.**

   Double-click the little speaker icon by your clock.

   Adjust the volume under the Line Balance settings. Make sure that the little box beneath the Line Balance area is checked.

4. **Turn on your sound source — start playing the album, turn on the camcorder, or whatever else you're recording — and quickly press the Record button on MusicMatch's Recorder.**

The program automatically transfers the incoming sound into MP3 format, skipping the WAV file in the process.

Creating CDs from MP3s

MusicMatch uses your computer's CD burner to create two types of CDs. Why two? It creates one type of CD for playing on your home or car stereo, and another type that's packed with hundreds of MP3 files for playing on your computer. It creates both types of CDs from any of the MP3 files in your collection. Feel free to mix and match your favorite MP3s to create your own Greatest Hits CDs.

Before you can create any type of CD, you need a CD-R drive (CD Recordable) or a CD-RW drive (CD Read/Write drive), and a pile of blank CDs. The CDs cost about a buck apiece if you buy them in bulk.

To create either type of CD in MusicMatch, follow these steps:

1. **Create a playlist of the songs you want to store on the CD.**

   Follow the steps in the section "Playing MP3 files" earlier in this chapter. Basically, you want to fill your Playlist window with the songs you want to copy to a CD.

   If you're creating a CD for your home stereo, start with about ten MP3s. You probably won't be able to fit many more songs, although you'll be given that chance later.

2. **Click the CD-R button beneath the playlist.**

   This button lives between the Clear and Shuffle icons. (I've put it in the margin so you won't miss it.)

   When you click the CD-R button, the Create CD from Playlist window pops up, as shown in Figure 11-13. You choose the Audio (default) button to create a CD for playing in your home and car CD player. You choose the Data (MP3, WMA, WAV) button to create a CD for storing bunches of MP3s to play back on your computer or on a portable MP3 player that can handle those CDs.

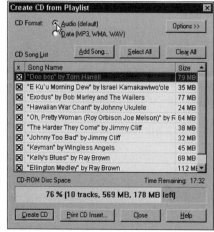

Figure 11-13: Ten MP3 songs consume about 75 percent of this audio CD.

3. Choose the type of CD you want to create from the window.

Clicking either button shows how much space you have left on the CD. In Figure 11-14, for instance, the ten MP3s have consumed 76 percent of the audio CD, leaving room for only two or three more songs.

When I click the Data button, however, the ten songs consume only 8 percent of the CD, leaving much more room. (That shows you how much MP3 compresses songs.)

4. Add or remove songs until the CD is filled.

Keep dragging or removing songs from the Playlist window until you're satisfied with the amount of songs stuffed onto the CD.

5. Place a blank CD into your CD-R or CD-RW drive and click the Create CD button.

MusicMatch converts the MP3 songs into audio format, if necessary, and copies them to the CD.

✔ When you purchase the upgrade version of MusicMatch, you can print CD covers to go with your newly created CDs. It can print any artwork you'd like on the cover, or it can tile the covers from the works you've placed on the CD (see Figure 11-14).

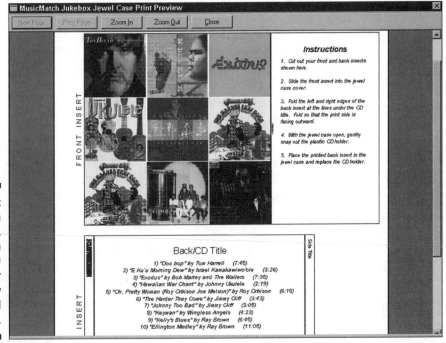

Figure 11-14:
When upgraded, MusicMatch prints CD covers for your newly created CDs.

✔ Some older computers or drives have difficulty creating CDs. To help them out, click the CD-R button beneath the playlist to open the Create CD from Playlist window (refer to Figure 11-13). Then click the Options button. Under Audio CD-R options, choose Use Hard Drive Cache. This lets MusicMatch decode the song and then write it to the CD. That keeps MusicMatch from trying to decode and write at the same time, which confuses some systems.

✔ You'll find more information about creating CDs from MP3s in Chapter 12.

Listening to Internet Radio through MusicMatch

Chapter 8 explains Internet Radio — a way to hear music Webcast through the Internet. Among its other duties, MusicMatch picks up Internet radio stations. It plays the stations in three different ways, as I describe in the following sections.

Listening to MusicMatch radio

MusicMatch contains a list of stations broadcasting in certain genres, from Adult Alternative to Rap & Hip-Hop. The songs coming from these stations are from top-name artists in their fields. To tune one in, follow these steps:

1. **Click the Radio Stations tab.**

   The Radio Stations window appears, as shown in Figure 11-15.

2. **Choose your connection speed.**

   Dial-up modems should click the Low button under Connection Speed. Faster modems (cable, DSL, ISDN, and their cousins) receive better sound when you choose the Hi button.

3. **Choose the type of station you want to hear.**

   Click the type of music that moves you. (You can switch stations at any time.) Rest your mouse pointer over each station to hear what type of artists it plays. Alternative Rock, for instance, plays artists such as Green Day, Incubus, and Fuel.

   The music begins playing — at the beginning of a song, unlike many other stations. To hear a different type of music, click a different genre of music.

Figure 11-15:
Click the
Radio
Stations tab
to hear pre-
sorted radio
stations.

Listening to other Internet radio Webcasts

MusicMatch radio isn't limited to its own prefab stations, thank goodness. If you're ready to hear other stations the Internet has to offer, follow these steps.

1. **Click the Radio Stations tab.**

   The Radio Stations window appears (refer to Figure 11-15).

2. **Click the More Stations button in the upper-right corner of the Radio Stations window.**

3. **When the diminutive Broadcast window appears, click the Station Selector box.**

   Yet another window pops up, shown in Figure 11-16, this time listing hundreds of radio stations sorted by format.

4. **Choose a genre under Format, choose a station that appears, and click the Play button.**

   When you choose a genre, the window's right side displays a bunch of stations fitting that description. Choose one, click the Play button at the window's bottom, and MusicMatch begins playing the station, usually in the middle of a song.

Looking for a particular station? Click the Search button at the bottom of the window (refer to Figure 11-16). Click in the little black stripe along the window's bottom, and type a word describing the station. Click the Search button, and MusicMatch tries to find that station.

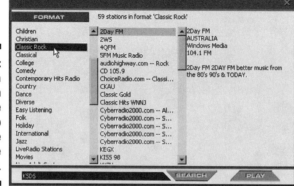

Figure 11-16: Choose a selection from the Format tab to see the available stations.

To visit a station's Web site, click the Go to the Station's Web site button from the Broadcast window that you saw in Step 3. Feel free to bookmark the station in your Internet browser so that you can easily find it later.

Creating a personalized station

MusicMatch offers several ways to create radio stations customized to your particular interest. First, you can simply choose your favorite type of music, and MusicMatch begins playing those types of songs.

Second, you can create your own station by mixing your favorite types of music. Click the Create New Station button from the Radio Stations tab (refer to Figure 11-15) and choose the Mix Stations button. Next, choose three of your favorite types of music (see Figure 11-17). Slide the bars from side to side to determine how often that music should appear in your mix. When you click the Save and Finish button, type a name for your new station in the Name Station box. Click Launch Station, and your new radio station plays.

Third, you can create a station based on your favorite artist. Click the Create New Station button from the Radio Stations tab, just as before, but choose the Artist Match button this time. Type your favorite artist — Sly and the Family Stone, for example — type a name for your station, and click the Launch Station button to hear your new station. You'll hear a mixture of songs by your favorite artist, as well as other songs by musicians similar to that artist.

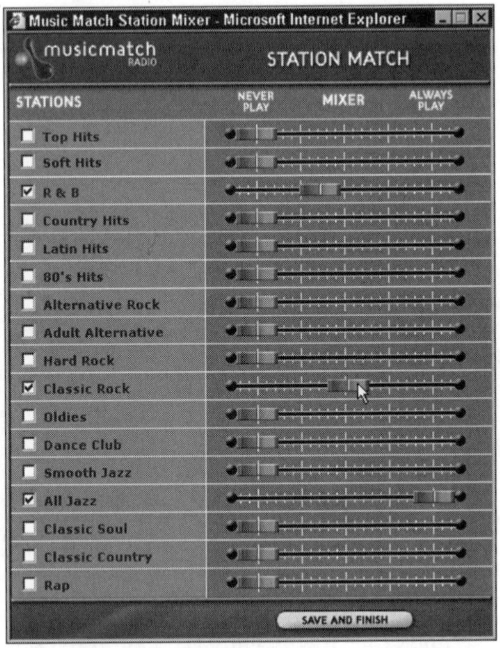

Figure 11-17:
Choose
three types
of music
and then
slide the
bars to
determine
their
placement
in the mix.

The fourth radio station option is the most fun. You can let MusicMatch "eavesdrop" on the song titles you listen to. At first, I was suspicious. But then again, all my next-door neighbors certainly know what I listen to, so it's no secret. I decided to let MusicMatch know, as well. By letting MusicMatch in on what kind of music you like, you enable MusicMatch to create a personalized station based completely on what you've been listening to on your computer.

To start a personalized station based entirely on your own listening habits, click the My Station button in the middle of the Radio Stations window (refer to Figure 11-16). If you've been listening to enough songs for MusicMatch to understand your listening preferences, the program will launch a new station, based on your musical tastes.

 ✔ To let MusicMatch know the song titles you play, choose Settings from the Options menu. At the bottom of the page, click the two boxes in the box labeled Permission to communicate with the MusicMatch server. The program then automatically uploads a list of your song titles to the MusicMatch database. (It checks for updated versions of the program, too.)

TIP

- Created a station you love? Click the Send to a Friend button, and your friends receive a link to that station, ready for playing in their own copies of MusicMatch.

- When a song comes up in the MusicMatch radio station, the album cover also appears, as shown in Figure 11-18.

Figure 11-18:
When a song plays on MusicMatch radio, the CD cover appears as well.

- When you're playing a bunch of songs, either through MusicMatch radio or your own playlist, click the Now Playing tab. If you're connected to the Internet, MusicMatch brings up a page displaying information about the currently playing artist — as well as a way to buy more music by that artist.

TECHNICAL STUFF

- When you base a station on a favorite artist, MusicMatch checks to see other artists listened to by fans of your selected artist. Then it bases your radio station on your artist, as well as songs by those additional artists.

- ***Bummer department.*** Although MusicMatch radio makes for great entertainment, it sticks in an annoying plug for itself between every eight or nine songs. It's only a sentence or two, but it's bothersome as all get out.

Chapter 12

Saving MP3 Songs on a CD

Compact discs may look the same, but they come in a wide variety of formats, each designed for a different task. You can't buy one disc that does it all. In fact, you can't even buy a compact disc drive — a *CD-ROM drive* — that does it all. There are too many different formats for a drive to understand.

This chapter explains the types of CD formats you'll encounter, and explains how to store MP3s on them in different ways.

Understanding CD Formats

The next few sections explain the types of CDs on the market, what you can do with them, and when they're simply not up to the task.

CD-R discs

Short for *CD-Recordable*, these have also been labeled *WORM* discs by the People Who Like Letters Department. WORM stands for Write Once, Read Multiple. That means data can be written to them once and then read many times.

For years, CD-R discs ruled the CD world. Music CDs, as well as software programs, came on CD-R discs. Although the discs themselves were relatively cheap, the machines that made them — the CD *burners* — cost oodles of dollars.

Today, many computers come with inexpensive CD-ROM drives that can write information to discs. Known as Read/Write drives, these drives copy or *burn* files onto a blank CD-R disc. They can also read discs, just like their predecessors.

These Read/Write drives can't sling data as fast as their predecessors, though. If you replace your 32X CD-ROM drive with a Read/Write drive for burning CDs, you'll notice it's slower at reading CDs. (And burning CDs takes much, much longer than reading them.)

When choosing a new CD-ROM drive — or when buying discs to feed it, keep the following points in mind.

- When a blank CD-R disc is full of information, the fun is over. The disc can't be reused, like a floppy disk. You can't erase the freebie CDs that America Online sends out and use them for storing your own data.

- Luckily, the price of CD-R discs keeps spiraling downward. You can buy a bag of bulk CD-R discs, which translates to less than a dollar per disc.

- MP3 users must choose between two formats when burning information onto CDs. They either store MP3 files onto the CD, or they store audio files. The two formats are completely different. One is a computer file, and can only be played back in a computer. The other is digital audio that can be read in any regular home stereo CD player.

- If you burn MP3 files onto a CD, you can fit several hundred songs onto the CD. However, that CD only plays back on your computer or a special player designed to read MP3 files. To play MP3 songs on your home stereo, you need to decompress the MP3 files and convert them to audio files. That means you can only fit about a dozen or so songs onto a CD.

- The CDs designed for playback on a home stereo are known as Red Book CDs. Why? Because those players use an oddly named standard called *Red Book*. The CD players sold in home stereo stores are designed to play CDs that use the Red Book standard — and nothing else.

- The market is slowly seeing a few home stereo MP3 players. These look like regular CD players, and they connect to your home stereo, but they play songs in the MP3 format. That means you can burn a few hundred MP3 files onto a CD, push the CD into the home stereo MP3 player, and hear several hours of songs. Figure 12-1 shows an $800 ARQ1 Request CD player (`www.request.com`) that handles both types of CDs.

- Keep an eye on the MP3.com hardware section for the latest developments on home stereo MP3 players.

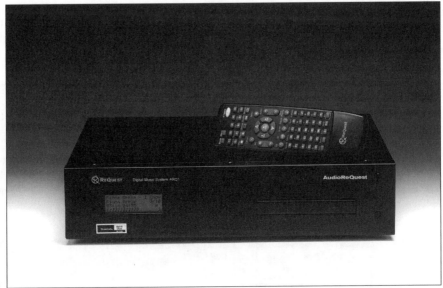

Figure 12-1:
The ARQ1
Request,
one of
several new
types of CD
players,
handles
both normal
CDs and
ones storing
MP3 files.

CD-RW discs

After a few years, computer technicians tired of discs that couldn't be reused like floppy disks. So they created a new technology called CD-Rewritable (CD-RW) discs. These discs can be written to, erased, and written to again.

Some older CD-R disc drives can't handle the new format, but it's quickly gaining acceptance among manufacturers. And all CD-RW drives can read CD-R discs.

However, CD-RW discs don't have much use among MP3 users because the discs cost so darn much — three to five times as much. And just as most people don't throw away their CD collections, little reason exists to erase a collection of MP3 files.

Besides, a home stereo can't read CD-RW discs, no matter how the information is stored.

✔ Although CD-R and CD-RW discs can both be written to, only CD-RW discs can be erased and written to again. CD-R is used for *permanent* storage; CD-RW is for *temporary* storage — yesterday's backup files, for instance, which are replaced with today's backup files.

✔ Some home stereo MP3 players can play CD-RW discs, as well as CD-R discs. They're few and far between, though. Before pulling out the credit card, be sure to check the specifications of the latest CD-reading gadget.

DAM CDs

Most CD-ROM drives can play CDs containing MP3s as well as the audio CDs from the music store.

But your home stereo probably isn't as versatile; it can only play audio CDs. However, MP3.com (www.mp3.com), the most popular MP3 Internet site, came up with a new method known as *DAM* — or Digital Audio Music — CDs. Figure 12-2 shows some of the site's available DAM CDs.

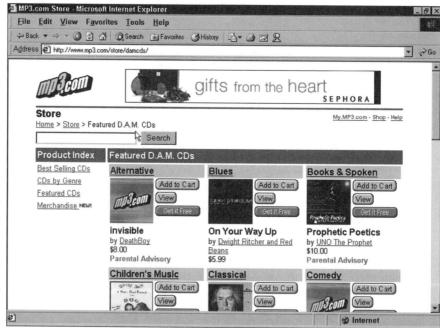

Figure 12-2: MP3.com's DAM CDs play in your home stereo's CD player, yet the discs also contain MP3 versions of the songs.

 These compact discs take advantage of an MP3 file's small size. MP3.com burns a CD with the audio files; then it fills the leftover space with those same songs in MP3 format.

That gives you the best of both worlds. You can put the CD in your home stereo to play the audio songs, or you can play both the MP3 and audio versions on your computer's CD-ROM drive. In fact, you can even copy the CD's MP3 files to your computer for playback on your hard drive, or copy them to your portable MP3 player.

Some older CD players and CD-ROM drives can't play DAM CDs. In fact, some CD-ROM drives won't be able to spot the MP3 files in the Windows Explorer File Manager. You may need to upgrade your CD-ROM drive to take advantage of this format.

Before buying a new CD-ROM drive, try the DAM disc on several computers. You may just have a bad disc.

✔ To store MP3s songs on your CD — or to convert them into CDs that will play on your home stereo — check out Chapter 11. MusicMatch software, which is included on the CD bound into this book, handles both those tasks. (It can't create DAM CDs, however.)

✔ You can find everything you need to know about CDs at Andy McFadden's highly regarded CD-Recordable FAQ at www.fadden.com/cdrfaq.

✔ No, you can't store your MP3s on a DVD. Well, you can, but you need a DVD writer, and they're still costing several thousand dollars. And you can't make copies of a DVD with your computer's writeable CD-ROM drive, either. They're two different formats. Even if you do find a way to copy it, you'll be stuck with a very low-quality copy because it will no longer be in the DVD format.

Part IV
MP3s for the Musician

The 5th Wave   By Rich Tennant

"It's not _great_ fidelity, but I'm surprised you can download an MP3 file into an electric pencil sharpener at all."

In this part . . .

Most people love MP3 because they can hear free music. But that's exactly why some musicians fear MP3. If it's free, how can I make a buck?

This part of the book is aimed at the musicians in the crowd — the people creating the music that's being tossed around on the Internet.

After anguishing for months to create an artistic masterpiece, why just give it away to people who probably won't even buy it? Why go through the hassles of creating CDs, boxes, and artwork? Why pay all that money?

In short, why bother at all?

This part of the book not only tells why, it tells exactly how. I interview four musicians, starting with a teenager who has earned more than $100,000 directly from giving away his MP3s. You'll hear about a band that created a musical CD designed for industrial use, but found a public eager to pay thousands to hear the songs streamed into their rooms.

You'll discover exactly how to record your CD, package it, promote it, and place it in the right retail channels. Finally, you'll find out how to decide into which MP3 sites to deposit your MP3s so that the public can discover just how good they are.

Chapter 13

Why Bother with MP3s?

*T*he musicians interviewed in this chapter all have a song or two on this book's CD, as well as spread across the Internet. At least one musician earned more than $100,000 directly from distributing his MP3s; another earned about $30,000; and another is still waiting on his first thousand.

Although money is certainly a prime incentive, some musicians use MP3 technology for other reasons. In this chapter, these musicians explain in their own words how they came to embrace MP3 as another tool in the working musician's arsenal.

Alex Smith's Trance Tunes

Site: www.mp3.com/cynicproject

One of the most successful MP3 artists on the Internet, 18-year-old Alex Smith, earned more than $100,000 directly through MP3.com's Payback for Playback program that I describe in Chapter 16. The site pays Smith based on the amount of activity his site generates. The popularity of his music often brings in several thousand dollars each month.

Even as a teenager at a Stillwater, Minnesota high school, Smith had no problem creating music. He'd been taking piano lessons since grade school, but turning his music hobby into a business seemed stifling. How could he expose people to his music, much less persuade them to buy it?

"I had produced music in the past," he said, "but never attempted to distribute it because I found no easy way of doing so. MP3.com made it possible for me to just upload the music, sit back, and watch the results."

In the summer of 1999, Smith created a site on MP3.com (see Figure 13-1), posted a few songs, and waited to see what would happen. Smith didn't expect much, but he was satisfied that he'd finally found a way for people to hear his music.

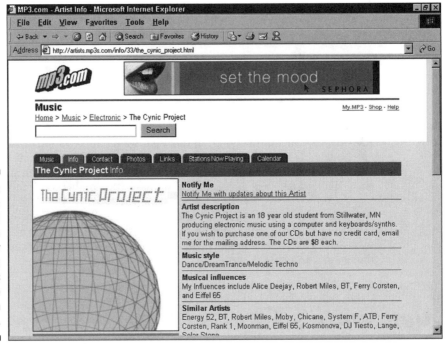

Figure 13-1: Alex Smith has earned more than $100,000 by releasing MP3s of his dance music on MP3.com.

"I got my first fan mail within weeks after publishing my music," he said. "Feedback from listeners was very inspirational and helped me write most of my music."

When MP3.com started its Payback for Playback program and the money started arriving, Smith finally quit his sales job at Office Max to concentrate on writing music full time.

Success came quickly. His first dance track hit number one on MP3.com's music charts in November 1999. As his earnings increased, he built a home studio and released his first CD a few months later. Today, he's sold CDs in more than 25 countries. Although he's saving and investing much of his money, he bought a new Toyota Celica and new music equipment. He's constantly updating his Web site at www.trancehits.net/tcp, doing all the HTML work himself.

"I was more interested in making music than distribution," admits Alex. "But when I heard about MP3.com, it motivated me. The process of becoming an MP3.com artist was so easy."

- ✔ Smith first became inspired to write electronic music after hearing Eurodance hitmaker Robert Miles's single, "Children." Soon, he began writing electronic music aimed at dance clubs. Smith's favorite artists include ATB, Ayla, BT, Ferry Corsten, Chicane, DJ Tiesto, Lange, DJ Sakin, Tomski, Rank 1, Energy 52, Kosmonova, and Solar Stone.

- ✔ Alex works on a Novation Supernova II 24 voice keyboard, an Alesis QS6.1 keyboard, a Korg Triton Rack, Roland JP8080, Roland XV-3080, Behringer Eurorack MX 1804X mixer, and a Midiman USB Midisport 4x4. He also uses a Pentium III with an SBLive! Value sound card running Cakewalk Pro Audio 9.0, Rebirth, and Fruityloops.

Buddy Blue's American Roots

Site: www.mp3.com/buddyblue

A popular Southern California musician, Buddy Blue doesn't mind laying down his guitar and picking up his computer keyboard every once in a while. It wasn't always that way.

When he first heard about MP3 technology, he was deeply skeptical. "I'm not exactly the most cyber-knowledgeable guy in the world," he admits, "so there was a sort of technophobia type of thing. I was one of the last guys in the world to get a CD player. I still listen to old 78s."

Buddy's music career spans 25 years, starting as a teenager playing covers at high school dances. After working on 15 CDs, he had "an inherent distrust of people getting your music and not having to pay for it."

"It seems philosophically wrong somehow," he said. "If I go to the dentist, I have to pay."

Taking the plunge, he made a Web site, added a few MP3s, and started getting e-mails from people who'd never have heard of him otherwise. Moving further, he posted a few of his songs on MP3.com (see Figure 13-2) to see what would happen. "I didn't think, 'Oh boy, this will put me on the map,'" he said. Still, he sold a few CDs and earned some money through the site's Payback for Playback program.

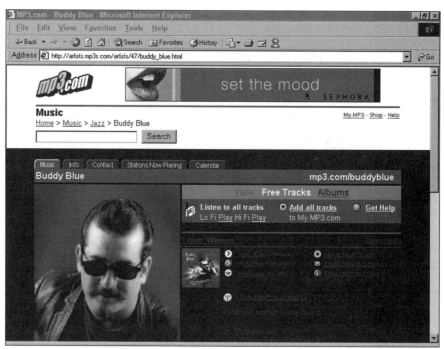

Figure 13-2:
Although skeptical of MP3 at first, Buddy Blue now finds it a useful tool for both promoting his own music and finding out-of-print songs by his musical heroes.

"I think I got a hundred some odd dollars that I wasn't expecting, so I can't complain," he said. MP3.com appeals to a younger and more cyber-savvy crowd than the older audiences attracted to his music.

Bowing to technology, Blue eventually converted his newsletter, formerly sent through the mail, to e-mail. Mass-mailings are much easier, and he often attaches links to photos or runs contests.

Even if MP3 isn't helping Blue sell oodles of albums, it's helping him in other areas: He uses the Internet to find MP3s of music he can't find elsewhere.

"Most of it is stuff I've looked for for a long time and been unable to find," he said. "Like there's nothing in print by Richard Berry, one of my musical heroes. I've got some vinyl on him, but nothing on CD. I've looked everywhere." Through Napster, he's found people who are willing to share their out-of-print oldies.

"I'm not a guy who'd download the latest Los Lobos stuff instead of buying the CD," he said. "Not only because I'd feel too guilty, but because I prefer CDs to MP3s, anyway."

He also subscribes to a '50s newsgroup (I talk about newsgroups in Chapter 4) to unearth rare, out-of-print stuff.

"There's this guy named Spade who posts on the '50s newsgroup," he said. "I had no idea so much rockabilly was out there. This guy posts nearly every day."

Blue's also pleased that his Web site now serves as a quick, multimedia business card.

"Now, if somebody's interested in booking you," he said, "you don't have to send them a CD, press kit, and photo. If they're interested enough in booking you, they'll take the time to check out your site on MP3.com or your own Web site. My computer has saved me a lot of money. It's ideal for people who want a band for their party."

✔ Although record stores usually file Buddy Blue's music in the Blues section, he doesn't consider himself a blues musician per se. He plays a wide mixture of bar-blast rockabilly, roadhouse blues, foot-stomping swing, and a little jazz thrown in for good measure.

✔ He plays a '70s Les Paul Custom through the same pre-CBS Fender Twin amp that he's used since high school. He also uses an early '60s Gibson ES-225, an Epiphone Joe Pass model, an old Guild F40-NT, and a wood-body dobro. He records at a nearby home studio www.vmusic.com/pseudocool/kitsch/.

Bill Sahner's Country Pop

Site: www.mp3.com/billysahner

Eager to promote his music, East Coast musician Bill Sahner placed a few snippets of his songs online back in 1998. Unfortunately, MP3 hadn't become mainstream, so he placed low-quality WAV files for his site's visitors to download. Because most visitors had 14.4 or 28.8 modems, few undertook the lengthy downloads, which led to little exposure for Sahner.

As MP3 grew in popularity, he converted his files to MP3. However, the site still didn't attract great numbers. Eventually, he heard about MP3 distribution sites like Audio Galaxy (www.audiogalaxy.com), ChangeMusic (www.changemusic.com), and MP3.com.

"They all made you agree to some scary legal mumbo jumbo," Sahner said, fearing he'd lose control of his copyrights and material. "Every story you hear coming out of the music business, from Elvis to Billy Joel, is about how someone wrangled control of their career, their material, or their money. You only need to watch *VH1 Behind The Music* two or three times to develop a paranoia about this. Unfortunately, I've watched it about 150 times."

Still, he decided the exposure was worth a chance. Soon after posting his songs, something exciting happened. "I could barely contain myself," he remembered. "People began to write reviews of my music. Someone was listening!" His songs earned good reviews on Listen.com, Audio Galaxy, and some MP3 E-zines.

When MP3.com began its Pay for Play program, he moved all his songs to that site (see Figure 13-3). One month later, his song "The Wild Ride" sat at the top of MP3.com's Country General charts for two weeks.

Figure 13-3: An early embracer of MP3, Bill Sahner enjoys the format's immediacy and ease of distribution.

A prolific songwriter, Sahner finds the immediacy of MP3 to be both a curse and a blessing. "Being able to release a song on the Web two minutes after you get your final mix can be a dangerous thing," he cautions. "Quite often you find yourself excitedly pushing your latest creation across the wires at 3 a.m., only to wake up the next morning and find you've posted a mushy mix with unintelligible lyrics.

"The beauty of Web distribution becomes apparent as you realize you can simply remix the song and post the improved version: No one has shipped 500,000 pieces of vinyl or plastic with your blurry song. I've remixed songs four or five times and re-released them."

Although his songs have been downloaded more than 70,000 times, he's only earned a few thousand dollars from MP3.com. Still, he enjoys the exposure and the feeling that he's appealing to a certain audience. "I feel I understand the art of the three-minute country pop song as well as anybody," he said.

- ✔ Sahner writes smooth country pop with a Tex Mex flavor, often with a humorous touch. He writes music for other artists, as well as recording his own tunes.

- ✔ Sahner plays Fender, Gretsch, and Rickenbacker guitars. He records on a Roland VS-880 hard drive recorder synced to Cakewalk software and MIDI devices, including an Alesis DM5 drum module and an Alesis QSR sound module. He mixes it all down through a small Mackie board to digital audio tape before moving the song to his computer for final touches using Cool Edit 2000. He uses MusicMatch to convert the final song to MP3 format.

Transoceanic's Relaxing Ambience

Site: www.mp3.com/transoceanic

Back in 1998, three Cambridge, UK musicians wanted to compose and record relaxing and uplifting music aimed for therapists specializing in relaxation techniques. They ended up with an hour-long CD, with a soft, New Age feel.

"We loved it," said Richard Jones, one of the three musicians, "and the masseuse we had worked with to develop it reported very positive feedback from her clients. But we didn't think it would be very commercial. How could relaxation music be 'successful' in the conventional sense?"

His feelings changed soon after reading about MP3 technology in a UK music technology magazine, *Sound on Sound* (www.sospubs.co.uk/).

"I thought, 'hang on, that's a way of sidestepping all this record/publishing company nonsense,'" he said. "And I did get quite excited. We had just finished a CD but had no outlet, so when MP3 just materialized from nowhere, it was quite exhilarating."

The band's expectations were initially quite low in September 1999, when they posted two tracks on MP3.com (see Figure 13-4). Four days later, Transoceanic's song "Celtic Stream" reached the Top 10 in MP3.com's Mood Music Charts. Within a month, more than a thousand MP3.com visitors had listened to the band's music.

Figure 13-4:
Although
Trans-
oceanic
originally
created its
music for
professional
massage,
aroma-
therapy, and
reflexology
therapists,
it's found a
huge
following on
MP3.com.

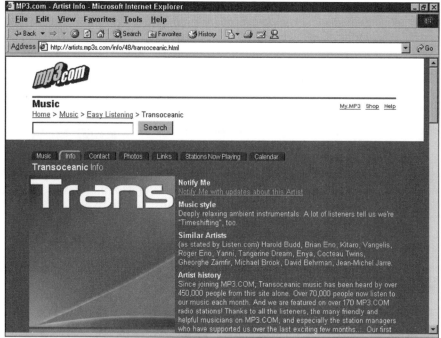

"Today, we've had more than a half-million listeners," he said, "we've made more than $30,000 through MP3.com's Payback for Playback program, and we are the number one MP3.com artist from the United Kingdom. Which is all really hard to believe given we recorded our music in a small bedroom."

Because Transoceanic's music is meant to be played in the background as a stress reliever, it's well suited for MP3.com's Payback for Playback program where artists receive money based on the activity generated by their songs. People simply log on to the site, click the Listen to All Tracks button, and hear the music cycle in the background.

Although designed and used by professionals as soothing background music during therapy, the music's audience has widened massively. People listen to the music at work, and parents play it when trying to put their small children to sleep; chronic pain sufferers play it to relax. Others listen to it while meditating or practicing Reiki.

"We've made far more money from people listening and downloading our music than from CD sales," he said. "People like getting free access to music much more than they like paying for music. It was initially quite a surprise that downloads were more profitable than CD sales. Once you realize that, you might decide that it's better to allow people free access to *all* your tracks. That's quite a difficult decision to make, though."

✔ Described as "mood music," Transoceanic creates gentle, melodic songs designed to unravel the binds of stressful situations. Among its influences the band counts Queen, Depeche Mode, Kraftwerk, Vangelis, NIN, Kitaro, Crowded House, Alanis Morrisette, Massive Attack, Moby, Radiohead, Badly Drawn Boy, Cowboy Junkies, Brian Eno, and many others.

✔ Transoceanic composes and records its music on a PC with Logic Audio, a Roland SH101, Korg TR-Rack, Ensoniq EPS16+, Yamaha 01v, Roland D110, Alesis Quadraverb, and a DAT Machine. The members are currently eyeing a Novation Supernova 2.

Chapter 14

Composing Songs for MP3

· ·

In This Chapter

▶ Working with analog recorders

▶ Using digital recorders

▶ Recording with MIDI

▶ Recording and editing with a digital workstation

▶ Composing and recording with your computer

· ·

A few years back, there weren't many options for recording songs. Everybody used tape.

Today, most people have switched to computers in one way or another. Computers record the sound, enhance it, and burn it onto a compact disc that's ready to play on the stereo.

This chapter examines the options available to musicians trying to release their tunes in MP3 format. It explains the most popular hardware and software options. Whether you're considering a four-track tape deck, a sexy Roland VS-2480, or some of the latest computer music software, check out this chapter for some general-purpose information about the format and its suitability for creating good quality MP3 recordings.

Analog Recording

For years, musicians recorded their music onto an *analog* tape recorder, ranging from a cheap cassette deck to a more expensive four-track or reel-to-reel machine.

To understand the word *analog,* you need some theory about sound waves; and because this involves physics, it gets boring fast. So here's the abbreviated version.

Sound travels through the air in waves of pressure. When somebody bangs a drum, the drumhead vibrates back and forth. This pushes the air back and forth in waves of pressure. The pressure bounces against our ears, vibrates our eardrum, and our brain translates the poundings into what we hear.

The air pressure bounces against microphones, too, which translate the waves of sound into waves of electricity. The tape recorder then stores a "picture" of the incoming waves as magnetic information on the tape's coating. When playing back an analog recording, the recorder uses the magnetic information to re-create the actual sound waves being played.

Analog's MP3 Rating: Good. Although cheap, portable, and relatively easy to use, analog quality suffers from occasional background hiss. Plus, the sound is recorded twice: once into your recorder, and then again into your computer. Each recording allows noise to creep in.

First, the good stuff:

- ✔ Analog tape recorders are inexpensive, starting at around $150 for a beginner's four-track model. Four tracks leave room for the drummer on one track, bass on the next, guitar or keyboard on the next, and vocals on the last one.

- ✔ Analog tapes don't cost much, either. Most recorders use the same cassettes you use in a boom box and can be found in any department or record store.

- ✔ Use a 30-minute tape when recording on an analog tape recorder. Longer-capacity tapes use thinner material, which doesn't record as well. You should also fast-forward the tape to its end and then rewind the tape completely before recording. This keeps the tape from being wound too tightly on its reels and improves quality.

- ✔ Want more than four tracks out of a four-track tape recorder? Try *bouncing:* Record three tracks and mix them all down to the fourth track. That leaves all the sounds on one track, and three more tracks to play with.

Now the bad news:

- ✔ Analog tape recorders tend to pick up a hiss in the background. The hiss increases as you bounce tracks. While analog tape recorders work great for recording song ideas and recording live shows, they're not the best audio workstations for professional-quality material.

- ✔ There's one last drawback to using analog tape recorders to create MP3s: To move the sound into your computer, you must route the sound through your sound card, adding even more hiss. That's why more people are turning to digital tape recorders (which I describe next) or creating their songs directly on the computer (which I describe later in this chapter).

Uh, what's a *track?*

Musicians rarely record songs live in the studio anymore. Instead, everything's recorded in layers. The drummer records the drum track, for instance. Then the bass player plays the bass line while listening to the drummer's recorded work. The guitar player puts on the headphones and lays down the rhythm or leads, followed by the vocalist, who sings over the completed instrumental version. Some musicians never actually meet each other while recording a song.

Every time a musician plays a part, it's recorded as a *track.* When each musician records on a separate track, it's easier to combine the layers into the finished product, or *mix.* The drum's volume can be lowered, and the bass can be punched up — all without interfering with anyone else's track.

The more tracks you can use, the better the final sound. For instance, everybody needs at least two tracks to record in stereo: the left track and the right track. Drummers are sound hogs; they sound best when each separate drum and cymbal are recorded separately on their own track. That way, the snare's volume can be increased, for example, without affecting the rest of the drum sounds, allowing more versatility in the final mix.

Digital Recording

Analog tape recorders take a "picture" of incoming sound waves and store the image onto magnetic tape. To play back the sound, the recorder reads the picture and re-creates the sounds from the image.

Digital audio works much differently. As sound waves enter the digital audio recorder, they're converted into a stream of numbers that represent the waves, as shown in Figure 14-1.

The recorder stores the numbers on Digital Audio Tape (DAT), a compact disc, a MiniDisc, a hard drive, or any other computer-savvy medium. When it's time to re-create the sound, the recorder reads the numbers and creates sound waves based on the digits.

Because digital sound is really just numbers, it's a natural for computers. In fact, everything is recorded onto a computer.

Digital's MP3 Rating: Very Good. It's expensive, but produces a high-quality recording. In addition, digital recorders come in a wide variety of formats, each tailored to a different recording requirement.

Figure 14-1:
Although it
displays an
image of the
sound
wave, the
Sonic
Foundry
Sound
Forge
software
records this
saxophone
riff as
numbers
stored on
your hard
drive.

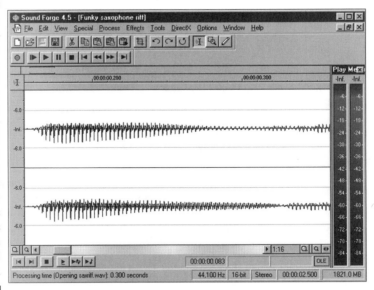

✔ The compact discs sold in stores have always used digital audio; they contain numbers, which a CD player uses to re-create sounds.

✔ When sounds become numbers, they're much easier to edit. They can be cut and pasted, just like words in a word processor. Best yet, different tracks can be moved around, mixed together, and bounced without adding any hum to the mix.

✔ The more numbers used to store a song, the higher its sampling rate. The *sampling rate* is a measurement of how frequently a recording device takes a reading of the sound it's recording. The MP3 standard sampling rate of 44 kHz, for example, means that the recorder splits the incoming sound into more numbers than a low sampling rate, such as 22 kHz.

✔ Don't use laptops for digital sound. Although some play back songs okay, they're simply not up to the task of recording music smoothly.

MIDI Recording

Sooner or later, you'll encounter the term *MIDI* when recording sound. Unlike analog and digital recording, however, MIDI doesn't contain any sounds or representations of sound waves. Instead, MIDI is a computerized instruction set that tells instruments how they should play.

MIDI works in two different ways. With the first, called *real-time sequencing,* the MIDI device listens to a musician play an instrument. For example, somebody sits at a synthesizer's keyboard, turns on the synthesizer's piano sound, and plays a song. The MIDI device listens to the person play and makes notes of which notes are played, when, and for how long. The resulting file is called a MIDI *sequence.*

Figure 14-2 shows a MIDI sequence of a bass line recorded in Cakewalk Pro. By changing the shape and location of the little lines, you change the placement and length of the notes. The software also translates the MIDI file into sheet music or notation.

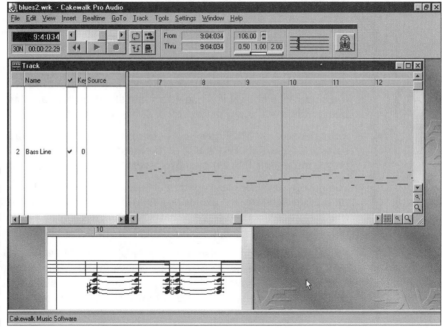

Figure 14-2: Cakewalk Pro displays a MIDI sequence of a bass line, with the sheet music below.

When the MIDI file is played back, it re-creates the sounds of the person playing a piano — mistakes and all. (Part of MIDI's charm is that you can edit files to remove the mistakes.)

The capability to edit a recording is where the second method of MIDI recording comes in. Called *step-time sequencing,* this laborious second method involves calling up an empty MIDI file and entering notes one by one. Not only do you have to record the individual notes, you also have to enter the duration of each note, as well.

But MIDI does much more. Because it keeps track of what instrument created what notes, you can also edit the type of instrument. Edit the MIDI file and assign the recorded instrument to a flute instead of a piano, for instance, and the MIDI file tells the synthesizer to sound like a flute when playing the file.

MIDI's MP3 Rating: Very good. You can use MIDI inexpensively on a home computer, using an existing sound card or linked to any MIDI-compatible synthesizer.

✔ MIDI files are very transportable — they just sound different on different synthesizers. A computer's cheap sound card, for example, can still play a MIDI file created on a $1,000 synthesizer. It won't sound nearly as good, but you'll hear the melody.

✔ Likewise, MIDI songs recorded on a cheap sound card can sound extraordinarily realistic when played back on an extraordinarily expensive synthesizer.

✔ Think of MIDI as sheet music. It contains instructions for which instruments to play, and at what times. By editing the sheet music, you change the sound of a song. Likewise, the same sheet music can sound completely different when played by different instruments.

✔ Most people edit MIDI files using computers and special MIDI editing software. Cakewalk Pro is one of the most popular; the latest version not only handles MIDI, but it can also insert up to 128 audio tracks, as well.

✔ You can chain MIDI files together. The *master* instrument — a keyboard on one synthesizer, for example — could be connected to a different synthesizer known as the *slave*. Whatever is played on the master instrument's keyboard is played back using the slave's sounds.

✔ For years, only keyboards could use MIDI; today, MIDI adapters work with guitars and other instruments. Now a guitar with a Roland GK-2A adapter and a Roland MIDI interface can also sound like a flute. (Just don't bend your strings, or the flute will sound damaged.)

Digital Studio Workstations

Roland blew open a new market in 1996 with its VS-880 digital studio workstation. Basically a hard drive in a box with input jacks, built-in software, mixing capabilities, and special effects, the VS-880 worked like a word processor of music.

Musicians could record their pieces straight onto the hard drive and then move them around into the right locations, adding effects where needed. If you made a mistake you could simply press the Undo button. Digital recording eliminated much of the background noise found in analog machines.

Today, Roland markets several digital workstations at varying prices. The top-of-the-line VS-2480, shown in Figure 14-3, features 24 tracks, stereo effects, a 64-channel mixer, a 30GB hard drive, and oodles of other gadgets.

Digital Studio's MP3 Rating: Very Good. Fantastic quality, but expensive and a very steep learning curve limits use by beginners.

- ✔ Although several other companies now market digital studio workstations, Roland still has a firm grasp on the market, outselling the others by a wide margin.

- ✔ Built from the ground up to record music, digital studios come with special shielding to keep any electrical noise from creeping into the mix. Computers, on the other hand, come with whirling fans, noisy power supplies, and other components. They're not particularly well shielded to protect sound.

- ✔ Now for the bad news. The least expensive Roland VS-840GX workstation sells for around $995 — and it substitutes an internal 250MB Iomega Zip drive for a hard drive. The VS-2480 sells for around $3,600, and the learning curve is very steep. Be sure to buy the instruction video and plan on attending all possible "how-to" classes at music stores.

Figure 14-3:
The Roland VS-2480 records songs directly onto its own hard drive, allowing for cut-and-paste editing and effects.

Composing and Recording on a Computer

Chapter 2 explains how to beef up your computer to create MP3s. To use that computer for actually composing your music, you need a few more items. Make sure that you're using the largest and fastest hard drive you can afford. You also want a CD-ROM drive that can write to CDs as well as read from them.

Finally, you have to make a couple of big decisions: which sound card and what software to buy. I help you gather information about both of these components in the following sections.

Choosing a sound card

Sound cards come in a wide variety of models and prices, each designed to fit a particular niche. Any sound card can work for creating MP3s. In fact, you don't even need a sound card to rip MP3s off an audio CD — the music flows onto your hard drive directly from the CD.

However, better sound cards translate into better sound, better effects, easier use, or all three. Here are some features to look for when you're shopping for sound cards, as well as a few recommendations. You'll encounter these terms when shopping, so you need to know how important they are to your work.

- **Digital Capable:** The best sound cards offer three types of digital sound, and you need all three. First, a *Digital to Analog Converter* (DAC) plays digital audio, like a recorded sneeze. An *Analog to Digital Converter* (ADC) records sounds from the card's Line-In or Microphone jacks. Finally, *Digital I/O* routes the card's digital output straight to a DAT recorder or CD burner, which keeps the sound digital as it moves from your computer to its storage area, bypassing any analog conversion where it can pick up noise.

- **Effects:** Most software can add effects, such as reverb, so it's not especially important for the card itself to have these built in.

- **Environmental Audio (EQ Presets):** Most software handles this feature, so it's not very important. These options shape your sound as if it were recorded in different places: a stadium versus a jazz club versus a church, for example. A band playing in each location sounds very different. Environmental Audio or EQ Presets mimic those locations by tweaking the sound.

- **Full-Duplex:** Everybody knows that a sound card plays sounds. But a Full-Duplex card can play sounds at the same time it records them, which is essential for musicians. You need to hear the drums and bass when you're recording the guitar or keyboard part, for example. A half-duplex card, by contrast, can either record or play, but it can't do both simultaneously.

✔ **Gold-plated Connectors:** The best cards plate their connectors with gold. Gold conducts electricity exceptionally well, and it's resistant to corrosion.

✔ **MIDI:** Described earlier in this chapter, MIDI is another essential. MIDI In and Out ports let you control other MIDI-compatible devices — even the ones you haven't purchased yet. Almost all cards have MIDI, so make sure that yours does. Some cards come with built-in MIDI-controlled synthesizers that create sound. Chances are, however, that you'll be connecting your own higher-quality MIDI instruments to the ports and letting the sound card send them instructions.

✔ **Music Synthesis:** Here's where the sound card creates musical tones, which can be played through its MIDI capabilities. When playing MIDI files on your computer, you hear these tones. A wide variety of built-in sounds is important for computer game players, but that variety isn't very important for musicians. Instead, musicians use the sound card's MIDI capabilities to control the sounds of their own keyboards, synthesizers, guitars, and other instruments. The quality of the sound card's built-in tones doesn't really matter.

✔ **PCI:** Sound cards plug into slots inside your computer. (Chapter 2 describes how to install a sound card.) PCI cards are much faster than ISA cards; make sure that yours is a PCI card, and make sure that you have an available PCI slot inside your computer. (You may have to shift some existing cards around in an older computer.)

✔ **Samplers:** Instead of making a synthesizer create synthesized tones for playback, other sound cards use _real_ sounds — actual recorded sound waves. People store _samples_ of these recorded sounds into the card's memory, and the card uses those as a basis for creating music. By adjusting a few samples, the card plays them in different keys. Creative Labs calls its samples _Sound Fonts_; Turtle Beach calls them a _sample store_.

✔ When installing a sound card, keep it as isolated as possible from other cards. If you can, keep an empty slot on both sides of the sound card. Or, connect it on an end slot, as far as possible away from the others — especially TV and video cards because they're the noisiest.

✔ Most computers come with a Soundblaster card or clone. These cards work fine for most computing chores, but they're not musician-quality. Look for something with multiple input and output jacks. The sound cards sold at computer stores are mostly for gamers. For a musician-quality card, shop at a music store. (Unfortunately, higher-quality cards cost anywhere from several hundred dollars to more than a thousand.)

✔ Just as musicians argue over the best guitar amplifier, computer composers argue over the best sound card. Ask your musician friends, and listen to as many cards as possible.

Choosing software

Just like sound cards, audio software comes with its own variety of bells and whistles. The software helps you create the music by recording what you play. Then it's time to edit out the mistakes, add in extra layers of sound, and sprinkle in some effects for aural interest. Finally, audio software saves the completed work in a format other people can listen to on various machines, be it CD player, cassette, or minidisc.

Here's a look at some of the features listed on the audio software boxes that you'll find out there on the shelves, along with some explanation of what the words mean:

- **Accompaniment:** Need a back-up band? Pick up some accompaniment software to play your backing tracks. The most famous, Band-in-a-Box, lets you type in chords, choose a style, and press Play. The software creates a MIDI backing band based on your chord progressions, even tossing in a few solos if requested.

- **Editing:** Editing packages often come with composing packages, ready to fix the mistakes. Did the vocalist's accidental blast of air leave a huge puff sound on the recording? Find the blast on the sound wave, isolate it, and trim it down to size so that it's not as noticeable.

- **Effects:** Just like guitar toys can add wah, flange, phase, echo, reverb, and other sounds to a guitar, audio software can add effects to the sound. The living room gospel band rehearsal can sound as if it performed in a huge hall.

- **Notation:** After creating a magnificent MIDI musical piece, it's time for everybody to learn it. But the bass player went to music school and she reads music. The solution? Buy a notation package. The software reads the MIDI file and prints out standard music notation (the little musical notes on charts) for each instrument. Yep, it's a real time-saver. Figure 14-4 shows a glimpse of Cakewalk Pro's notation software.

- **Recording:** Some software is dedicated to only certain parts of music; notation packages create only sheet music, for instance. Composing software, however, writes down the notes as you play them so that you can edit them later. The more tracks of digital audio your software can handle, the better. Beware, however — your computer's processing power is often the limit, not the software.

Cakewalk Software (www.cakewalk.com)

An industry veteran, Cakewalk puts out a large collection of music software to meet a wide variety of needs. The beginning package, Cakewalk Home Studio 8, records four tracks of audio with MIDI, prints notation, and tosses in effects, such as chorus and reverb. Cakewalk Pro Audio Deluxe, the top-of-the-line product, handles 128 tracks, 256 effects, and just about everything else you can think of.

Figure 14-4 shows Cakewalk Pro Audio displaying a MIDI track, four layers of digital audio tracks, and music notation down below.

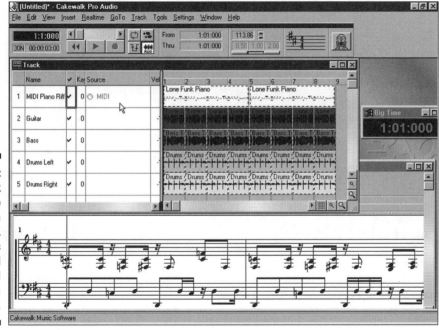

Figure 14-4:
Cakewalk Pro Audio displays a MIDI track, four layers of digital audio, and music notation.

Acid Software (www.soundforge.com)

Sound Forge creates several popular packages. Acid Pro, shown in Figure 14-5, comes with pre-created musical loops, ready to be arranged into your own, royalty-free creations. After you've set down a base, you can add your own loops, instruments, or vocals to create original tunes.

The company's sound editor, Sound Forge (refer to Figure 14-1), records and processes sounds, as well as creating loops for Acid Pro.

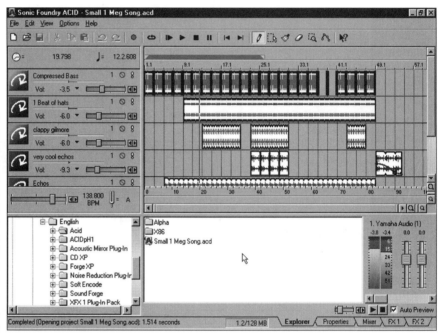

Figure 14-5: Acid Pro software by Sound Forge creates music when you arrange "loops" of sound into musical compositions.

Band-in-a-Box (www.pgmusic.com)

Band-in-a-Box, shown in Figure 14-6, serves as a creative inspiration and back-up band. Select the type of music you're interested in, and the software creates a complete song in that style, with its own chords, melody, and solos. Tweak a few settings, click the Play button, and Band-in-a-Box creates a different song matching your requirements.

Or, if you prefer a little more input into your songs, add your own chords, and Band-in-a-Box creates your backing track by adding bass, drums, and whatever other instruments you want to toss in. It works in MIDI, so it'll play on your computer's sound card. Or connect it to a professional synthesizer for professional-sounding tunes.

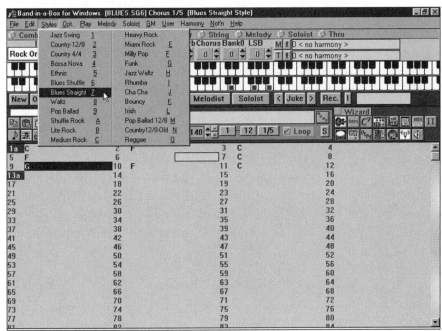

Figure 14-6: Band-in-a-Box creates backing tracks for your works.

Chapter 15

Musician's Guide to Turning Songs into MP3s

*N*ow that MP3 has grabbed the public's curiosity, MP3 files are pouring into the virtual record bins. With hundreds of thousands of musicians uploading their work, listeners won't have time to listen to them all — even when the songs are free.

Following MP3's "road to riches" may bypass the evils of a record company, but it eliminates a record label's conveniences, too. In addition to their practice chores, musicians must now handle recording, mixing, packaging, distribution, sales, and promotion.

In this chapter, I show you how to make a song sound the best when issued as an MP3, giving you that much more of an edge over the competition. I also give you some suggestions about how to package your music effectively, putting the prettiest package on your work.

Doing Everything Yourself

In order to make money from your MP3 files, you almost always need to sell a CD — it's as simple as that.

That leaves you with two options. You can handle all the chores of creating, packaging, and manufacturing your own CDs, or you can pay somebody to handle everything for you.

Each side has its advantages. You save money by doing it yourself, but it takes time away from your music. Lacking experience, you're never sure if you're giving your music its best shot.

If you pay a CD packager to handle everything, you're assured of a reasonably good final product. Plus, digital music is growing in popularity, so CD packagers are lowering prices to attract customers.

In this section, I show you how to create a professional-looking CD yourself, starting with recording your tunes and guiding you through placing the CD in stores. And don't worry if it gets too difficult. Do all the work you can, and let an all-in-one packager pick up where you leave off.

Preparing the computer for recording

Here's a secret: Computers don't store your files neatly onto your hard drive. They break them into little pieces and stuff them into any available empty nook. After a few months, your hard drive becomes cluttered with stray file pieces, slowing it down as it retrieves files.

To combat the problem, Windows includes a defragmenter program, shown in Figure 15-1. It realigns the little file pieces until they sit next to each other. When they lie together in neatly aligned rows, plenty of empty, uncluttered space on your hard drive becomes available for laying down new material. (Macintosh users can defragment their hard drives with Norton Utilities or Tech Tool Pro.)

Figure 15-1:
Open My Computer and right-click your hard drive; choose Properties, click Tools, and click Defragment Now.

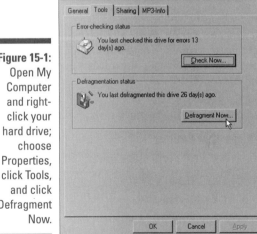

Empty, uncluttered space is just what you need to create MP3s and record audio. Uncompressed audio grabs about 10MB of space each minute. If your computer can work uninterrupted as it lays down the incoming audio in one long strip, the recording sounds that much better.

To defragment a drive, right-click its icon from either My Computer or Explorer. Choose Properties from the menu and then choose the Tools tab. Click the Defragment Now button and follow the on-screen instructions.

- ✔ While the hard drive churns away at its lengthy defragmentation ritual, take the time to clean the heads of your tape recorder. Some folks use rubbing alcohol and a Q-Tip. Others buy high-quality tape-head cleaner at music stores. Either way, rub a little of the liquid where the recorder's protruding silver bulges rub against the tape, and let it dry completely before use.

- ✔ Finally, forget about the thin audio cables that came with your computer or Soundblaster card. Although many types of patch cords dangle from the music store's walls, head for the thick, durable, and very expensive ones with "Monster Cable" (www.monstercable.com) printed along one side. Monster Cables, shown in Figure 15-2, might not be the very best, but they're a good step in that direction.

Figure 15-2:
Monster Cables might cost a lot, but they last much longer than the competition — and sound better, too.

Routing the cables into the computer

Did you create your song on your PC? Then your song is already inside the PC, ready for conversion. Take your nice clean sound to the next section and start setting recording levels.

Everybody else, whether you recorded in a studio, on a four-track player, or with a DAT recorder, must route the sound into the computer.

Analog tape recorders plug into the sound card's Line In jack. Use your sound recording program to save it as a WAV file. (A Macintosh stores sound as an AIFF or SDII sound format.)

DAT recorders might get lucky. A sound card with digital inputs (the Soundblaster Live, for example, offers inexpensive digital inputs) allows recording of the song while staying digital.

Chapter 9 explains the connection process; the next section explains how to set the levels before you finally push the record button.

Don't plug anything but a microphone into the sound card's Mic input jack. That jack is intended for more sensitive sound levels than the ones from a tape player.

For the best sound from a Digital Audio Tape (DAT) player, plug its output into a professional-level sound card featuring DAT input jacks.

Setting the recording levels

Nosy sound recorders want to know the *sampling* rate to use when converting the incoming sound to numbers. The higher the sampling rate, the more the computer pays attention to the incoming sound, resulting in higher sound quality. However, the higher the sampling rate, the more disk space is taken up.

There's something else to consider. Divide a sampling rate by two to see its *cycles*. The human ear can detect only about 20,000 cycles. That leaves little reason to sample at a rate higher than the MP3 standard of 44.1 kHz — most people wouldn't be able to hear the difference anyway. (Besides, MP3 eliminates most of those frequencies during compression.)

Cables connected? Levels set correctly? Push the record button on your recording software, and then push the play button on your tape player, in that order. (You can easily edit out any blank spots later.)

The idea here is to get as clear a representation of your work as possible stored into your computer. Add any effects later so that you can reverse the ones that somehow sound silly the next day.

Processing the sound

Rev up your sound-editing software's package and start editing. Start by trimming the empty spots at the beginning or end, as I describe in Chapter 9. Next, the amount of work you have to do depends on your budget and how happy you were when you recorded the sound.

If you have the cash, burn a CD and take it to a mastering specialist. These folks work with the best equipment, and give your work a fresh ear. They adjust the levels, tweak the mix, fix mistakes, run the sound through the proper equalizers, compressors, and limiters, and generally make your songs sound more alive.

If you're a working-class musician, or simply want to learn about home recording, try some subtle tweaks. Are the vocals loud enough? Bass too loud? Would the song sound better fading out in different places? Use your software's Fade effect in several different spots, using different rates. Does the song sound better? Or just different? Stick with the ones that sound better.

You may want to leave your song alone, especially if you've recorded it in a professional studio. But if your computer *is* your studio, experiment with different effects in different parts of your song. (Always locate the software's Undo button first, and be sure to save a copy of your clean WAV file as a backup.)

✔ Mixing is quite an art. You'll find plenty of home studio books at the music store. Picking one up is a very . . . ah . . . sound investment.

✔ For some intensive information on mixing and mastering, check out The Voodoo of CD Mastering (`www.essrl.wustl.edu/~adl/mastering/`). (Yeah, that's a long one to type in. Good thing all the links mentioned in this book are included on a links page on this book's CD.)

✔ When you're finished editing, it's time to punch your software's Normalize button — especially if you're uploading several pieces from the same CD. Normalizing makes your file play as loud as possible without distortion. By normalizing all your MP3s to the same value, listeners won't have to reach for the volume knob when switching between songs.

Duplicating and packaging your CD

Today, burning your own CD is relatively easy. Chapters 11 and 12 cover the finer points. But selling your own CDs creates more work.

The CD itself needs artwork (and barcodes on the packaging, if you're planning sales through larger retail outlets such as record chains). You need a plastic CD case (known as a *jewel case*) or sleeve. The CD case needs to be wrapped in tooth-shattering plastic wrap. Some companies handle these chores for you. Just mail them the disc, and they mail back your professional-looking copies.

Other companies do bits and pieces of the work, forcing you to make more decisions. No matter which method you choose, here's a look at the chores necessary to professionally package your CD.

Mastering

After recording and mixing the songs, you're not finished. In which order will they play on the CD? Is there a natural progression between them? Do the songs have the right amount of delay between them? Should some songs fade into each other?

Should the bass, treble, or midrange be adjusted on some tracks? Did you put too much reverb on the vocalist?

And most important, are you too involved in your own composition to predict what will sound best to others?

That's where mastering comes in. A sound engineer listens to your work using a different studio environment, different speakers, and different equipment. The mastering engineer tweaks your mix until it sounds the best according to his or her professionally tuned ear.

When the mastering is complete, you have a CD that's ready to be duplicated.

If you don't have your CD mastered, the folks at the pressing plant will master it. Though they might be great at duplicating thousands of CDs in a hurry, they may not be the best ones to add the fine finishing touches to your music.

But I *like* being abnormal!

Normalizing is necessary for even antiestablishment musicians. To *normalize* sound means to adjust its peak values to a certain level. That cuts down the screams, boots the whispers, and makes everything audible.

When normalizing a song, set the software for –0.5 dB. Normalizing means something a little different when preparing a set of songs for a CD. In this case, normalizing adjusts the average volume of all the songs so that they don't differ wildly.

One caveat, however: When ripping a song from a CD and creating an MP3 file, don't bother with the normalizing option. Keep the song at the same levels as it was originally recorded. (The record company paid somebody a lot of money to set those recording levels. Don't mess with them.)

Designing the cover

First impressions count. And your audience's first impression won't come from your music, it will come from your CD's cover artwork.

So start thinking about your cover as soon as you begin songwriting. Take pictures of jam sessions, band members, or early morning reflections in pools of water on terra cotta tiles. Try to find something stating the mood of your music.

Draw up a rough picture of what you want, and then spend time trying to add in the details. Then hire a graphic artist.

- ✔ That doesn't necessarily mean you have to pay somebody. Check the local schools for beginning graphic artists. Some may exchange work for credit on the CD.

- ✔ Some CD packagers recommend graphic artists in your area, but you still save money by creating as much of the cover yourself. Graphic designers charge much less for smoothing out an idea than for creating something themselves.

- ✔ When hiring a graphic artist, make a contract stating who is responsible for artwork, layout, typesetting and film (if applicable), and printing.

Manufacturing

A computer's CD-ROM drive burns numbers into a compact disc when creating a music CD. Mass-produced CDs come to life through a different process known as *injection molding*.

Also known as replication, the second method is less expensive in bulk, and more reliable.

When looking for a company to replicate your CDs, make sure that it's rated with an ISO-9002 certification. That's an industry standard.

If you tour a lot, make a few cassettes, as well. Some people still don't like CDs. Plus, plenty of people have cassette players in their cars, and they'll want to hear your tunes on the drive home.

Letting Somebody Else Package Your Music

If you'd rather make music than manufacture CDs, hire an all-in-one CD packager to handle the details. They'll take care of the artwork, mastering, and manufacturing of your masterpiece.

Check out the Information Database at www.musicianassist.com for a list of CD packagers. Here are some you can start with:

✔ **Oasis Recording, Inc.** (www.oasiscd.com), shown in Figure 15-3, offers one of the most comprehensive CD creation packages.

Oasis offers its services in stages, picking up where you left off. No cover design? It helps you find a designer. It creates both CDs and cassettes from your work. Finally, it offers advice and programs to promote your music. Be sure to check out the great links on the Oasis Web site for more information.

✔ **Global Express Media** (www.globalexpressmedia.com) offers pressing, design, film, proofs, all printed materials, and polywrap packaging (see Figure 15-4).

✔ **CD-Lab** (www.cd-lab.com) hails from Glendale, Arizona. As shown in Figure 15-5, the company offers anything from a quickie 24-hour turnaround for CD duplication to printed and packaged full-color covers. Be prepared to turn in your own artwork according to its specifications or be charged extra. (Use its handy Web page calculator to check the prices.)

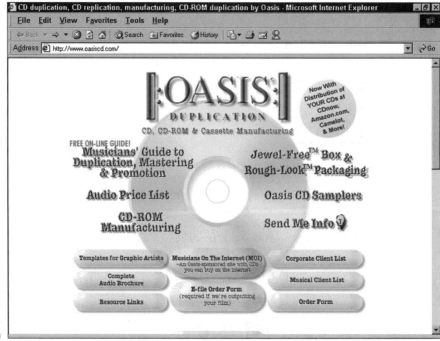

Figure 15-3:
Oasis Recording offers mastering duplication, promotion, and sales through CDnow, Amazon, and more.

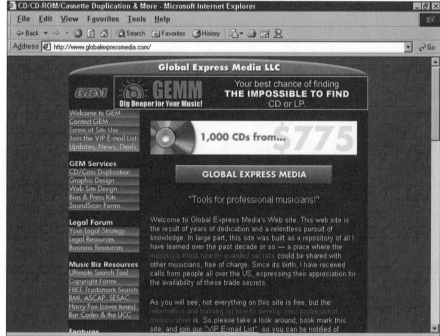

Figure 15-4:
Global
Express
Media
offers an
estimate
calculator
for CD
production
on its
Web site.

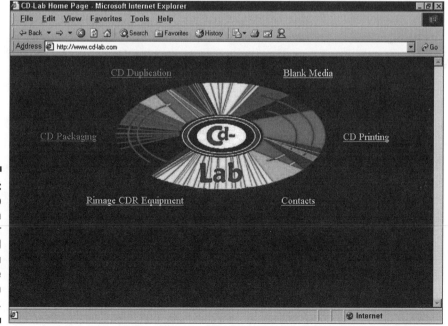

Figure 15-5:
CD-Lab
offers a
24-hour
turnaround
when you
need those
copies in
a hurry.

Chapter 16

Making Money from Your MP3s

*A*t this point, you've created a product to sell — your music has moved from inside your head onto stacks of CDs. It's time to convince the public to buy your music, and the first step is to convince them to listen to it. This chapter shows several ways to put your music into the public's ears.

Remember, there's no such thing as too much marketing and promotion. Marketing doesn't always cost money. It can be as simple as wearing a band T-shirt during the day and carrying a stack of promotional CDs in the trunk.

Marketing is work, though. It involves lots of phone calls, keeping track of hundreds of people, and eating up lots of time away from your music. You might want to turn the job over to somebody else — a topic I also cover here.

Either way, after reading this chapter, you'll know how musicians turn their music into money.

Plugging Your Band with Press Releases

Don't forget the simple, traditional channels of promotion. Write up a press release — a single-page letter describing your band, your music, and when/if you'll be playing live. Send the press release, a free copy of your CD, and a photo of the band to any writers covering music. Stay local for a better chance of coverage.

Mail copies to local radio stations, too. It might hurt inside to give away your precious CDs, but if nobody's talking about them, nobody will know to buy them. The best publicity is word of mouth.

Try to turn your press release into news by taking an "angle" on your band. Are you holding a CD-release party? Use that for the first paragraph. Have you written a song about a current event? That's news, too.

Keep in mind the following things when writing a press release. Remember that this small sheet of paper represents your band. If it's ignored by the media, your band will have a much harder time getting noticed.

✔ Always put contact information at the top of your press release. People usually like to speak with the person who sent in the list, either to verify the facts or to find out more information. Be sure to add an e-mail address and Web page address, if you have one. (And you should.) Does a member of the band carry a cell phone? Include that number. Many media people work on a tight deadline, and ease of accessibility can determine who gets coverage.

✔ Start with a headline announcing the newsworthiness of your event. Then, in the first paragraph, answer the questions of who, what, where, when, and why.

✔ If you can't afford to send out CDs with your press releases, direct the recipients to your Web site that carries MP3 versions of some of your songs.

✔ Been reviewed in a newspaper or magazine? Add a few quotes from the review, no matter how small. Media people follow each other like cattle; if you get coverage in one place, other media people are likely to follow.

✔ If marketing seems foreign to you, hit the library or bookstores. CD Baby (www.cdbaby.com) recommends *Guerilla P.R.* by Michael Levine. Easy-to-read and thorough, Levine explains how to get your name into the media with little or no budget.

✔ If you're not much of a writer, find a friend to write it up for you. Make sure that the press release is short and to the point. News people receive dozens of press releases each day. A quick glance tells them whether they've found something they can use.

✔ Search the Internet for college radio stations and Internet radio stations. The Radio-Locator (www.radio-locator.com), shown in Figure 16-1, can help you get started. Those stations are much more receptive to new material than commercial stations. Find any stations or DJ shows that play material like yours, and send in a copy of your CD.

✔ Can't afford to send out CDs? Don't have any CDs? Then put MP3s of songs on your Web site and put the Web site address at the top of the press release.

 ✔ Send out a press release at *every* opportunity — a new gig, when you sign up that hundredth fan for your mailing list, or a live interview on a radio station (even if it's only a Webcast from a next door neighbor's house). Keep your band in the public eye as much as possible. If you don't stand out, you'll lose out.

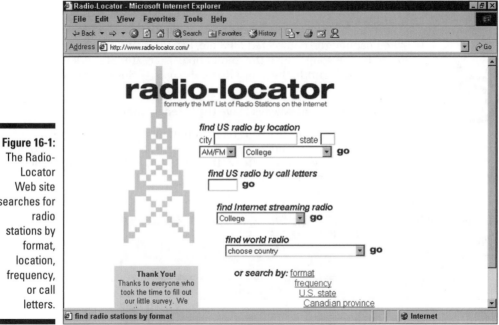

Figure 16-1:
The Radio-Locator Web site searches for radio stations by format, location, frequency, or call letters.

Creating High-Quality MP3 Files

Encoding means transforming your recording into an MP3 file. (Encoders get maximum coverage in Chapter 10, so head there for the basic mechanics.) And musicians want the highest-quality MP3s possible. To ensure the best quality when encoding your own compositions, keep the following things in mind:

 ✔ If your encoder program offers an HQ option, use it. HQ stands for *High Quality,* and it means that the encoder reads the entire file before choosing the best encoding scheme. When HQ is turned off, the encoder tests only part of the file.[Q]

✔ Don't use Variable Bit Rate (VBR) encoding unless you're sure you can get away with it. Most encoders grab files at the Constant Bit Rate (CBR) of 128 Kbps. VBR gives the encoder more leeway when converting files. A pause within a song doesn't need much encoding. A finger-bleeding guitar solo could need more than average encoding to preserve the quality. VBR sometimes creates better MP3s with less file size, but it occasionally increases file size, too. The clincher? Some MP3 players can't handle the VBR format.

✔ A sure sign of professionalism is to fill out the MP3 file's tag immediately after encoding. Enter the title, artist, album, year, genre, and comment, as shown in Figure 16-2. Stick your band's Web site in the comments area to allow for instant feedback and, hopefully, CD sales.

✔ When naming the completed MP3 file, use the band or artist's name followed by the song title. If the Red Cabbages create "Shredder" for the Cole Slaw CD, entitle the song "Red Cabbages — Shredder.mp3."

✔ *Never* offer MP3 versions of your entire CD. Just choose two or three of the strongest songs. Always leave the listener wanting to hear more.

You're in charge of promoting your band. If that means giving away some of your music for free, try to smile while gritting your teeth. You need exposure. And be *sure* to place your Web site on the MP3 file's ID tag so that listeners can contact you for more music.

Figure 16-2:
Always fill
out your
MP3 file
tags with
information
for your
band, and
remember
to include
your Web
site where
people can
contact you.

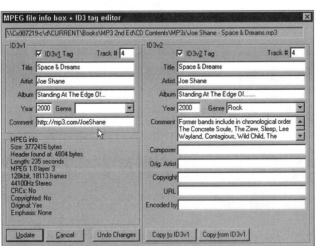

Create a Web Site — and Fast

A musician definitely needs a Web site. It's a multimedia business card aimed at the media. It's a place for people to turn if they need a band for a party. It's a place to sell your music. Your fans need it to keep track of the latest news.

It's no surprise that one of the most popular bands, Radiohead, keeps up one of the best Web sites. Full of odd photos, toothsome animations, diaries, bizarre trapdoors, politicking, message boards, poetry, scribblings, and odd ravings, the site can keep visitors entranced for hours. When they tire of audio/visual bombardments, they can head to the online shop, shown in Figure 16-3.

MP3.com creates a Web page for you on its site when you sign up as a new artist. The page it creates follows a standardized format, but it's customizable — provided you have a few Web-building skills.

✔ With a Web site, you can sell other promotional items, such as T-shirts and posters, along with your CDs. These other items often make more money than the CDs. Most MP3.com sites offer links to the posting band's own Web pages, providing quick access for curious listeners.

✔ Be sure to post all reviews you receive, both positive and negative. That shows visitors that if nothing else, you're honest. That's an invaluable quality in the mail-order business.

✔ Put your Buy This CD! link on every page of your Web site so that it shows up easily. This isn't the time to be modest. The easier you make it for people to buy your CD, the more copies you'll sell.

✔ Let Web site visitors sign up for a mailing list, and then send frequent e-mails full of announcements, show dates, quizzes, and other information to the list. Keep people enthusiastic about your music so that they'll tell their friends about it.

✔ Don't know how to make a Web site? Then at least have MP3.com set one up for you. That gives you a spot to direct people who inquire about your band.

Selling and Distributing Your Music

Convincing people to exchange money for music is one of the toughest parts of musicianship. The first step is providing easy access to your work.

Always carry a batch of your CDs in the trunk. When you see a music store or chain, drop by, introduce yourself, and ask the manager to carry your stuff on *consignment*. That means you drop off the CDs; if they sell some, they send you part of the money. If they don't sell any, they return the CDs after a given period of time.

Your music gains more legitimacy when its in the bins. And larger stores often carry a "local artists" section that they try to fill.

If you'd rather spend time creating music than selling it, consider some online consignment. One popular online consignment store for independent music is CD Baby (www.cdbaby.com), shown in Figure 16-4.

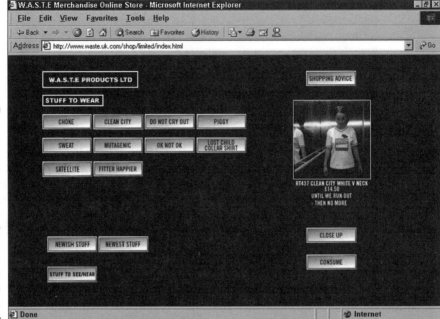

Figure 16-3:
After entertainingly visitors for hours, Radiohead's enchantingly esoteric Web site offers them a place to shop.

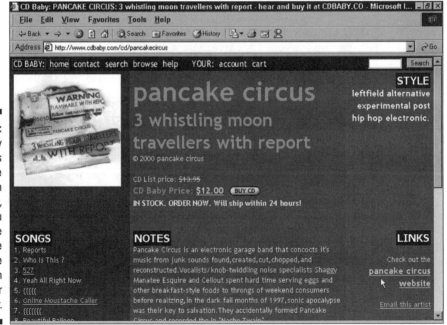

Figure 16-4:
CD Baby handles online distribution of your CDs, letting you continue your online sales while away from your computer.

It works like this: Send CD Baby five of your band's CDs to start with, and a $35 setup fee. CD Baby creates a cool Web site for your band (like the one in Figure 16-4), with RealAudio sound clips, links to your own Web site, and all the text and descriptions you want.

Your Web address is easy for people to remember: www.cdbaby.com/yourband. Plus, CD Baby sticks your page in the site's search engines, ready to be accessed by visitors looking for their favorite types of music.

The online company accepts all credit card payments through its Web site or 800 number. Fans listen to a few of the tunes using RealAudio; if they like the CD, they buy it, and CD Baby ships it to them within 24 hours.

Attracting 200,000 visits each day, CD Baby sells an average of 200 CDs each day from its stable of 8,000 independent artists.

- ✔ To sell your CDs through your Web site, just put a link to your CD Baby page, which takes care of the mechanics of payment and sample listens. That keeps your own Web site sales active while you're on the road or in the studio. (And, unlike MP3.com, CD Baby sends checks each week.)

- ✔ Oasis, one of the full-service CD packagers that I cover in Chapter 15, handles distribution in several national retail chain stores through Valley Media, the largest full-line distributor in the nation. So if you hire Oasis to do your distribution, your CD appears on Amazon.com (www.amazon.com), among other online stores.

- ✔ You'll find more information at IndieCentre (www.indiecentre.com), a site devoted to helping people create their own labels to sell records. Although the site is no longer being updated, it's still full of information.

Earning Money from Freebie MP3 Sites

Today, lots of Internet sites beg musicians for uploads. Most work pretty much the same. You sign up for an account, and fill out the online legalese that spells out everybody's expectations. You upload your MP3s, address information, pictures, band stats, and other information.

This section profiles several of the most popular sites. How did they become the most popular? Because after you upload your songs to them, they pay you money. Well, almost. Each site has different criteria for payment, however, so don't expect to get rich quick.

Here's a look at MP3.com, Ampcast.com, and the Internet Underground Music Archive — IUMA for short (www.iuma.com).

The MP3.com Payback for Playback program

Being one of the first (and certainly the largest) sources of MP3 songs and information, MP3.com has brand-name recognition. Soon after going online in early 1999, its legal troubles placed it all over the news, boosting its popularity as the scourge of the entrenched record industry.

After you sign up for the MP3.com New Artist program by sending in your band information and MP3 songs, MP3.com creates a Web site for you on its site, cataloged by both location and genre. Visitors sift through the MP3 databases, finding bands in their hometown, if they want, or just listening to tango music from Brazil.

Who's listening? As shown in Figure 16-5, you can log on to MP3.com with your artist's password to see a tracking sheet of your downloads and listens. You can tell your bar buddies that you've had 1,626 downloads in the past two weeks.

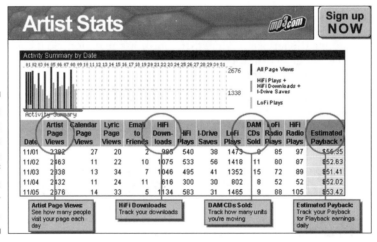

Figure 16-5: MP3.com lets artists track the number of downloads for their songs.

Best yet, MP3.com pays artists based on their account's activity through its Payback for Playback program. MP3.com places a million dollars in a pot each month and distributes it to qualifying musicians based on the amount of user activity on an artist's MP3.com Web site.

✔ Like almost all MP3 distribution sites, MP3.com accepts only original songs — no remixes or covers. You must have either written the song or hold the song's copyright. Feel free to remix your own stuff, but don't remix other people's songs. You'll find more information on legal rights and copyrighted material through The Harry Fox Agency, Inc. (www.nmpa.org/hfa.html).

✔ Too busy jamming to create, package, distribute, and sell your work?
Make MP3.com handle the chores. Send them a CD with less than 57
minutes of music, and MP3.com creates a *DAM* CD. As I describe in
Chapter 12, a DAM CD contains both an MP3 version and a regular audio
version of all the songs, so the CD can be played either on a computer or
in a regular CD player. Your fans purchase the DAM CD directly from
MP3.com, and MP3.com sends you 50 percent of the proceeds.

Rolling in royalties from Ampcast.com

Around the same time that MP3.com began smelling MP3's cash potential,
Ampcast.com caught a whiff, too. The sites opened within a few months of
each other. Yet, MP3.com quickly rose to the top of the podium, leaving the
competition in the orchestra pit. Why? Well, it certainly didn't hurt that
MP3.com had the "MP3" domain name in its favor, bringing immediate credi-
bility, traffic, interested musicians, and investor dollars.

Ampcast.com hasn't given up, though. In fact, Eric Briceno, one of the
founders, says he's glad that he didn't get oodles of financing a few years
back, blow through it like so many other Internet companies, only to go bank-
rupt during the dot-com dive in late 2000.

Instead, Ampcast.com has kept a low profile, sticking to its goal of entertain-
ing "Generation Y" through independent music and video. The plan has
attracted a stable of 2,000 artists and a collection of around 7,000 songs.

DAM, money talks

A band sets its own price on its DAM CDs,
although they usually sell for under $10. For
each sale, MP3.com pays the artist 50 percent
of the gross revenue.

Don't expect checks to come in every week.
MP3.com tabulates the proceeds on a quarterly
basis. If it owes you more than $50, expect a
check within two more months. If it's less than
$50, wait three more months. That means that
you're paid about five months after your sales
reach $50 (which is better than the book busi-
ness, actually).

Artists who can't wait for the cash are opening
CompuBank accounts, however. As described
on MP3.com (www.mp3.com/service/
compubank.html), artists with a CompuBank
account receive access to their earnings
immediately — even if they've earned less than
$50. The catch? — you have to make an initial
deposit of $100 in your CompuBank account
before the company activates your account.

How does Payback for Playback *really* work?

There's no denying that artists make money through the MP3.com Payback for Playback program. Alex Smith has made more than $100,000 through the program. Check out Chapter 13 for the profile on Smith.

But how does it work? Well, MP3.com cryptically states the following:

"Your portion is calculated daily based on a formula of user activity. Due to the inclusion of all MP3.com member artists and the fact that this number changes daily with new member artist sign-ups, payment amounts will vary from day to day even if user activity (stats) remains fairly consistent. Likewise, due to the complexity of the formula, there will be no direct correlation between your stats and your payment."

Here's a basic rundown of who qualifies for payment:

✔ The program only applies to musicians who have signed up with MP3.com and have their music available on the site at the beginning of a month.

✔ One or more of the musician's songs must be "streamed" or downloaded by at least 15 separate users within that month. (Being played on the My.MP3.com program counts toward the goal.)

✔ Musicians meeting the first two conditions are eligible for that month's "monthly pot," which averages one million dollars. That pot is divvied up between the qualified musicians according to MP3.com's formula, which "takes into account the number of times music and/or other content from Qualified Artists and My.MP3.com Artists is played by different users of the MP3.com Web site."

So, there's no real way of knowing how much you'll make. But if your songs are played a lot in comparison to everybody else's songs, you can count on making more money than the competing musicians.

"There are about five of us working for the company," Briceno said. "We're working out of our basements. We do it because we love it, and we pay attention to our artists. The community is built *by* the community, not by a bunch of corporate bean counters."

When Ampcast.com heard its artists' loudest request — to be paid for their music — it obliged with a royalty system paying six cents for each download (see Figure 16-6). Of course, there are a few catches. Like MP3.com, Ampcast.com accepts only original work. Visitors can download the same song bunches of times, but only the first download by a particular visitor counts toward royalties. In fact, the payment plan is remarkably similar to the MP3.com Payback for Playback program, which I describe in the sidebar "How does Payback for Playback *really* work?" Its formula of six cents per download, however, is much easier to figure out.

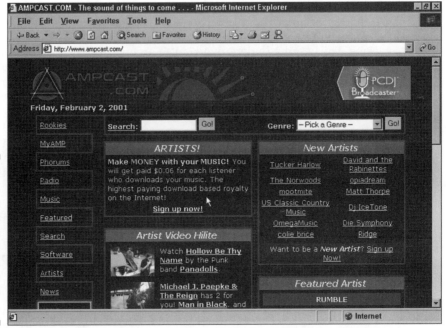

Figure 16-6:
Ampcast.
com pays
musicians
six cents
for each
individual
listener who
downloads
their music.

✔ Ampcast.com plans to launch a CD program, printing and manufacturing CDs for artists, selling them both online and to artists in bulk.

✔ Founded by a group of acoustic engineers who quit their jobs, Ampcast.com prides itself on staying small and accessible to its group of artists.

✔ Unlike many similar sites, Ampcast.com also carries artists' videos in QuickTime. (Ampcast.com has partnered with Apple Computer, creators of QuickTime.)

✔ Ampcast.com is not connected to the AmpCast MP3 player for the Macintosh.

✔ The Ampcast.com target audience, "Generation Y" — the sons and daughters of the Boomers — is a huge group of teens born between 1979 and 1994. Cash rich, technologically savvy, and 60-million members strong, they've got businesses salivating.

Sharing the profits with IUMA

Note: Shortly after this section was written, IUMA suspended operations. The site still exists, but not at the level that I discuss in this section. Don't be afraid to visit the site, however, as IUMA might have found new financial legs since the time of this writing.

Who first started delivering music on the Internet? MP3.com? Ampcast.com? Rollingstone.com?

Nope. The Internet Underground Music Archive (www.IUMA.com) (see Figure 16-7). Known as IUMA (pronounced eye-U-ma), the Archive began dishing out Internet music in 1993 from founder Jeff Patterson's dorm room in Santa Cruz. Back then, IUMA started as a small FTP site on the school's servers, using 14.4 modems.

IUMA eventually evolved into a Web site that offered MP3 downloads, CD sales, and individual Web pages for its members. Today, it showcases 20,000 bands, offering a springboard to success that's helped launched the career of Sublime, among others.

IUMA may not be as well known as MP3.com, but it's certainly more hip and offers easy access to tomorrow's stars.

But where's the money? Well, IUMA chose the Strategic Partnership route. By allowing itself to be purchased in 1999 by Emusic.com (known as Goodnoise back then), it received enough funding to focus on promoting independent musicians.

Figure 16-7:
IUMA, the first Internet site to distribute digital music, pays artists based on their downloads, streams, ad revenue, and through special promotions.

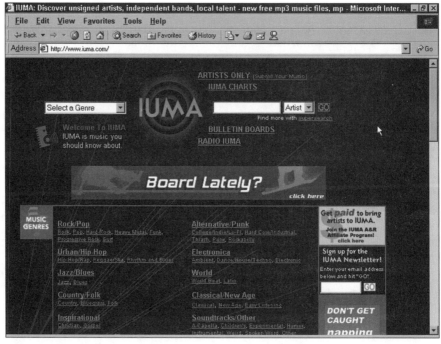

Today, IUMA shares the wealth with its musicians in several ways, from downright zany to incredibly fair. Here's how to convert your creativity to cash:

- ✔ IUMA lets you sell your CDs on its site. Create a Web site for your band on IUMA, describe your CDs, and send five copies of each one to IUMA, stating your price, band name, and CD name. When IUMA receives your goods, it puts a "Buy-It!" button on your Web site, where visitors can purchase your CDs. When you sell a CD, IUMA takes five bucks off the top; you get the rest.

- ✔ Like most sites for musicians, IUMA runs ads on its pages. Unlike most artist sites, however, IUMA shares the ad revenue it makes from your Web pages. IUMA pays approximately 0.25 cent (that's ¼ of a penny) each time your page is viewed, as well as for each download or stream of your songs. Although less than a penny sounds like chicken feed, remember that you're earning money each time your page is *viewed*.

- ✔ Pregnant? Then keep your eyes open for a repeat of IUMA's "Name Your Baby IUMA" contest. In November 2000, IUMA awarded $5,000 to ten parents who named their babies "Iuma." The winners? Iuma Thornhill, Iuma Ross, Iuma Becht, Iuma Carlton . . . you get the idea.

Even when IUMA isn't handing out cash for baby names, song downloads, or ad revenue, it's helping promote bands in other ways. Here are a few:

- ✔ IUMA creates a chart measuring each artist's popularity on the site by streams, downloads, and sales. Every month, the top-ranked artists earn a spot on a list that's sent to 1,700 industry people at more than 600 labels. It may not be wallet money, but it's sure a great way to get noticed.

- ✔ The site sponsored an "I-Candy" contest, awarding $5,000 for the best music videos. Visitors vote to choose the three winning artists.

- ✔ IUMA is also involved with MusicOMania!, a competition among college bands. Visitors vote on their favorite bands, narrowing the competition to four. In 2000, those four were flown to a final live competition, where the national champion took home a $10,000 grand prize, a record demo deal with a professional producer, and 5,000 CDs from the demo.

- ✔ Finally, IUMA pays artists $15 for every new artist they bring to IUMA's site.

- ✔ IUMA, like most other Web sites that pay musicians, calculates royalties on a quarterly basis. IUMA sends out checks within 45 days of the quarter's end.

Looking at the others

But wait, there's more . . . musicians might want to give these other MP3 sites a click or two to see what's up. Sites like these pop up — and disappear — every few months. To find out the latest crop, head for www.google.com and search for several names at once: IUMA, garageband, and Ampcast, for starters.

EMusic

No doubt, EMusic (www.emusic.com) pays its artists well. The site, shown in Figure 16-8, charges visitors 99 cents for every MP3 song they download. Starting to drool over the cash potential for your own band? Grab a sponge.

That's because EMusic.com signs only major-league artists, with a roster that includes Elvis Costello, Creedence Clearwater Revival, They Might Be Giants, Duke Ellington, and Bob Marley, among others. EMusic.com sloughs its unsigned or independent artists off to its partner, IUMA.com, which I describe in the preceding section.

Will visitors pay nearly a buck a song for an MP3 tune they can download for free from Napster or someplace else on the Internet? That's the problem plaguing EMusic.com's business plan.

EMusic also provides unlimited downloads of its artists for a monthly fee — $9.99 per month for a yearly contract; $14.99 for three months. Although its sizable roster of artists includes Phish, Merle Haggard, Green Day, George Clinton, Johnny Winter, and Louis Armstrong, it's by no means a comprehensive segment of the music industry.

Figure 16-8:
EMusic charges shoppers 99 cents for each MP3 they download from a major artist.

garageband.com

garageband.com, shown in Figure 16-9, lays the teaser on the home page: Join our site and compete to win a $250,000 recording contract!

Keep a few things in mind, however. First, bands compete against thousands of other bands for the big pie — they're not awarded tiny pieces of it, like bands at other sites. Also, don't join with the expectations of recording your pro-quality CD and then pocketing all the profits.

The money's basically a loan, like it is with all recording contracts. After an on-site competition every few months, one band wins a recording contract worth $250,000. When the session's done, the band has a hot new CD that sounds pretty darn good. Like any other contract, however, a portion of the proceeds go to paying back the costs incurred by the recording session.

- ✔ garageband.com uses a formula for calculating winners that's so complicated it's patented as the Lathroum Preference Engine (LPE). Registered members listen to a few songs whenever they log on, and vote on their merits. After all the songs have been listened to, some several times, the site holds a final competition with the top 50 bands, and the LPE calculates a final winner for the recording session.

- ✔ Co-founded by Jerry Harrison of the Talking Heads, garageband has attracted a wide variety of people to its advisory board, including Brian Eno, Sir George Martin, Steve Earle, and many recording and engineering technicians. In fact, it bills itself as the only Internet site "created by musicians for musicians."

- ✔ With so many musicians reviewing each other's material, garageband.com is a great place for feedback on your tunes. Just remember that you're there for feedback, not cash, and you'll be happy.

Jimmy and Doug's Farmclub.com

For all its faults, garageband.com has good intentions. Even though its lure of a quarter-million dollar contract can be deceiving, the site is trying to promote new musicians to the world.

Not so with Jimmy and Doug's Farmclub, shown in Figure 16-10. This site is basically a front for a major record label pushing its own talent. There's no hiding it, really. "Jimmy" is Jimmy Iovine, co-chair of Universal's Interscope label. And "Doug"? Doug Morris, CEO of Universal music.

Nothing new here.

Figure 16-9: garageband .com runs a contest that awards the winner with a $250,000 recording contract.

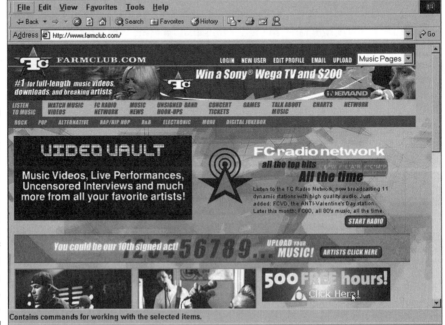

Figure 16-10: A front for Universal Records, Farmclub. com features "all your favorite artists" — if they hail from Universal, that is.

Streaming Your MP3 files from Your Web Site

It's important for musicians to turn their Web sites into multimedia business cards for potential customers, bookers, or talent searchers. The best way to do that is to let people hear your MP3 songs directly from your site.

Sure, they can download the MP3 songs and listen to them, just like any other file. But some people don't want to wait for a song to download before they can hear it. Wouldn't it be nice if they could hear your music immediately simply by clicking its title?

Actually, it's fairly easy to make an MP3 file stream from your Web site. If you've built your own Web site — no matter how simple — and you know a little about HTML editing, just follow these steps:

1. **Create a text document in Notepad that contains the name and Web address to your MP3 file.**

   For instance, if your MP3 is called `Jam.mp3`, and you're storing it on your Web site at `www.andyrathbone.com`, add this line into your Notepad file:

   ```
   http://www.andyrathbone.com/jam.mp3
   ```

   Make sure that you type the complete path to the file, as it exists on the Web. Be sure to press Enter at the end of the line.

2. **Save your newly created text document as "`jam.m3u`".**

   To make sure that you've saved your file correctly in Notepad, save it with quotation marks around it: "`jam.m3u`".

   You need the quotation marks so Notepad saves the file with the extension `.m3u` instead of its usual `.txt`.

   You've created a file that contains only the path to your MP3 file. A file ending in `.m3u` is a *playlist* file. Most MP3 players, including Winamp and MusicMatch, recognize that file as containing a list of locations to MP3 files.

3. **Using your Web page editor, create a hyperlink to that M3U file somewhere on a Web page.**

   For example, create a Web page that includes this line:

   ```
   Play my jam with Steve and Jeff from last summer
   ```

   Then use your Web page editor to add the hyperlink to the word jam. In my case, I'd add this hyperlink to the word jam:

   ```
   http://www.andyrathbone.com/jam.m3u
   ```

When a visitor clicks <u>jam</u>, the browser opens the playlist file, finds the MP3 file's location, and starts playing the song through that person's default MP3 player.

In fact, a visitor can simply type **www.andyrathbone.com/jam.m3u** to make the song start streaming.

4. **Upload your MP3 file, your newly created M3U file, and your edited Web page to your Web site host.**

This trick seems simple enough. But here are the reasons why this little procedure doesn't always work.

✔ You must be handy enough with HTML editing and Web site creation to create and upload the three files: the MP3 file, the M3U playlist, and the HTML file containing the link.

✔ The biggest problem, by far, is modem speed. Standard MP3 files come encoded at 128 Kbps. Unless you're using a cable modem or faster, the file won't download nearly fast enough to play smoothly. People with dial-up modems will hear part of the song, a pause while the browser downloads the song's next portion, a little more of the song, and so on. To avoid this problem, you must shrink the file by re-encoding it at a lower rate.

✔ MP3 players always battle each other for the privilege of playing your MP3 files when you click them. If you've installed more than one player, Windows may be confused about how to open streaming Internet files. You must make sure that your MP3 player is set up to play M3U files.

Now, the solutions to those problems:

✔ If you're not handy with editing or creating Web pages, head for MP3.com or CD Baby. They'll build Web pages for you with streaming songs, allowing you to avoid the hassle.

✔ To combat the encoding problem, use MusicMatch to re-encode your Web page's MP3 files from 128 Kbps to 24 Kbps. That lets an MP3 file stream smoothly to a 28.8 modem. Choose Convert from the MusicMatch File menu and select your MP3 file from the left side. Choose a new folder for it on the left side, and slide the bar to the left until it reads 24 Kbps. Click the Start button to re-encode the file to the lower rate. The songs encoded at 24 Kbps won't sound as good as they did when encoded at 128 Kbps, but they'll give the listener a taste of what's to come if they take the time to download the 128 Kbps version.

✔ If you can't figure out how to set up your MP3 player to play .m3u files — or if Windows is causing the problem, head to MP3.com and download the MP3Fix program. It automatically resets everything so that your favorite MP3 player handles streams correctly.

✔ Always give Web site visitors *three* ways to hear your music, using a different button for each: Offer a low-fidelity, 24 Kbps version that streams to dial-up modems; offer a standard, 128 Kbps version for streaming to fast modems; and offer a button for visitors to simply download the 128 Kbps version of the MP3 file. (MP3.com offers these choices on every artist's Web site: Lo Fi Play, Hi Fi Play, and Download.)

✔ Do you have an account on MP3.com? Use the hyperlink from *those* songs on your own site. That helps boost your Payback for Playback rankings. To get the hyperlink, right-click the Lo Fi Play or Hi Fi Play button and choose Properties. Copy the hyperlink, and use it on your page instead of making your own playlist. Be sure to copy the hyperlink from the button marked Listen to All Tracks. Then when a visitor clicks on the link in your site, it streams *all* your music from MP3.com. (This trick only works when visitors have an account on MP3.com, however, so if visitors start to complain, knock it off.)

✔ Some servers put limits on the amount of space you can use for storing files. Because MP3 files average about 3 to 4MB, they quickly eat up space on a server that allows only 10MB storage. Be careful that you don't try to pack too much onto your server.

Part V
The Part of Tens

The Tubmans successfully download an entire multimedia MP3 file of Gustav Holst's composition,"The Planets".

In this part . . .

Sometimes chapters simply turn into lists. When that happens, they're shuttled off to a special part of the book: The Part of Tens.

It's full of lists: "The Ten Best MP3 Sites," for instance, details exactly where to go for MP3 songs and information. Musicians enjoy the "Ten Ways MP3 Helps Musicians." (It's full of tricks like how the Rio MP3 player helps you learn Steve Vai riffs.)

Looking for more practical stuff? Check out "The Ten Most Useful MP3 Utilities," along with how to grab them. Confused about the legalities of all this stuff? Head for "Ten Things to Know about Copyrights."

MP3 technology is still new enough to spawn rumors. Can the Rio really dial long-distance calls — and for free? This chapter reveals the truth to the MP3 oddities you read on the Web sites.

Finally, the last chapter in the book might be the most important of all to today's impatient music fans. "Ten Quick Ways to Use MP3" shows the fast and easy way to get something done.

Chapter 17

The Ten Best MP3 Sites

*N*ew MP3 sites pop up daily; some list MP3 files, others carry utilities, and still others carry news about the latest MP3 happenings. For the current day's list of sites, head for www.google.com and search for the term MP3. Believe me, you'll be flooded with thousands of sites to explore.

But for a quicker way to fish for sites, start with the ones that I list here. No, there aren't exactly ten — but I'm going for quality here, not quantity. Besides — many of these sites list other sites, which list other sites, which list . . . well, you get the idea.

MP3.com

Site: www.mp3.com

As you can tell by the way that it snagged the rights to the MP3 domain name, MP3.com, shown in Figure 17-1, grabbed hold of the MP3 explosion before most people even heard the boom.

In December 2000, the site served up around 50 million listens from its collection of 800,000 MP3 songs posted by more than 125,000 artists and record labels.

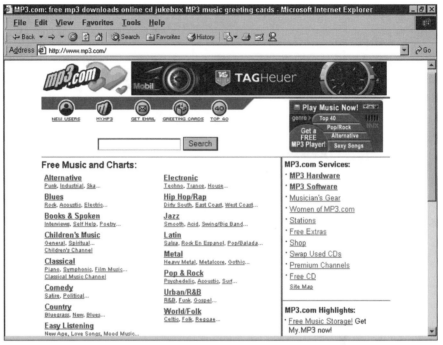

Figure 17-1: Although some users complain it's gotten too big, MP3.com still offers the most songs, best payment system for musicians, and best reviews of MP3 hardware and software.

You won't find illegally traded MP3s here; there's no room for them. Instead, you'll find professionally produced songs by bands around the world. Less than one percent of all bands makes it onto the charts. MP3.com lets you hear what the other 99 percent sound like.

If you're a musician, upload your songs to MP3.com for maximum exposure. (Plus, the site's Payback for Playback program gives away $1 million dollars each month, distributed to bands with the most activity on the site.)

But be prepared to market your stuff, as I describe in Chapter 16, or you'll get lost among the roar. Simply uploading your tunes isn't enough.

Listen.com

Site: www.listen.com

MP3.com offers 800,000 songs from 125,000 bands and labels. How do you know the difference between Melt-Banana and The Cross Movement? Or any of the other MP3 songs on the Net? Drop by Listen.com, shown in Figure 17-2, one of the largest directories to online MP3s.

Figure 17-2:
A one-stop
shop,
Listen.com
provides
links to
radio
stations,
MP3s and
videos, and
also offers
reviews of
MP3 tunes.

At Listen.com you'll find a description and short reviews of Japanese noise rockers Melt-Banana, as well as Christian Rap artist The Cross Movement. Listen's full-time staff of reviewers has cataloged more than 200,000 artists in 500 genres scattered across more than 1,200 Web sites.

Listen.com tells you where to find the MP3s posted legitimately by the Big Artists, as well as the up-and-comers that belong in tomorrow's CD collection.

It's a great first stop when you're looking for a particular song or type of music.

DailyMP3

Site: www.dailymp3.com

As the name says, DailyMP3, shown in Figure 17-3, updates its massive content daily, adding news, MP3 searches, price lists of MP3 players, and MP3 FAQs (known as answers to Frequently Asked Questions in the trade).

Add in the huge directory of players, encoders, rippers, playlist makers, plugins, and skins, and DailyMP3 becomes a site worthy of visiting on a . . . er . . . daily basis.

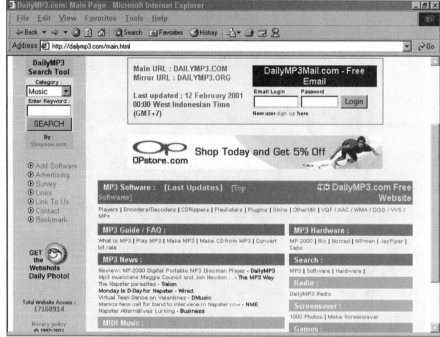

Figure 17-3:
DailyMP3 updates its content daily to include the latest bits of MP3 news, software, and hardware price lists.

Gnutella News

Site: www.gnutellanews.com

Napster constantly wobbles on its hotly debated legalities. But as it started to tip over, dozens of similar file-sharing programs sprouted up across the Internet to replace it. How can you keep track of them all? Which Napster clones are still alive?

And what's this about Gnutella? After all, Gnutella isn't a program — it's just a technology, as I explain in Chapter 5. Dozens of programs use Gnutella technology to swap files. Which program puts Gnutella's technology to work most efficiently?

Gnutella News, shown in Figure 17-4, does a fine job of keeping its anxious public informed. Although obviously warped toward the merits of Gnutella, a search of its News Headlines area often turns up tidbits about Aimster and other Napster alternatives that I describe in Chapter 5.

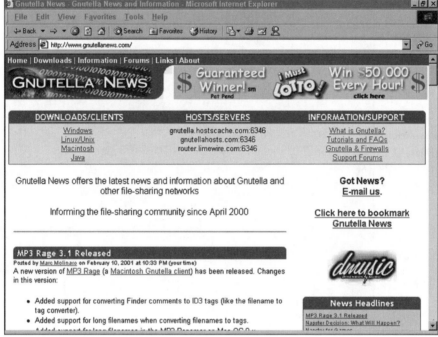

Figure 17-4:
Wary
Napster
fans should
keep an eye
on Gnutella
News,
which
tracks the
progress of
Gnutella
and other
file-sharing
sites.

AskMP3

Site: www.askmp3.com

You'll find oodles of information for both the newbie and the techie at the AskMP3.com site, shown in Figure 17-5. The site deals with all types of media compression, including video, DVD, audio, and streaming. If that stuff bores you, just click the word MP3 along the top of the screen to visit the MP3 section.

The site claims to have the best MP3 resources, and it's not kidding. It lets you search for the latest in MP3 news at the top MP3 sites, gives history and background on the MP3 format, answers FAQs, searches for MP3 songs, locates search engines and newsgroups, and lists both portable and software players.

If that's not enough, it details MP3 technical resources and test sites and discusses patents and licensing details.

In short, if you have a question about MP3, you'll find the answer — or a pointer to the answer — here.

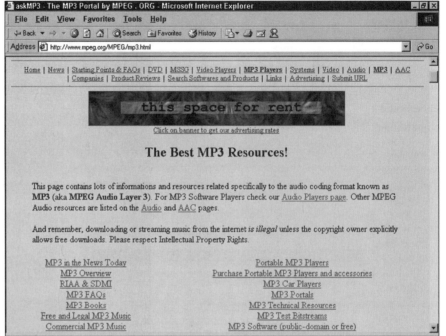

Figure 17-5: Although this site deals with all types of media compression, it boasts a huge depository of MP3 information.

CNET.com

Site: www.cnet.com

CNET.com, online since June 1995, quickly grew to become one of the Internet's largest sources of technology information. Today, it serves up Web sites in 25 countries and 16 languages.

But enough of the hype. CNET's Web site, shown in Figure 17-6, tucks a wealth of MP3 information inside its thousands of pages.

Head for the CNET Music Center to find information on how to play, organize, find, and create MP3s. Check out the information about MP3 radio stations, portable MP3 player ratings, and MP3 downloads, and you find enough information to stay busy for the afternoon. (And the next afternoon, too, because the content changes so quickly.)

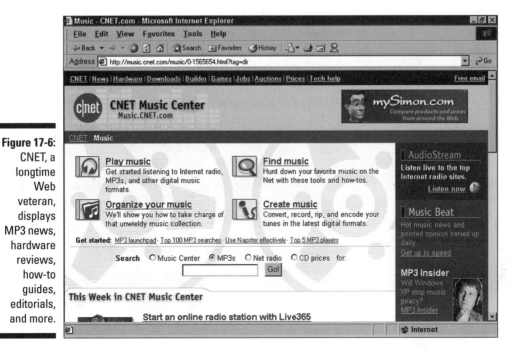

Figure 17-6:
CNET, a
longtime
Web
veteran,
displays
MP3 news,
hardware
reviews,
how-to
guides,
editorials,
and more.

Yahoo!

Site: `http://search.news.yahoo.com/news?p=mp3`

It's hard enough to keep track of who's hip in the music scene. When you combine the fast-paced music scene with the hustle-bustle in the technology world — MP3, in particular — it becomes increasingly difficult to keep track of the main players in MP3.

Who's got the best new MP3 player? Where's the best site? What's going on with this copyright stuff?

Wouldn't it be nice to have somebody filter the news and display all the articles relating to MP3? Yahoo! (`www.yahoo.com`), shown in Figure 17-7, is glad to do it for free.

When I typed the link `http://search.news.yahoo.com/news?p=mp3`, Yahoo! quickly displayed 1,045 news articles mentioning MP3. It searched through dozens of sources, including the Associated Press, CNET, ZDNet, Rolling Stone, the San Jose Mercury News, and many more.

Figure 17-7:
Yahoo!
filters the
news to
display any
articles that
mention
MP3.

If you *really* want to be on the cutting edge, choose the page's Alert Me option. That way Yahoo! e-mails you whenever new MP3-related articles appear in the news.

Note: If `http://search.news.yahoo.com/news?p=mp3` doesn't work because Yahoo! changed its site, go the long route: Head for `www.yahoo.com` and choose News from the crowded menu along the page's top. Type the word **MP3** into the Search News box and click the Search button to see MP3-related articles. (Click <u>Advanced</u> to customize where Yahoo! searches when digging up its news.)

Chapter 18

Ten Ways MP3 Helps Musicians

. . . .

In This Chapter

▶ Practicing with the Rio

▶ Recording quick music ideas on the Nomad

▶ Collaborating on song ideas

▶ Removing vocal tracks

▶ Adding sounds to live shows

▶ Exchanging rough production tracks

. . . .

MP3s bring a "get-rich-quick" promise to musicians, who post their songs on sites like MP3.com and wait for the talent agents to knock on their door.

But while waiting for that to happen, musicians can use these practical MP3 tips to hone their craft.

Practicing with a Portable MP3 Player

Like many musicians, guitar player Sean Cusiter of San Jose, California, doesn't read music. While listening to a song, he grabs a guitar and plays along until he figures out the sound. This works fine for some songs, but others aren't as easy to pick up on the fly.

For years, musicians taped songs they needed to learn. Then their fingers moved rapidly between the fretboard and the Rewind button until they either learned the guitar parts or wore out the tape.

When Sean bought his Rio portable MP3 player, he found a new way to learn songs.

"I discovered by accident that the Rio can record and loop sections — or entire songs — that have been recorded to MP3 format," Sean said. "I found that by pushing the Rio's A-B button once, and then pushing it again after a few seconds, that the Rio would replay the section of music over and over."

He picked up an acoustic guitar, pressed the Rio's A-B button, and within about five minutes he had nailed down two simple songs: Everlast's "What It's Like" and Sugar Ray's "Every Morning."

"I've probably added 30 or more songs to my list of songs that I can play," he said, "and have definitely improved on some of the ones that I already knew."

✔ To sneak in some extra listening, Sean also bought a CD-to-cassette-player adapter (which I cover in Chapter 5) for listening to his Rio's songs while driving.

✔ Although the Rio PMP300 has the A-B feature, many other portable MP3 players do not. Luckily, the Rio PMP300 is one of the least expensive players. In fact, it's often auctioned off on eBay (www.ebay.com) for about $75.

✔ Don't have a portable MP3 player? Check out the Winamp plug-in on this book's CD. It loops sections of songs to make them easier to learn — especially the guitar solos. Combine it with another Winamp plug-in, Pacemaker, to change the tempo and pitch, and you won't have to keep tuning your guitar to match the music.

Recording Quick Music Ideas on the Nomad

It happens to every musician. You're strumming a guitar at the beach or playing saxophone at a friend's house. One thing leads to another, and you stumble across a great riff or a catchy phrase to start a new song.

But how can you possibly remember it the next day? If you're near a telephone, you can play it onto your answering machine — but that's kind of awkward and draws stares in public places.

Instead, try turning on the Voice Record mode of your Creative Labs' Nomad or other record-capable portable MP3 player. Record your tune, and save it onto the machine.

Later, when you play it back, see if your musical idea still sounds workable or just sounded great at the time. . . .

Swapping Song Ideas with Band Members

Brian McLeod, a 30-year-old Miami musician, met another musician, Vancouver-resident Eric Schafer, on a mailing list for the Roland VS series digital audio workstations. One day, Eric posted an MP3 and QuickTime file so that members could compare the codec's quality.

"I sucked down his MP3," said Brian, "flew it into my recorder digitally, added my guitar tracks, and then mixed it back into the Macintosh."

Brian encoded the result and posted it back onto the Internet. Eric liked his work, and the two began a series of projects, swapping MP3 files and adding to each other's work. Although they've never met, they've worked on several projects over the Internet.

"It's an incredibly powerful thing to be able to send files back and forth like this to geographically opposite ends of the country," he said, "nearly instantly, and mostly for free. Federal Express costs 15 bucks and takes a day."

Even when shrunk down, MP3 files are usually too large to send through e-mail. Brian and Eric overcame this problem by using WhaleMail (www.whalemail.com). Brian uploads his MP3s to the WhaleMail site and addresses them to Eric. Eric subsequently receives an e-mail message about Brian's upload. Eric clicks a link in the e-mail and begins downloading Brian's files.

The duo has worked around another MP3 limitation: The fact that MP3s simply don't provide enough quality for professional-level songs.

"MP3s encoded at 128 Kbps sound pretty crappy compared to the source audio," Brian admits. "192 Kbps and above, though, can sound *very* good. I have done some 256 Kbps bitrate MP3s that are virtually indistinguishable from the original master."

"Guitars and keyboards tend to survive MP3 encoding fairly well intact. It's transient high-pitched sounds like a hi-hat or bells or such that get swishy from the encoding."

Removing Vocal Tracks

The DeFX Winamp plug-in, which you can find at www.winamp.com, removes vocal tracks from MP3 files. Guitar players can tune out David Lee Roth when trying to pick up some of Eddie's more manic shreds.

The sound editor performs its magic by cutting out the "middle" track, which is where the vocals usually lie. *Usually* is a key word, however. Although the software completely erases the vocals from some songs, other times it merely turns down the volume on everything.

Still, it's a valuable tool when it works. Lead singers can also use it to practice singing with a backing band. To find the DeFX plug-in, head to www.winamp.com, search for DeFX, and click Download when the page appears.

Adding Sounds to Live Shows

The Spice Girls give it a bad rap, but plenty of other bands perform live to prerecorded backing tracks. Got a bar gig playing a single guitar? Adding some sound effects to the show? For years, bands used prerecorded sounds to synchronize with the live performance. This was either expensive and delicate (Digital Audio Tape) or unreliable (the all-too-skippable CD-Rs).

MP3 brings a reliable, skip-proof format to bring on tour for live concerts. Plug a laptop into the soundboard and make sure that the sound guy isn't reading e-mail instead of playing back the required explosions.

No laptop? For almost two years now, this book's tech editor, Rich Barker, has successfully used a Rio to spice up his band's live performances.

Exchanging Rough Production Tracks

Derek Sivers sometimes works for Nike and VH1 to compose and record music for commercials. Because commissioned projects like this need several rounds of approval, Sivers used to FedEx the Digital Audio Tapes of his work to his clients' offices.

With MP3, he creates a rough mix of the music as he goes, encoding it into MP3 and e-mailing it to the company for feedback on the composition or even on the balance of the final mix.

For Sivers and many other freelance musicians, MP3 has reduced a week-long process into a day-long process, impressing deadline-driven corporations along the way.

Chapter 19

The Ten Most Useful MP3 Utilities

Soon after MP3 flooded the Internet, thousands of MP3-struck programmers began churning out MP3 utilities. (Chapter 6 covers the MP3 players; Chapter 9 handles the CD rippers; and Chapter 10 covers the encoders.)

This chapter describes some of the useful MP3 utilities you see listed under <u>Miscellaneous</u> at sites such as www.dailymp3.com or www.mp3.com.

Winamp Plug-ins

The popular MP3 player Winamp enthusiastically embraces modifications. The program creates a folder for user-created plug-ins — software tidbits that customize Winamp to give it more power. To use a plug-in from the Internet, download the file, unzip it (a process I describe in Appendix A), and, if the plug-in doesn't install itself, copy it into Winamp's plug-ins folder. (Chapter 6 describes Winamp and its plug-ins.)

Here are a few favorite Winamp plug-ins to start playing with; most are free or shareware. (Many are included on this book's CD.)

✔ **MuchFX2:** With hundreds of Winamp plug-ins to choose from, sometimes it's hard to choose just one. This plug-in lets you stack several Digital Signal Processing plug-ins. Add effects to your SHOUTcast radio station Webcasts, for instance. Fun!

✔ **Nullsoft Crossfading output plug-in:** Written by Justin Frankel, the driving force behind Winamp, this plug-in fades one song into the next when playing from a list. Smooth stuff.

✔ **WildTangent Visualizers:** Whereas most Winamp visualizers bring swirling colors to the screen, WildTangent's plug-ins fill the screen with dancers, games, and spaceships that move to the grooves.

✔ **WinAlarm:** Here's the perfect way to wake up to your favorite song playing on the home stereo. (Chapter 6 explains how to hook up your computer to your home stereo.) Give the program your wake-up time, and leave your computer and stereo turned on. Choose a song to set the mood you'll need that day.

To find the best plug-ins currently on the site, head to www.winamp.com, click the <u>Skins & Plug-ins</u> link, and choose <u>Five Star</u> beneath the Plug-ins category. That reveals the top-ranked plug-ins as rated by Winamp's reviewer.

Diamond Rio Enhancers

The Rio's earliest customers were computer-savvy folk who wanted *more* from their expensive new toy. Most wrote Rio software from necessity, curiosity, or laziness.

Here's a look at some of the best programs available for wringing the most out of your Rio, as well as where to find them:

✔ Dreaming of Brazil earns top name accolades, as well as top feature list for Rio programs. Brazil uploads or downloads *any* file to the Rio 300, adding file transporter to the Rio's musical workload. The program reformats SmartMedia cards to original specifications so that they'll work again in digital cameras. The program is at www.parkverbot.org/harald/download/. (And it works with Windows NT.)

✔ To replace the "stinky" RioPort software that came with the Rio 500, check out RIOFXP at http://duncanthrax.net/riofxp/. It uploads and downloads files and folders in batches, rearranges files, supports tags, lets you upload any file, and — best of all — it's free.

✔ For the best places to find Rio-related utilities, head to www.dailymp3.com and search under the Other Utils link for Portable MP3 Utilities. Last look showed more than a dozen.

ID Taggers and Renamers

MP3 files include more than music. They contain the artist's name, the song's title and album, the recording date, and other interesting tidbits. Known as the ID tag, this information comes lodged inside every MP3 file — *if* the MP3's creator took the time to fill out the form when making the file.

Unfortunately, many don't bother with this descriptive information. But there's a second problem. File names for the same song often differ drastically. The same Grateful Dead show might be stored as `dead110673.mp3` by one person and `Grateful_Dead_-_11_6_73.mp3` by another.

To solve these problems, programmers wrote two sets of programs — *renamers* and *ID taggers*. Renamers let you choose a standard setting for your file name: Artist — Song, for instance. When you select your MP3 file names, the program renames each file according to your own standards. (Or, it can grab information from the file's tag and use that for the file name.)

ID taggers also examine your selected files and compare the tag, if any, with the file name. It fills in any empty tags, grabbing the artist and song title from the file name. Or, if you've created the MP3s, you can fill in the tag yourself. By using renamers and ID taggers together (or using an all-in-one renamer/tagger), your MP3s stay neatly tagged and named.

Dozens of these programs exist; head for the software sections of `www.mp3.com` or `www.dailymp3.com` to find a current version of one you like.

Sound Enhancers

Many utilities help wring as much sound as possible from your MP3s. Sometimes sound-fixing is as easy as copying Winamp's MuchFX2 plug-in to your hard drive. Described earlier in this chapter, the MuchFX2 plug-in lets you combine several Winamp plug-ins to enhance the audio.

- ✔ **Normalizers:** Different CDs play back at different volumes — whatever sounded good to the record producers at that point. When you hear lots of MP3 songs shuffled around on a hard drive, the volume difference stands out. *Normalizing* software fixes the problem by maximizing your MP3 file's volume to a certain rate without distorting it. By normalizing the WAV files before burning them onto a CD, each song on the CD will play back at a constant volume.

- ✔ **MP3 Mixer/DJ Utilities:** DJ programs aren't only for people who bring their laptops to the dance clubs. Many programs help radio stations mix their songs. Some utilities let you blend the end of one song into the beginning of another. Others remove any silence between songs as they play, letting them run into each other. (Those work great for playing recordings of concerts that have been separated into several MP3 files.)

- ✔ **Pop Removers:** These programs repair the aural oddities left in WAV files ripped from CDs. To remove the pop or tick sounds from a WAV file, look for a Pop Remover program; some also clean up scratchy records. (Pop Removers are different than the Pop-Up Remover programs that remove annoying pop-up advertisements that appear on Web sites.)

WinZip

One of these days, you'll download a file that doesn't seem to do anything — it's a Zip file. Think of a Zip file as a box; it's usually a collection of files that have been compressed and stuck together with a program called WinZip.

WinZip can zip files into a single convenient file, and unzip the files back into their normal state.

People zip files for two reasons. First, if a program consists of several files, it's easier to download a single file and unzip it than to download each file separately. Second, zipped files are compressed, making them faster to download. Zipping MP3 files rarely saves space, however, because the files are already compressed in the first place. Instead, programs usually find themselves zipped before distribution.

WinZip is included on this book's bundled CD, and you'll find installation instructions in Appendix A.

Chapter 20

Ten Things to Know about Copyrights

- -

In This Chapter

▶ Top ten myths by the RIAA about online piracy

- -

The Recording Industry Association of America (the RIAA at www.riaa.com) represents companies and people in the recording industry. Based on its own interpretation of copyright laws, the RIAA considers these to be the top myths regarding online piracy.

You can find this list and more information at the RIAA SoundByting Web site (www.soundbyting.com).

The RIAA and the recording industry are against MP3s.

The RIAA has received comments from a number of Internet users who support the MP3 format and have suggested that the recording industry "be more receptive" to new technologies. Fact is, the recording industry is supportive of new technologies and practices, including electronic distribution over the Internet. Indeed, most of our member companies are already providing music on the Internet. They're offering promotional singles, Webcasts, or streaming-audio jukeboxes so that users can preview new recordings. We just know there is a difference between "*free*" music that is deliberately given away and "*stolen*" music that is put online without authorization. With users like you asking for more music via the Net, this trend — of companies offering their copyrighted recordings online — will only increase.

However, whether or not people use the MP3 format is not really the issue. MP3 is only a compression technology. It is what you do with it that matters. Whether music is encoded in the MP3 format or some other format doesn't matter if the sound files are not authorized by the artist or record company.

The recording industry is certainly embracing technology, not running away from it. If you would like to learn more about what RIAA members are doing to further the electronic distribution of sound recordings via the Internet, check out www.riaa.com/audio-intro.cfm.

The goal of SoundByting is to explain the legal issues related with the use of recorded music online. Unfortunately, the reality is that many of the MP3 sites on the Internet are unauthorized. Like you, we hope this will change.

If a Web site doesn't display a copyright notice for the music, the music isn't copyrighted, and it's okay to download.

In the United States, almost every work created privately and originally after March 1, 1989, is copyrighted and protected whether or not it has a notice.

An Internet site operator can offer music for download from his or her site, without permission from the copyright owners, so long as one or more of the following disclaimers are posted to the site:

- ✔ If you download a sound file, you must delete it from your hard drive in 24 hours.

- ✔ You must already own these CDs to legally download the sound files.

- ✔ This site is for promotional purposes only.

- ✔ Please support the artist and buy the CD.

It doesn't matter how many disclaimers you put on a site. If you reproduce, offer to distribute, and/or distribute full-length sound recordings without a license, you are violating copyright law.

Moving my unauthorized music site to a server outside the United States would make it legal.

First, U.S. law applies when the uploading and downloading takes place in the United States, even if the server is physically located in another country. Second, the copyright laws of foreign countries are, in many cases, similar to those in the United States.

So I offer full-length sound recordings for download without the copyright owners' permission. The "Fair Use" doctrine and the "First Amendment" protect me.

Before we explain why the "fair use" doctrine may not protect you in this case, let's explain what "fair use" is. "Fair use" is a principle under federal copyright law that allows people to reproduce, distribute, adapt, display and/or perform copyrighted works under certain circumstances, without explicit authorization from the copyright owner. "Fair use" is actually a defense that can be raised in an infringement lawsuit. When determining whether a particular use is a "fair use," a court will typically look to:

- ✔ The nature of the use (i.e., was it for commercial purposes or not)

- ✔ The length of the excerpt (i.e., how much of the whole work; does the excerpt use the most distinctive part)

✔ How distinctive the original work is

✔ How the use will impact the market for the original work

Short excerpts for educational purposes or for the purpose of criticism or comment may be considered "fair uses," however, there is no set formula for determining at the outset whether your use will qualify for this defense. Though some uses may be "fair," uploading and downloading full-length recordings without permission almost certainly is not "fair use."

As for the First Amendment to the U.S. Constitution, it does protect freedom of speech and religion. This does not include the right to infringe on copyright. As a matter of fact, copyright itself was written into the Constitution before the Framers ever even got to the first ten amendments.

Though it may be illegal to operate a site with unauthorized sound files, it's okay to have a site that links to a number of unauthorized files. So long as the actual files aren't on my server, it's legal.

Liability for copyright infringement is not necessarily limited to the persons or entities who created (or encoded) the infringing sound file. In addition to being directly liable for infringing conduct occurring via the site, a linking site may be contributorily or vicariously liable for facilitating copyright infringement occurring at the sites to which it links.

Contributory liability may be imposed where an entity knowingly and materially contributes to the infringing activity. In the case of a linking site, we believe that providing direct access to infringing works would constitute material contribution to infringing activity.

Vicarious liability may be imposed where an entity has the right and ability to control the activities of the direct infringer and also receives a financial benefit from the infringing activities. Liability may be imposed even if the entity is unaware of the infringing activities. In the case of a linking site, we believe that providing direct access to infringing works may show a right and ability to control the activities of the direct infringer and that receiving revenue from banner ads may be evidence of a financial benefit.

If I just download sound recordings from an illicit music site or if I make sound files on my computer from my CDs, it's just a copy for personal use and not a violation.

Personal use copying was considered by Congress when it enacted the Audio Home Recording Act of 1992 (AHRA). The AHRA was a legislative compromise to deal with certain, specifically defined, categories of digital audio copying. Attempting to balance the various competing interests, among other things, the AHRA provides that manufacturers of covered devices must (1) register with the Copyright Office; (2) pay a statutory royalty on each device and piece of media sold; and (3) implement what is known as a serial copyright management system (or SCMS), which prevents all but first generation copies. In exchange for this, the manufacturers of the devices, which might have otherwise found themselves subject to liability for contributory copyright infringement (among other things), received a statutory immunity from suit.

Consumers also received something. As long as the copying is done for non-commercial use, the AHRA gives consumers immunity from suit for all analog music copying, and for digital music copying with AHRA covered devices. It is important to note that the AHRA does not say that such copying is lawful; it simply provides immunity from suit.

The difference between copying to cassette (for instance) as opposed to a computer hard drive is that audio cassette players (as well as Minidisc and DAT players) are devices covered by the AHRA, and a computer is not. The specific reasons are technical but boil down to this: The AHRA covers devices that are designed or marketed for the primary purpose of making digital musical recordings. Multipurpose devices, such as a general computer or a CD-R drive, are not covered by the AHRA. This means that they do not pay royalties or incorporate SCMS protections. It also means that neither the devices nor the consumers who use them receive immunity from suit for copyright infringement.

If I upload music from a CD that I own, I'm not violating copyright law.

Just because you own the CD doesn't mean you "own the music." You can't put full-length sound recordings on the Internet for others to download without permission of the copyright owners of the sound recording and the musical composition.

If I don't charge people for downloading music from my site, the activity is legal.

If you don't hold the copyright, you can't sell or even give away unauthorized copies of the sound recording. In addition, the No Electronic Theft ("NET") Act, which amended Section 506 of the Copyright Act, clarified that even if a site barters or trades in infringing materials or doesn't charge or otherwise make a profit, there still may be criminal liability.

Uploading music on the Internet doesn't hurt anybody. In fact, it's promotional and free advertising.

As a matter of fact, that's also "Myth No. 9" of Brad Templeton's Ten Big Myths About Copyright. He states, "It's up to the owner to decide if they want the free ads or not. If they want them, they will be sure to contact you. Don't rationalize whether it hurts the owner or not, *ask* them. Usually that's not too hard to do. Time past, ClariNet published the very funny Dave Barry column to a large and appreciative Usenet audience for a fee. But some person didn't ask, forwarded it to a mailing list, got caught, and the newspaper chain that employs Dave Barry pulled the column from the Net, . . . [ticking] off everybody who enjoyed it. Even if you can't think of how the author or owner gets hurt, think about the fact that piracy on the Net hurts everybody who wants a chance to use this wonderful new technology to do more than read other people's flamewars."

Chapter 21

(Almost) Ten Rumors about MP3

*F*or all practical purposes, MP3 lives on the Internet. That's where you find MP3 players, file-search engines, MP3 utilities, and the songs themselves.

Because rumors always spread along the Internet like ants after cheeseballs, MP3 technology is rife with rumors. What's true and what's false? This chapter holds the answers.

The Rio Makes Free Long-Distance Calls

True. You can make long-distance phone calls from the Rio, and they're free. By playing back the sound of coins dropping into public telephones, the Rio fools the phone into thinking you really paid for the call. A device that does this is called a "redbox" in the hacker's trade.

This Rio rumor is nowhere near unconditionally true, however, and here's why:

✔ It's illegal. Possession of a redbox is a felony in the United States.

✔ Any portable MP3 player can do it, not just the Rio.

✔ The trick only works on older public phones. The newer phones recognize the trickery and aren't fooled.

✔ You need to fiddle with a sound editor to create the precise "beep beep" tones heard when coins slide down the chute.

✔ Headphones aren't up to the task. You need to attach a speaker to the Rio or other MP3 player, making your acts pretty obvious in a public place.

✔ Finally, when you're caught holding a Rio with a speaker and the contraband tones, it's difficult to deny your intentions to the FBI. (By the way, a Palm Pilot can do the same thing, and it comes with a built-in speaker.)

The SDMI Group Is Creating Copy Protection to Wipe Out MP3s

False. The recording industry, upset over the growing power of MP3, joined with several technology companies to create the secret Secure Digital Music Initiative (SDMI). The SDMI Web site (`www.sdmi.org`) remained closed to the public while the group held its first batch of meetings. It eventually opened its cyberdoors last year.

The SDMI adopted an ARIS Technologies digital watermark to be embedded in all newly recorded music. Most portable MP3 players released by the end of the year 2000 were to be SDMI-compliant and able to recognize the digital watermark.

So, what does all this stuff mean? It means the record industry wants to embed secret, inaudible codes into its recorded music. By examining the digital codes in any piece of music, the record industry can tell which master the CD was made from, making it easier to catch the counterfeits.

What does it all *really* mean? Well, not much. First, the SDMI missed its deadline to create the technology, so the MP3 players released for the 2000 Christmas holiday season didn't use the watermark. Second, the group hasn't created an un-breakable code to thwart piracy. Third, the group's executive director recently resigned, leaving the organization without a leader. Finally, the group's members are so diverse, they're having a difficult time agreeing on anything substantial.

Even if they do create a watermark system that works on MP3 files, it will work only on newly released songs. Just about every song released before the year 2000 will still play fine.

To keep abreast of SDMI achievements — or lack of them — head to `www.wired.com` and search for SDMI.

Some Mainstream Artists Let You Record Their Concerts and Trade MP3s

True. Although many artists forbid the taping of their live shows, many not only allow it, they help the fans place the microphones. They let fans trade tapes or MP3s of their live shows, and they don't mind if the MP3s of the live shows are posted on the Internet.

For the best list of the MP3-friendly bands, check out the mammoth Bands That Allow Taping Web site (`www.enteract.com/~wagner/btat/`), maintained by Kurt Kemp and Mike Wagner.

The site lists dozens of bands and their policies. Some allow audio taping, others allow videotaping, and some invite fans to plug into the soundboard to make copies. In some cases, the site lists the name of the soundman for on-site information.

Some of the bands listed as allowing taping of concerts include the Allman Brothers Band, Arlo Guthrie, The Black Crowes, The Dave Matthews Band, Dire Straits, Henry Rollins, Jefferson Starship, Little Feat, Los Lobos, Mike Keneally, and dozens of bands that are too young and hip for me to recognize.

Before lugging your gear to the show, however, keep these things in mind:

✔ Just because a band allows fans to tape and trade its concerts doesn't mean that it allows people to make MP3s of its released CDs and trade them — or sell them, especially. These guys have to make a living somehow.

✔ Don't try to bring a microphone stand unless the list says it's acceptable. And even then, try to check with the venue beforehand to see whether it's allowed.

✔ Finally, even though a band may allow taping, the venue may not be as friendly. When you tell the security guard you're allowed to bring in your reel-to-reel, you may be greeted with a blank stare. Your best bet is to buy a portable DAT recorder and carry it in discreetly.

✔ A friend of mine hid her DAT recorder under her belt, ran the microphone wires beneath her shirt above her back, and hid the tiny microphones in her hair, one microphone above each ear. Then, to keep the background crowd noise to a minimum, she glared at anybody who came within five feet.

Winamp Has Two Hidden "Easter Eggs"

True. By clicking certain areas in the program, you can see the program's logo pop up. Earlier versions showed the programmer's face and cat. These digital signatures left by the programmer are often called *Easter Eggs.* Turn to Chapter 6 to see which keys to press, and in which order.

MP3 Files Record in CD Quality

False. MP3 files are compressed versions of audio files. To compress the files, MP3 technology removes some of the information from the file — the upper and lower frequencies.

It filters out other sounds found in "CD-quality" audio. Although many of these sounds aren't audible to the human ear, they're still missing from the MP3 version of the song.

So, when you see MP3 touted as "CD-quality" sound, you know that it's just not true. It should always be described as "near CD-quality" sound.

Proprietary Audio Files from SDMI, Microsoft, and Liquid Audio Are Secure

False. The proprietary systems proposed by the SDMI and currently used by Microsoft and Liquid Audio are meant to keep users from copying the files. Although designed to keep people from making illegal copies of the songs, these formats also keep people from making legal copies of songs they've purchased.

Frustrated programmers quickly put their keys to the keyboards, and all the proprietary formats released so far have been defeated by programmers. For example, on the same day Microsoft released its copy-protected MS Audio 4 technology, an anonymous programmer announced a release of another program: One that removes the security from MS Audio files. The program takes Microsoft's registered WMA files and outputs them as WAV files. The program then re-encodes the WAV files into an unprotected WMA file.

Two other programs, AudioJacker and Total Recorder, defeat copy-protection schemes from Liquid Audio, the SDMI, and a2B music. Both programs work similarly: They record any sound generated by another computer program and save it as a WAV file. The WAV file can then be converted to an MP3 file.

The point? The battle will be left up to the courts as to whether these programs can legally convert protected MP3s, as long as the conversion is for noncommercial and personal use. After all, the major movie studios tried to declare VCRs illegal because they could be used to make illegal copies of tapes. But in 1984, the U.S. Supreme Court legalized VCRs because the devices had legitimate, legal uses.

Actually, the movie industry is now pleased at the court's decision: It's now making huge profits by releasing movies on videotape.

Chapter 22

Ten Quick Ways to Use MP3

In This Chapter

▶ How do I convert MP3s so that they play on my home stereo?

▶ How do I find out my IP Address?

▶ How do I edit an MP3 file?

▶ How do I convert albums, WAV files, or speech into MP3s?

▶ How many of my CDs will fit in 10GB of hard drive space?

▶ How do I separate my recorded concert into several MP3s?

▶ How can I convert RealAudio or streamed audio into an MP3 file?

*W*hile I researched this book, the same questions came up over and over. I've given them long, detailed answers throughout this book. But who wants to read something long and detailed when you're just trying to copy your Bjork MP3s onto a CD that you can play in your car's CD player?

Bookmark this chapter because it contains the short and dirty answers to the most frequently asked questions about MP3s.

How Do I Convert MP3s so That They Play on My Home Stereo?

You can fill a CD with hundreds of MP3s, but they won't play on your average home stereo. Unfortunately, home stereos prefer a different music format that only fits about a dozen songs onto the CD. So, here's how to convert the MP3s to the right format and burn them onto a CD — all in one step:

1. **Load MusicMatch from this book's CD, choose File from the top menu, and choose Create CD From Playlist. When the window appears, choose the CDs you want to load onto your CD, and press the Create CD button.**

   • MusicMatch automatically calculates how much space you have left on the CD, letting you juggle songs until you fill the CD.

   • You can find out more about MusicMatch in Chapter 11.

How Do I Find Out My IP Address?

If you ever want to Webcast an Internet radio station, you'll eventually come across The Big Question: What's your IP Address? To find out, follow these steps:

1. **Click the Start button.**

2. **Choose the Run option.**

3. **Type** winipcfg **in the Open box and click OK.**

A technically challenging box appears, listing your IP Address in the IP Address box.

Have a Mac? Open the TCP/IP control panel, and the IP Address will be hiding in there.

How Do I Edit an MP3 File?

You can edit an MP3 file in a number of ways, but the best way is to edit the file while it's still in MP3 form.

Editors such as MP3Trim (`www.logiccell.com/~mp3trim/`) cut off parts of MP3 files that you'd like to discard — great for editing long concert recordings into individual songs. It also changes the volume and fade-in/outs of MP3s, and best yet, it's free.

For more vigorous editing, though, you need to convert the MP3 to a WAV file and edit from there by using Cool Edit, which you can find on this book's CD.

To convert an MP3 into a WAV file, follow these steps:

1. **Load MusicMatch and choose Convert from the File menu.**

2. **Select your MP3 file and select WAV as the Destination Date type.**

3. **Click the Start button.**

The problem? An MP3 file, by nature of its compression, has lost some sound quality. By converting it to WAV and recompressing it to MP3, you lose even more sound quality. Avoid editing this way whenever possible.

How Do I Separate My Recorded Concert into Several MP3s?

If your concert is one long WAV file, use Cool Edit (included on this book's CD) to separate the songs. When you load the WAV file into Cool Edit, you'll notice changes in the waveform as the songs change. Edit out each song, and encode the resulting WAV file into an MP3.

If your concert is one long MP3 file, check out the MP3 editors at www. mp3machine.com/win/EDITORS/. At least one of them should do the trick.

As a last resort, convert the entire show to a WAV file with MusicMatch, and then use Cool Edit to separate the songs. Finally, use MusicMatch to convert the songs back into MP3s.

How Do I Convert Albums, WAV Files, or Speech into MP3s?

Start by converting the albums or speech into WAV files: Hook up a microphone or run cables to your sound card's MIC or Line In jacks and record the incoming sound, be it from the album or voice.

After you record the sounds as WAV files, use MusicMatch to convert the WAV files as MP3 files using the steps in the previous section.

I've filled Chapter 11 with more detailed information.

When Converted to MP3, How Many CDs Fit in 10GB of Hard Drive Space?

I can average about 230 MP3s in 1GB of hard drive space, so 10GB will hold about 2,300 MP3s. If your CDs average 11 songs, that's 209 CDs.

Of course, your mileage may vary.

How Can I Convert RealAudio or Streamed Audio into an MP3 File?

It's difficult to convert RealAudio or streamed audio for a reason: You're not supposed to be able to convert these types of files for legal and copyright reasons. RealAudio is a proprietary format, and streamed audio isn't designed to be saved.

It isn't a big deal, though, because both formats are designed for easy, real-time transport across the Internet, not high fidelity.

If you're dead set on converting these files, though, head for www. highcriteria.com and check out Total Recorder. It captures any audio aimed at your sound card and saves it to your hard drive.

Part VI

Appendixes

The 5th Wave   By Rich Tennant

"Get the cannon ready kids! Your Mom's almost got the '1812 Overture' downloaded!"

In this part . . .

By now, you've probably digested most of this book. Therefore, it's time to add a little tidbit to the end of the digestive tract: the appendixes.

You've probably noticed the CD bound inside the back cover of this book. Appendix A, dubbed the special "About the CD" appendix, describes all the cool MP3 players, encoders, and other programs included on the CD (as well as installation instructions, where appropriate). Mac user? Linux user? You're not left out; the disc includes programs for both those platforms.

The CD appendix also describes bunches of freebie MP3 songs for listening, as well as information about the bands creating them. You'll find information about the latest versions of Web browsers — Netscape and Internet Explorer — and a special HTML file. Give this file a click to open it with your Web browser, and you'll have quick and easy access to every Web page that I mention in this book.

And if any technical terms left you burping, head for the glossary in Appendix B, where you'll find explanations for all the book's multi-syllabic terms and acronyms.

Appendix A

About the CD

● ●

*H*ere is some of what you get on the *MP3 For Dummies,* 2nd Edition, CD-ROM:

- ✔ Internet Explorer, Commercial version for browsing the Web
- ✔ Netscape Communicator, Commercial version for browsing the Web
- ✔ WinZip, shareware version for unzipping files ending in the letters ZIP
- ✔ MP3 players for Windows, Linux, Macintosh, and Windows CE
- ✔ Sample MP3 songs
- ✔ Winamp skins and plug-ins
- ✔ FreeAgent, freeware version for accessing newsgroups
- ✔ CuteFTP, shareware version for accessing FTP sites
- ✔ Cool Edit 2000, shareware version for editing audio

System Requirements

Make sure that your computer meets the minimum system requirements detailed in the following list (If your computer doesn't match up to most of these requirements, you may have problems when using the contents of the CD.):

- ✔ A PC with a fast Pentium processor, or a Mac OS computer with a 68040 or faster processor.
- ✔ Microsoft Windows 98 or later, or Mac OS system software 7.6 or later.
- ✔ At least 16MB of total RAM installed on your computer. For best performance, I recommend at least 32MB of RAM installed.
- ✔ At least 300MB of hard drive space available to install all the software from this CD. (You'll need less space if you don't install every program.)
- ✔ A CD-ROM drive — double-speed (2x) or faster.

✔ A sound card for PCs. (Mac OS computers have built-in sound support.)

✔ A monitor capable of displaying at least 256 colors or grayscale.

✔ A modem with a speed of at least 28,800 bps.

If you need more information on the basics, check out *PCs For Dummies,* 7th Edition, by Dan Gookin; *Macs For Dummies,* 7th Edition, by David Pogue; *The iMac For Dummies,* 2nd Edition, by David Pogue; *Windows 98 For Dummies,* 2nd Edition, or *Microsoft Windows Me Millenium Edition For Dummies* both by Andy Rathbone (all published by IDG Books Worldwide, Inc.).

Using the CD with Microsoft Windows

To install items from the CD to your hard drive, follow these steps:

1. **Insert the CD into your computer's CD-ROM drive.**

2. **Click the Start button and choose Run from the menu.**

3. **In the dialog box that appears, type** d:\start.htm.

   Replace *d* with the proper drive letter for your CD-ROM if it uses a different letter. (If you don't know the letter, double-click the My Computer icon on your desktop and see what letter is listed for your CD-ROM drive.)

   Your browser opens, and the license agreement appears. If you don't have a browser, Microsoft Internet Explorer and Netscape Communicator are included on the CD.

4. **Read through the license agreement, nod your head, and click the Accept button if you want to use the CD.**

   After you click Accept, you're taken to the Main menu. This is where you can browse through the contents of the CD.

5. **To navigate within the interface, click any topic of interest to take you to an explanation of the files on the CD and how to use or install them.**

6. **To install software from the CD, simply click the software name.**

   You'll see two options: to run or open the file from the current location or to save the file to your hard drive. Choose to run or open the file from its current location, and the installation procedure continues. When you finish using the interface, close your browser as usual.

Feel free to keep the CD inside your CD-ROM drive and play its MP3 files from there. The songs play from the CD just as well as they do from your hard drive. When you find your favorites, feel free to copy them to your hard drive, portable MP3 player, or anyplace else you want.

Using the CD with Mac OS

To install the items from the CD to your hard drive, follow these steps:

1. Insert the CD into your computer's CD-ROM drive.

In a moment, an icon representing the CD you just inserted appears on your Mac desktop. Chances are, the icon looks like a CD-ROM.

2. Double-click the CD icon to show the CD's contents.

3. Double-click `start.htm` **to open your browser and display the license agreement.**

If your browser doesn't open automatically, open it as you normally would by choosing File⇨Open File (in Internet Explorer) or File⇨Open⇨ Location in Netscape (in Netscape Communicator) and select *MP3 For Dummies*. The license agreement appears.

4. Read through the license agreement, nod your head, and click the Accept button if you want to use the CD.

After you click Accept, you're taken to the Main menu. This is where you can browse through the contents of the CD.

5. To navigate within the interface, click any topic of interest to take you to an explanation of the files on the CD and how to use or install them.

6. To install software from the CD, simply click the software name.

You'll see two options: to run or open the file from the current location or to save the file to your hard drive. Choose to run or open the file from its current location, and the installation procedure continues. When you finish using the interface, close your browser as usual.

Using the CD with Linux

The following sections show how to read the CD's directory in Linux.

Reading the directory with Linux

Before grabbing the programs off the CD, you need to see them on the disc. Follow these steps to read the disc's directory.

1. **Insert the CD into your computer's CD-ROM drive.**

   Give your computer a moment to take a look at the CD.

2. **When the light on your CD-ROM drive goes out, go to the command prompt and type the following:**

   ```
   mount -t iso9660 /dev/cdrom /mnt/cdrom
   ```

   Then type:

   ```
   cd /mnt/cdrom
   ```

3. **Type 'ls' to list the files in the CD's contents.**

   The 'ls' command will list the contents of the CD for you.

Viewing the disc's information and using the files

Here's how to view the disc's information and use the files.

1. **To view the licenses in their respective directories, type** vi **and the file name of the license (either** gpl.txt **or** IDG_EULA.txt**).**

   This file contains the end-user license that you agree to by using the CD.

   In Linux, the most convenient way to read this file is to use the vi editor.

   When you're done reading the license, exit the program by typing **'Esc'** and then typing **:q!**.

2. **Use the 'cp' command to copy the program you want to run from the** /cdrom **directory to where you want to store it.**

   For example, if you want to copy 'mon' from /cdrom to your /etc directory, type the following:

   ```
   cp mon /etc
   ```

3. **Use the 'cd' command to change directories to the directory you placed the program.**

   For example, if 'mon' is in the /etc directory, type the following to get to the /etc directory:

   ```
   cd /etc
   ```

4. **Type the name of the program you want to run and press Enter if you want to run it.**

> *Note:* On some systems, Linux may claim that it can't find the program. If it acts this way, it's just being fussy. Type a period and a slash in front of the program that you want to start and press Enter. This tells Linux that you want this specific program, right in the current directory.

What You'll Find on the CD

The following sections are arranged by category and provide a summary of the software and other goodies you'll find on the CD. If you need help with installing the items provided on the CD, refer to the installation instructions in the preceding section.

Shareware programs are fully functional, free, trial versions of copyrighted programs. If you like particular programs, register with their authors for a nominal fee and receive licenses, enhanced versions, and technical support. *Freeware programs* are free, copyrighted games, applications, and utilities. You can copy them to as many PCs as you like — for free — but they offer no technical support. *GNU software* is governed by its own license, which is included inside the folder of the GNU software. There are no restrictions on distribution of GNU software. See the GNU license for more details. *Trial, demo,* or *evaluation* versions of software are usually limited either by time or functionality (such as not letting you save a project after you create it).

Web browsers

Internet Explorer, from Microsoft.

For Mac and Windows. *Commercial product.* This is the popular, powerful Web browser packed with all the latest features for today's cybertravels. It's also free, which makes it a true bargain. This program is updated frequently, so check out the Microsoft Web site at `www.microsoft.com`.

Netscape Communicator, from Netscape.

For Windows, Mac, and Linux. *Commercial version.* This free suite of programs includes a full-featured browser (Navigator), e-mail program (Messenger), and an HTML editor (Composer). This program is updated frequently, so be sure to check out `www.home.netscape.com`.

WinZip: A handy tool for Windows

For Windows. *Shareware.* WinZip, from Nico Mak Computing, is an invaluable file compression and decompression Windows shareware utility. Many files that you find on the Internet are compressed, or shrunken, in size via special programming tricks, both to save storage space and to cut down on the amount of time they require to be downloaded. You may also occasionally receive compressed files (ZIP files) as e-mail attachments. After you have a compressed file on your hard drive, you can use WinZip to decompress it and make it useable again. For more information, check out www.winzip.com.

MP3 players and tools

This CD includes MP3 players for several types of computers and operating systems. Make sure that you use the correct one for your particular computer setup, or the player won't work.

Audion, by Panic Software.

For Mac. *Demo.* Everything works in this trial version for the first 15 days. After 15 days, everything still works — but for only 30 minutes at a time. Audion plays CDs, MP3s, and streaming network audio. It also encodes, edits, and mixes your audio, as well as manages your music collection. Audio 2 requires Mac OS 8.1 or later, Power Macintosh with a 604 processor; a G3 or higher is recommended. For more information or to update to the full version, visit www.panic.com/.

Hum, from UtopiaSoft.

For Windows CE. *Shareware.* Take a PocketPC out of the box, and it can start playing MP3 files. That's not true of the older Windows CE palmtops and handhelds, though. But when you install this copy of Hum and plug in your earphones, your old Windows CE computer can play your favorite tunes.

Like Nullsoft Winamp, Hum supports skins. Hum sounds best on the Casio Cassiopeia E-100 series. To license your copy, load Hum, choose Help from the program's menu, select License Info, and enter the following key *exactly,* including hyphens:

KAGI-32631465-7A28A74B86B75F5E

For the latest information, head to www.utopiasoft.com.

MusicMatch Jukebox, from MusicMatch

For Windows, Mac, and Linux. *Shareware.* MusicMatch gets complete coverage in Chapter 11. It's an "everything" system that creates, plays, and categorizes your MP3s. To create MP3s, put a music CD into your CD-ROM drive, select the tracks you want to record, and click Start.

Register the program for $29 to receive the enhanced version that turns CDs into MP3s 25 percent faster, burns CDs up to 12 times faster, creates and prints CD covers for your jewel cases, and more. Check out www.musicmatch. com for more information.

SoundJam MP, by Casady & Greene.

For Mac. *Shareware.* SoundJam MP is the first full-featured, all-in-one, MP3 player and encoder for the Macintosh. SoundJam MP converts music quickly into high-quality MP3s from CD, AIFF, QuickTime, and WAV formats. SoundJam requires Mac OS 8.1 or later, Power Macintosh with a 603 processor at 100 MHz or faster; a G3 is recommended.

This copy is a seven-day trial; for more information or to update to the full version, check out .

Winamp, by Nullsoft, Inc.

For Windows. *Freeware.* If you haven't installed Winamp on your Windows computer, install this copy, and quickly. One of the first high-fidelity MP3 players, Winamp is fast, highly configurable, and supports MP3, CD, WMA, Audiosoft, Mjuice, MOD, WAV, and other audio formats. It also accommodates feature adding "plug-ins" and decorative skins.

If you're an arty type, slip some decorative software called "skins" onto Winamp to change its appearance. Special software (plug-ins) changes the Winamp audio and visual effects. (This CD also contains some of the most useful skins and plug-ins.) Check out www.winamp.com for more information.

Xaudio

For Linux. *Freeware.* Xaudio creates MP3 decoders for a wide variety of platforms. When a decoder is properly installed, it plays MP3 files.

This particular decoder runs on Linux. For more information, head to www. xaudio.com/downloads/#linux.

For more basic Linux information, you can also check out *Red Hat Linux For Dummies,* 3rd Edition, by Jon 'Maddog' Hall and Paul Sery.

Sound utilities

Cool Edit 2000, from Syntrillium Software Corp.

For Windows. *Shareware.* Newcomers to audio recording might want to start with Cool Edit 2000. It records through your sound card from a microphone, CD player, or other source. It allows editing of audio with professional digital tools and adds sound effects. This unregistered version reads and writes MP3s, but only saves one minute of the audio file when converting to MP3. Once registered for $69, that limitation is removed. Cool Edit 2000 contains five additional plug-in options not available in the Pro product.

Cool Edit Pro, from Syntrillium Software Corp.

For Windows. *Demo.* A full-featured program for audio professionals, Cool Edit Pro mixes up to 64 tracks together, using just about any sound card. Cool Edit Pro costs $399 plus shipping. This demo is fully functional with the following exceptions: It has a 30-minute time limit per session, it doesn't save any work nor offer Clipboard support, there's no RealAudio support, and it doesn't integrate with Cakewalk.

CuteFTP, from GlobalSCAPE, Inc.

For Windows. *Shareware.* CuteFTP makes it easy to upload and download files from FTP sites and servers. This version works for 30 days, after which time you must register it for $39.95. For more information, visit the company's Web site at www.globalscape.com.

FreeAgent, from Forte, Inc.

For Windows. *Freeware.* Free newsgroup reader, updated for Y2K. With FreeAgent, it's easy to keep track of conversations on the Usenet newsgroups, as well as upload and download binary files. For more information, head to the company's Web site at www.forteinc.com.

Winamp skins and plug-ins

Winamp, the popular and ultra-configurable Windows MP3 player included on this CD, allows users to create "skins" and "plug-ins." Skins change the look and feel of Winamp, allowing users to drape the program in wild colors, shapes, and textures. Plug-ins change how Winamp sounds or behaves.

Table A-1 shows the skins contained on this CD. Table A-2 shows the plug-ins.

Table A-1		Winamp Skins on the CD	
Creator	*Skin Name*	*Description*	*Comments*
Claire Williams	Immortals II	Cool science-fiction/ mechanical/ organic skin packs it all in `www. claire. immortals.co.uk/`	
Silvio Dell'Acqua	Mediterraneo	Fantastic Mediterranean artistry theme	Great piece of work by Italian Silvio Dell'Acqua
John Ambro	FlareTech AcidAmp	Swirls, muted colors, and hot buttons John Ambro, inspired by the music of his friend DJ FlareTech, created this skin	
David Tryse	42	Ultra modern, with incredible use of transparency	
Edward Sadler	Reptalien V1, version 1.2	Way cool textured skin of purple alien flesh	
Javier Ontiveros	"Looking For Myself"	Darkly surreal and abstract `http:// orbita.starmedia. com/~bloodlesskins/ index.html`	
Kauko Mikkonen	Moonsilver	Steel blue and dark, it looks like a winking robot	
Kauko Mikkonen	Sepish	Stylish, curved, and transparent as all get out	
Kevin Bonzerelli	Yellow Submarine, version 1	Nothing is real — except for these fantastic colors and shapes	
Masayoshi Nishiura	Salamander II	Ouch! Hot and grating, yet smooth and cool `http://www. ne.jp/ asahi/ma-kun/ ore/ e-index.html`	

Table A-2	Winamp Plug-ins on the CD		
Creator	*Plug-in Name*	*Description*	*Comments*
Brian Stuart	WinAlarm (Shareware)	Wake up or fall asleep to Winamp as it plays your favorite tunes. Supports multiple alarms and can shutdown the computer at the end of the alarm.	WinAlarm is shareware; register it for $10. For more information, visit the creator's Web site at `www.magma.ca/ ~bstuart/index. html`.
Curtis Mathews	Loop Master Musician's Tool Plugin (Freeware)	A great tool for musicians learning tunes and licks, this plug-in lets you select start and stop points within a tune and then loop between the points.	
Ianier Munoz	Chronotron (Freeware)	Changes the tempo of the music without changing the pitch.	`www.gmixon.com`
M. Dallongeville	Space	Watch nebulas burst across the screen in this stellar visualization.	`www.multimania. com/scalpel`
Marc S. Ressi	MuchFX2	Have too many favorite plug-ins? Then use this plug-in to "stack" them so they run simultaneously.	`www.ressl.com.ar/`

Creator	Plug-in Name	Description	Comments
Peter Petrov	RockSteady	MP3 songs often differ widely in volume. Instead of lunging for the volume control when each song starts, grab this plug-in. It monitors the volume level and automatically adjusts each song to play at approximately the same level.	`http://piettropro.cjb.net/`
Tomas Lusk	NT Pitch (Freeware)	Great for MP3 DJs, this plug-in speeds up or slows down your music.	`http://nt.home.webjump.com`
WildTangent, Inc.	Bear-O-Matic (Freeware)	Visualizer that mixes an Indie film feel, a hidden message, and dancing bears.	`www.wildtangent.com/candy/visualizers.html`
WildTangent, Inc.	FaceOff (Freeware)	An odd head twitches his face in time to the music.	`www.wildtangent.com/candy/visualizers.html`
WildTangent, Inc.	TechnoWarp (Freeware)	A spinning 3D-frequency graph dances on a stage of flashing lights.	`www.wildtangent.com/candy/visualizers.html`
WildTangent, Inc.	Whack-A-Note (Freeware)	Notes appear on-screen as the music plays. Click the notes to gain points.	`www.wildtangent.com/candy/visualizers.html`

(continued)

Table A-2 *(continued)*

Creator	Plug-in Name	Description	Comments
WildTangent, Inc.	Speedway (Freeware)		
WildTangent, Inc.	Space Rocks (Freeware)		
WildTangent, Inc.	Blaster Ball (Freeware)		
WildTangent, Inc.	Dream Pack: Four visualizers in one package (Freeware).	Four way-cool visualizations ranging from a flying spaceship to vibrating atoms.	`http://www.wildtangent.com/candy/visualizers.html`

Links to resources

The CD contains links to every Web site that I discuss in this book, and many of these links take you to places that can provide you with tutorials and lots more technical information. By clicking <u>Web Links</u> on the CD interface, you have access to many resources that can help you learn and use MP3.

Songs category

What fun is having all these MP3 players if you don't have some music to listen to? The CD also includes 30 sample MP3 files contributed by artists throughout the United States and Canada. Table A-3 lists the artists, their songs, and the musical style of each track. Please use these files to try out any of the MP3 players included on this CD.

Some artists list their own Web sites and e-mail addresses. If you find a song you particularly like, visit the artist's site or send him an e-mail message. You might find more MP3 files from that artist, buy one of his CDs, or find out where you can see the artist perform live. Artist Web sites and other cool links are included on the CD. Check out `links.htm` at the root of the CD.

Table A-3		MP3s on the CD	
Artist	*Song Title*	*Music Style*	*Web Site / Other Info*
Art Faccio	"Timeline"	Finger-burning guitar instrumental	Art's been playing guitar for almost 20 years and taught guitar for 10 years. He's had endorsement deals with several companies.
Art Faccio	"Storm the Gates"	Guitar instrumental ballad with a few flurries	Art's been playing guitar for almost 20 years and taught guitar for 10 years. He's had endorsement deals with several companies.
Billy Sahner	"So Sincere" "Carelessly"	New Country	Billy Sahner is one of several artists that I feature in Chapter 13. The CD *Best Of Billy Sahner* can be ordered from his MP3.com site at http://www.mp3.com/billysahner. "So Sincere" copyright 2000 by Billy Sahner.
Brian McLeod	"SG-Anything"	Pop/Rock	Brian's music can be found at www.pisces.com/mp3.
Brian McLeod	"OhMyGodMix"	Flashy guitar instrumental	Brian's music can be found at www.pisces.com/mp3.
Buddy Blue	"Drunk Again"	American Roots	Buddy Blue is one of several artists that I feature in Chapter 13. Order his music from www.buddyblue.com.
Dan Egan	"Glance at the Moon"	Guitar-based instrumental	Look for information about Dan Egan's music at www.eganmusic.com.

(continued)

Table A-3 *(continued)*

Artist	Song Title	Music Style	Web Site / Other Info
Dan Egan	"Sunset"	Guitar-based instrumental	Look for information about Dan Egan's music at www.eganmusic.com
Dave Freden	"I Hate My Job"	Pop/Rock	Dave's music can be found at www.mp3.com/davefreden.
Dave Freden	"Fragile Creatures"	Pop/Rock	Dave's music can be found at www.mp3.com/davefreden.
Derek Loux	"I Dreamed of You"	Rock	To purchase "Endangered Species," the debut release from Manic Thirst, visit them online at www.manicthirst.com or send a check or money order for $16.00 (+ $2.00 shipping and handling) to Manic Thirst, 6210 Newberry Rd., #307, Indianapolis, IN 46256. **Copyright Info: "I Dreamed of You" words and music by Derek Loux and Heather Loux, copyright 2000 Buddy Bear Music / BMI & House Frau Music / BMI, used by permission."
Doug and Sandy McMaster Aloha Plenty	"Kelii's Slack Key Jam"	Hawaiian	Find more information about Doug and Sandy McMaster at www.alohaplentyhawaii.com/index.htm
Jamie Reno	"Reunion"	Pop	Jamie Reno can be reached at these locations: PO Box 420876, San Diego, CA 92142; jreno@san.rr.com; www.jamiereno.com.

Artist	Song Title	Music Style	Web Site / Other Info
Jari Riitala	"If You Want Me"	Jazz	Jari Riitala can be reached here at www.dlc.fi/~riitala.
Jari Riitala	"Solarium"	Jazz	Jari Riitala can be reached at www.dlc.fi/~riitala.
Joe Shane	"When I First Saw You"	Pop	Joe Shane can be reached at www.mp3.com/joeshane.
Joe Shane	"Space and Dreams"	Pop	Joe Shane can be reached at www.mp3.com/joeshane
Rascalin Music	"Lyin' Eyes"	Reggae	Rascalin music can be reached at www.rascalin.com.
Smokin' Dave and the Premo Dopes	"Van Willin'"	Rock 'n' Roll	Find more information about Smokin' Dave and the Premo Dopes at www.disgraceland.com/smokindave.htm.
Sweet Nancy Productions	"Joyous Exaltation"	Instrumental piano	Sweet Nancy Productions can be reached at www.sweetnancy.com.
The Cheeksters	"Beautiful Lie"	Pop/Rock	Find more information about The Cheeksters at www.disgraceland.com/cheeksters.htm.
The Common	"China Tiger"	Pop	I'm keeping my Acquisitions Editor happy by including a song from his band. Find out more about The Common at www.thecommononline.com.

(continued)

Table A-3 *(continued)*

Artist	Song Title	Music Style	Web Site / Other Info
The Cynic Project	"Eurodance Megamix"	Trance	The Cynic Project, one of the bands profiled in this book, can be reached at `http://mp3.com/cynicproject`
The French Broads	"Hook"	Rock and Roll with a catchy riff	Find more information about The French Broads at `www.disgraceland.com/frenchbroads.htm`
The Ghosts	"Rock The Joint"	Rock 'n' Roll	Find more information about The Ghosts at `www.disgraceland.com/.htm`.
the magical attraction of Booty!	"Trans-Lucy"	Pop/Alternative	A high-tech alternative band with music, videos, and all things "booty" online at `www.magicbooty.com`.
The Opposable Thumbs	"Hit List"	Rock 'n' Roll	Find more information about The Opposable Thumbs at `www.disgraceland.com/thumbs.htm`
Transoceanic	"Celtic Stream"	Relaxing Ambience	Transoceanic, a band profiled in this book, can be reached at `www.mp3.com/transoceanic`. This song was co-composed by Terry Donoghue.
Wonderdrug	"Star Trip"	Pop	Written by Marc and Eric Johnson. © 2000 Wonderdrug Music. Wonderdrug can be reached at `www.wonderdrug.net`.

If You've Got Problems (Of the CD Kind)

I tried my best to include programs that work on most computers with the minimum system requirements. Alas, your computer may differ, and some programs may not work properly for some reason.

The two likeliest problems are that you don't have enough memory (RAM) for the programs you want to use, or you have other programs running that are affecting installation or running of a program. If you get an error message, such as Not enough memory or Setup cannot continue, try one or more of the following suggestions and then try using the software again:

- **Turn off any antivirus software running on your computer.** Installation programs sometimes mimic virus activity and may make your computer incorrectly believe that a virus is infecting it.

- **Close all running programs.** The more programs you have running, the less memory is available to other programs. Installation programs typically update files and programs; so if you keep other programs running, installation may not work properly.

- **Have your local computer store add more RAM to your computer.** This is, admittedly, a drastic and somewhat expensive step. However, if you have a Windows 95 PC or a Mac OS computer with a PowerPC chip, adding more memory can really help the speed of your computer and allow more programs to run at the same time. This may include closing the CD interface and running a product's installation program from Windows Explorer.

If you still have trouble installing the items from the CD, please call the Hungry Minds, Inc. Customer Service phone number at 800-762-2974 (outside the U.S.: 317-572-3993).

Appendix B

Glossary

● ●

access time: The number of milliseconds a drive takes to find and grab a piece of information. Buy a drive with a low access time for the best recording.

AIFF: Short for Audio Interchange File Format, it's the Macintosh format for digital sounds.

analog: Naturally moving things, such as waves, sounds, and motion — things that computers turn into numbers for storage. (See also *digital.*)

analog-to-digital converter (ADC): A device that records sounds and converts them into numbers for ease of copying.

bootleg: An illegally traded or recorded file. Bootleggers are also known as *pirates*.

burning: The process of writing files onto a CD-R (CD Recordable) or CD-RW (CD Rewriteable) disc.

cardioid microphone: A microphone designed specifically to record sounds that are created in front of the mic while ignoring other sounds. (See also *omnidirectional microphone.*)

CD Digital Audio (CD-DA): A CD-ROM using an early '80s standard for recording sound on CD. Musical CDs use this standard. (This standard is also called *Red Book*, for some corporate reason.)

CD-quality sound: A phrase describing sound recorded at 16 bits, 44.1 kHz. (That's the rate used to record your musical CDs.)

CD-R: Short for *CD Recordable*. These discs can be written to as well as read from. Because they can't be erased and reused, they're also called WORM discs, short for *Write Once, Read Many*.

CD-ROM: *Compact Disc Read-Only Memory*. A fancy name for a CD.

CD-RW: Short for *CD Rewriteable.* These discs let you erase and reuse them. Although all CD-RW drives work with both CD-R and CD-RW discs, not all CD-R drives work with CD-RW discs. Some CD-based MP3 players don't work with CD-RW discs, only CD-Rs.

codec: Short for *compression/decompression.* A program that compresses sound or video files for storage or transmission and then decompresses the file when playing it back. MP3 files use different codecs to compress files to the MP3 standard.

compression: A way of making files take up less space.

condenser microphone: These battery-powered guys work best when recording sensitive sounds, such as light-touch pianos and whispers.

copyright: A legal term defining ownership rights of a created work. In the case of a song, a copyright can be established for the tune's composer, the lyrics, and the band's performance of the song.

DAM CD: Short for *digital automatic music.* DAM CDs are used by the MP3.com Web site to stuff both MP3 songs and standard CD audio format songs onto the same CD. As a result, the CDs play on your regular stereo, and you can easily copy the MP3 files to your hard drive or into MP3 players.

data buffer: A way to temporarily store information, leading to smoother transfers. Streaming sound often uses a buffer. Increase the buffer size if the sound breaks up upon arrival.

daughterboard: A small card that pops onto a sound card to give it new capabilities. For example, plugging a digital daughterboard onto a Sound Blaster Live card adds digital in/out capabilities.

decibel: A way to measure the volume of a sound.

decoder: A program that reads an encoded file and decompresses it for use. Winamp, for instance, contains a decoder for playing MP3 songs.

digital: Computerized things; collections of numbers that represent pictures, sounds, text, or video. (See also *analog.*)

digital signal processor (DSP): A bit of computer mechanics for adding echoes, reverb, and other effects to sound.

digital-to-analog converter (DAC): A sound card that can play recorded sounds stored in a file.

distortion: Although electric guitarists spend hundreds of dollars trying to create it, most sound card owners consider it unwanted noise.

dubbing: Touching up recorded material by adding new pieces of audio.

dynamic microphone: The best mic for recording loud, powerful stuff, such as heavy metal bands or arguments on the Larry King show.

encoding: With regard to MP3 technology, the process of converting an audio WAV file into an MP3 file.

equalization: The art of changing a song's recorded frequencies to enhance its sound.

filter: To remove an undesirable quality, such as removing a hiss from a recording.

freeware: Programs freely available to the general public.

frequency: Without getting complicated, an annoying mosquito whines at a *high* frequency; a foghorn rumbles at a *low* frequency.

FTP: Short for *File Transfer Protocol.* It's a simple way to transfer files online.

General MIDI (GM): A MIDI numbering sequence with all the instrument sounds lined up in a designated order, starting with pianos and ending with sound effects.

High Sierra: A format for placing files and directories on CD-ROM so that DOS can read them. (Named after the High Sierra Hotel and Casino in Lake Tahoe, Nevada, High Sierra is based on its predecessor, *ISO 9660*).

ID3 Tag: A space at one end of a sound file for adding information about the song — the artist, title, band name, genre, year, and other information. Constantly in flux, the ID3 tag has undergone several changes to include lyrics and artwork.

IRQ (Interrupt Request): A computerized "tap on the shoulder" used by sound cards and other components when they need the CPU's attention. Your computer has only a few of these "shoulders," and cards trying to use the same IRQ usually won't work right.

ISO-9660: An older format for placing files and directories on CD-ROM so that DOS can read them. Replaced by the *High Sierra* format.

jewel case: The cheap little plastic cases that CDs come packaged in. It's sometimes referred to as a jewel box.

jukebox: Large CD-ROM drives that hold several CDs, thereby letting you switch among discs easily and expensively. Not to be confused with the MusicMatch *Jukebox* — software for creating and playing MP3s.

leech or **leecher:** A semi-derogatory description for people who download all the available MP3 files without posting any in return.

lossy compression: A compression technique used for files such as MP3. Lossy compression cuts out some of the sound in order to save space.

MIDI (Musical Instrument Digital Interface): A way to store music as a series of computerized instructions; the resulting tiny files can be played back on a wide variety of computers and electronic instruments.

MP3: A method of compressing audio files to about one-tenth their normal size while still keeping near CD-quality sound. MP3 stores about one minute of audio in 1MB of space when using the standard 128 Kbps bitrate.

MPEG 1 Layer 3: The official term the Moving Picture Expert Group chose for MP3.

multisession CD-R: A newer type of CD-R drive that lets you add data to a disc on different occasions. (Older CD-R drives made you burn all your data onto the disc in one session.)

multi-voice: The capability to mimic more than one instrument simultaneously, found in most sound cards.

newsgroups: A large grouping of Internet discussion areas formed around individual topics. Outlook Express and other programs locate, read, and download files posted on newsgroups. (The `alt.binaries.sounds.mp3` newsgroup is a large outlet for song piracy.)

omnidirectional microphone: A microphone that can pick up sound from all sides, not only those sounds emitted in front of the mic. (See also *cardioid microphone, dynamic microphone.*)

Orange Book: A standard for CDs that use the WORM (*Write Once, Read Many*) format. Big companies use this standard to back up boring computerized paperwork.

Philips: A huge company that developed CD technology with Sony.

phono cable: Cable used mostly for connecting audio equipment and sound cards.

playlist: An ordered list of MP3 files and their locations used by MP3 players or Internet radio stations to play songs in certain sequences.

plug-in: A file that enhances an application, such as Winamp, when placed in Winamp's plug-ins directory and selected. One plug-in displays flashy on-screen graphics that twitch in time to the tunes. Another fades songs into each other as they play. Head for `www.winamp.com` to see them all.

public domain: Works no longer under copyright, so they may be freely copied and distributed. They enter the public domain when the copyright expires or the copyright holder gives his or her material to the public domain.

RCA audio cable: Commonly found on most home stereos, this cable ends with a little round metal "Hat" that slides onto a little round metal "head."

RealAudio: Another popular sound format, but usually used for streaming — *Webcasting* — over the Internet. It lacks the sound quality of MP3.

RIAA: Short for the *Recording Industry Association of America.* The RIAA is a trade group of record industry companies formed to foster "a business and legal climate that supports and promotes our members' creative and financial viability around the world." Visit the RIAA at www.riaa.com.

Red Book: Nothing to do with the magazine, this term simply means a CD containing music (such as a Rolling Stones album) and no computer programs. Another name for *Compact Disc Digital Audio,* or *CD-DA.*

ripper: A program that digitally copies the contents of an audio CD onto your hard drive where it can be encoded into MP3 files.

sampling rates: When computers listen to a sound or watch a video to store the information into a file, they're *sampling* the information. The *higher* the sampling rate, the better the quality, the closer the computer pays attention to the information, and the bigger the resulting file.

SCSI (Small Computer System Interface): A way to link several computer gadgets.

SCSI port: A special connector required by some CD-ROM drives and other devices, it comes on a special SCSI card.

SCSI/2: Same as SCSI, but with a new and improved format.

skins: Cosmetic enhancers for programs such as Winamp. Insert a skin file into Winamp's skins file and select it to give Winamp a wood grain appearance, for example, or cover it with pictures of rock stars.

shareware: Programs given away under the condition that you'll buy it if you like it. Evaluation times differ, but the cost is usually under $40.

SHOUTcast: An Internet radio station Web site founded by the creators of Winamp. Listen to it at www.shoutcast.com. (See *Webcasting.*)

SoundBlaster-compatible: A sound card that works with any software written for the SoundBlaster card. (That's about 90 percent of the programs on the market.)

synthesized: Sounds created by computer circuitry.

tray-loading: A type of CD-ROM drive that sticks out a tray to accept CDs, like a tongue asking for a mint.

tweaking: Fiddling with knobs until everything finally looks or sounds right.

VBR: Short for *variable bit rate.* Songs encoded at a variable rate, using lots of encoding for sensitive parts and little encoding for pauses in songs. Not all MP3 players (including Creative Labs' first Nomad) can handle VBR encoding.

VQF: Short for *vector quantization format.* Another freebie codec that some claim works better than MP3. It's not compatible with MP3, however, and works a computer harder when encoding and decoding.

voice: Another word for a musical instrument sound. A 20-voice synthesizer won't necessarily produce 20 instruments, however, because many cards mix two or more voices when creating chords and complex instrument sounds.

Webcasting: Playing radio stations across the Internet, usually by playing MP3s through computer servers.

Winamp: The most popular MP3 player by far, Winamp offers regular updates, easy customization, great sound, and integration with the SHOUTcast Webcasting system.

Windows CE: A miniature version of Windows that runs on tiny Personal Digital Assistants. The latest PocketPCs run Windows CE version 3.0 and can play MP3s.

Windows Media Audio (WMA): The Microsoft response to MP3. Some say it sounds better, others say it sounds worse. Nevertheless, WMA files can be encoded at 96 Kbps with the same sound quality as a 128 Kbps MP3 file. That makes them smaller and popular for portable MP3 players that can play the WMA format.

Yellow Book: A standard for compact discs containing computer programs and data.

Index

• D •

• *N* •

• *O* •

• *P* •

• S •

• *T* •

Notes

Hungry Minds, Inc.
End-User License Agreement

READ THIS. You should carefully read these terms and conditions before opening the software packet(s) included with this book ("Book"). This is a license agreement ("Agreement") between you and Hungry Minds, Inc. ("HMI"). By opening the accompanying software packet(s), you acknowledge that you have read and accept the following terms and conditions. If you do not agree and do not want to be bound by such terms and conditions, promptly return the Book and the unopened software packet(s) to the place you obtained them for a full refund.

1. **License Grant.** HMI grants to you (either an individual or entity) a nonexclusive license to use one copy of the enclosed software program(s) (collectively, the "Software") solely for your own personal or business purposes on a single computer (whether a standard computer or a workstation component of a multi-user network). The Software is in use on a computer when it is loaded into temporary memory (RAM) or installed into permanent memory (hard disk, CD-ROM, or other storage device). HMI reserves all rights not expressly granted herein.

2. **Ownership.** HMI is the owner of all right, title, and interest, including copyright, in and to the compilation of the Software recorded on the disk(s) or CD-ROM ("Software Media"). Copyright to the individual programs recorded on the Software Media is owned by the author or other authorized copyright owner of each program. Ownership of the Software and all proprietary rights relating thereto remain with HMI and its licensers.

3. **Restrictions On Use and Transfer.**

   (a) You may only (i) make one copy of the Software for backup or archival purposes, or (ii) transfer the Software to a single hard disk, provided that you keep the original for backup or archival purposes. You may not (i) rent or lease the Software, (ii) copy or reproduce the Software through a LAN or other network system or through any computer subscriber system or bulletin-board system, or (iii) modify, adapt, or create derivative works based on the Software.

   (b) You may not reverse engineer, decompile, or disassemble the Software. You may transfer the Software and user documentation on a permanent basis, provided that the transferee agrees to accept the terms and conditions of this Agreement and you retain no copies. If the Software is an update or has been updated, any transfer must include the most recent update and all prior versions.

4. **Restrictions on Use of Individual Programs.** You must follow the individual requirements and restrictions detailed for each individual program in Appendix A of this Book. These limitations are also contained in the individual license agreements recorded on the Software Media. These limitations may include a requirement that after using the program for a specified period of time, the user must pay a registration fee or discontinue use. By opening the Software packet(s), you will be agreeing to abide by the licenses and restrictions for these individual programs that are detailed in Appendix A and on the Software Media. None of the material on this Software Media or listed in this Book may ever be redistributed, in original or modified form, for commercial purposes.

5. **Limited Warranty.**

   (a) HMI warrants that the Software and Software Media are free from defects in materials and workmanship under normal use for a period of sixty (60) days from the date of purchase of this Book. If HMI receives notification within the warranty period of defects in materials or workmanship, HMI will replace the defective Software Media.

   (b) HMI AND THE AUTHOR OF THE BOOK DISCLAIM ALL OTHER WARRANTIES, EXPRESS OR IMPLIED, INCLUDING WITHOUT LIMITATION IMPLIED WARRANTIES OF MERCHANTABILITY AND FITNESS FOR A PARTICULAR PURPOSE, WITH RESPECT TO THE SOFTWARE, THE PROGRAMS, THE SOURCE CODE CONTAINED THEREIN, AND/OR THE TECHNIQUES DESCRIBED IN THIS BOOK. HMI DOES NOT WARRANT THAT THE FUNCTIONS CONTAINED IN THE SOFTWARE WILL MEET YOUR REQUIREMENTS OR THAT THE OPERATION OF THE SOFTWARE WILL BE ERROR FREE.

   (c) This limited warranty gives you specific legal rights, and you may have other rights that vary from jurisdiction to jurisdiction.

6. **Remedies.**

   (a) HMI's entire liability and your exclusive remedy for defects in materials and workmanship shall be limited to replacement of the Software Media, which may be returned to HMI with a copy of your receipt at the following address: Software Media Fulfillment Department, Attn.: *MP3 For Dummies,* 2nd Edition, Hungry Minds, Inc., 10475 Crosspoint Blvd., Indianapolis, IN 46256, or call 1-800-762-2974. Please allow four to six weeks for delivery. This Limited Warranty is void if failure of the Software Media has resulted from accident, abuse, or misapplication. Any replacement Software Media will be warranted for the remainder of the original warranty period or thirty (30) days, whichever is longer.

   (b) In no event shall HMI or the author be liable for any damages whatsoever (including without limitation damages for loss of business profits, business interruption, loss of business information, or any other pecuniary loss) arising from the use of or inability to use the Book or the Software, even if HMI has been advised of the possibility of such damages.

   (c) Because some jurisdictions do not allow the exclusion or limitation of liability for consequential or incidental damages, the above limitation or exclusion may not apply to you.

7. **U.S. Government Restricted Rights.** Use, duplication, or disclosure of the Software for or on behalf of the United States of America, its agencies and/or instrumentalities (the "U.S. Government") is subject to restrictions as stated in paragraph (c)(1)(ii) of the Rights in Technical Data and Computer Software clause of DFARS 252.227-7013, or subparagraphs (c) (1) and (2) of the Commercial Computer Software - Restricted Rights clause at FAR 52.227-19, and in similar clauses in the NASA FAR supplement, as applicable.

8. **General.** This Agreement constitutes the entire understanding of the parties and revokes and supersedes all prior agreements, oral or written, between them and may not be modified or amended except in a writing signed by both parties hereto that specifically refers to this Agreement. This Agreement shall take precedence over any other documents that may be in conflict herewith. If any one or more provisions contained in this Agreement are held by any court or tribunal to be invalid, illegal, or otherwise unenforceable, each and every other provision shall remain in full force and effect.

Installation Instructions

The *MP3 For Dummies,* 2nd Edition CD offers valuable information that you won't want to miss. The following sections tell you how to install the items from the CD.

Using the CD with Microsoft Windows

To install items from the CD to your hard drive, follow these steps:

1. **Insert the CD into your computer's CD-ROM drive.**
2. **Click the Start button and choose Run from the menu.**
3. **In the dialog box that appears, type** d:\start.htm.
4. **Read through the license agreement, nod your head, and then click the Accept button if you want to use the CD.**
5. **To navigate within the interface, click any topic of interest to take you to an explanation of the files on the CD and how to use or install them.**
6. **To install software from the CD, simply click the software name.**

   Choose to run or open the file from its current location, and the installation procedure continues.

Using the CD with a Mac

To install items from the CD to your hard drive, follow these steps:

1. **Insert the CD into your computer's CD-ROM drive.**
2. **Double-click the CD icon to show the CD's contents.**
3. **Double-click** start.htm **to open your browser and display the license agreement.**

   If your browser doesn't open automatically, open it as you normally would. Choose File⇨Open File (in Internet Explorer) or File⇨Open⇨ Location in Netscape (in Netscape Navigator), and select *MP3 For Dummies.*
4. **Read through the license agreement, nod your head, and then click the Accept button if you want to use the CD.**
5. **To navigate within the interface, click any topic of interest to take you to an explanation of the files on the CD and how to use or install them.**
6. **To install software from the CD, simply click the software name.**

   You'll see two options: to run or open the file from the current location or to save the file to your hard drive. Choose to run or open the file from its current location, and the installation procedure continues. When you finish using the interface, close your browser as usual.

For instructions about using this CD with a Linux system, or for more detailed instructions on installing the software to a Windows or Mac OS machine, see Appendix A, "About the CD."

FOR DUMMIES
BOOK REGISTRATION

Register This Book and Win!

We want to hear from you!

Visit **dummies.com** to register this book and tell us how you liked it!

✔ Get entered in our monthly prize giveaway.

✔ Give us feedback about this book — tell us what you like best, what you like least, or maybe what you'd like to ask the author and us to change!

✔ Let us know any other *For Dummies* topics that interest you.

Your feedback helps us determine what books to publish, tells us what coverage to add as we revise our books, and lets us know whether we're meeting your needs as a *For Dummies* reader. You're our most valuable resource, and what you have to say is important to us!

Not on the Web yet? It's easy to get started with *Dummies 101: The Internet For Windows 98* or *The Internet For Dummies* at local retailers everywhere.

Or let us know what you think by sending us a letter at the following address:

For Dummies Book Registration
Dummies Press
10475 Crosspoint Blvd.
Indianapolis, IN 46256

™
BESTSELLING BOOK SERIES